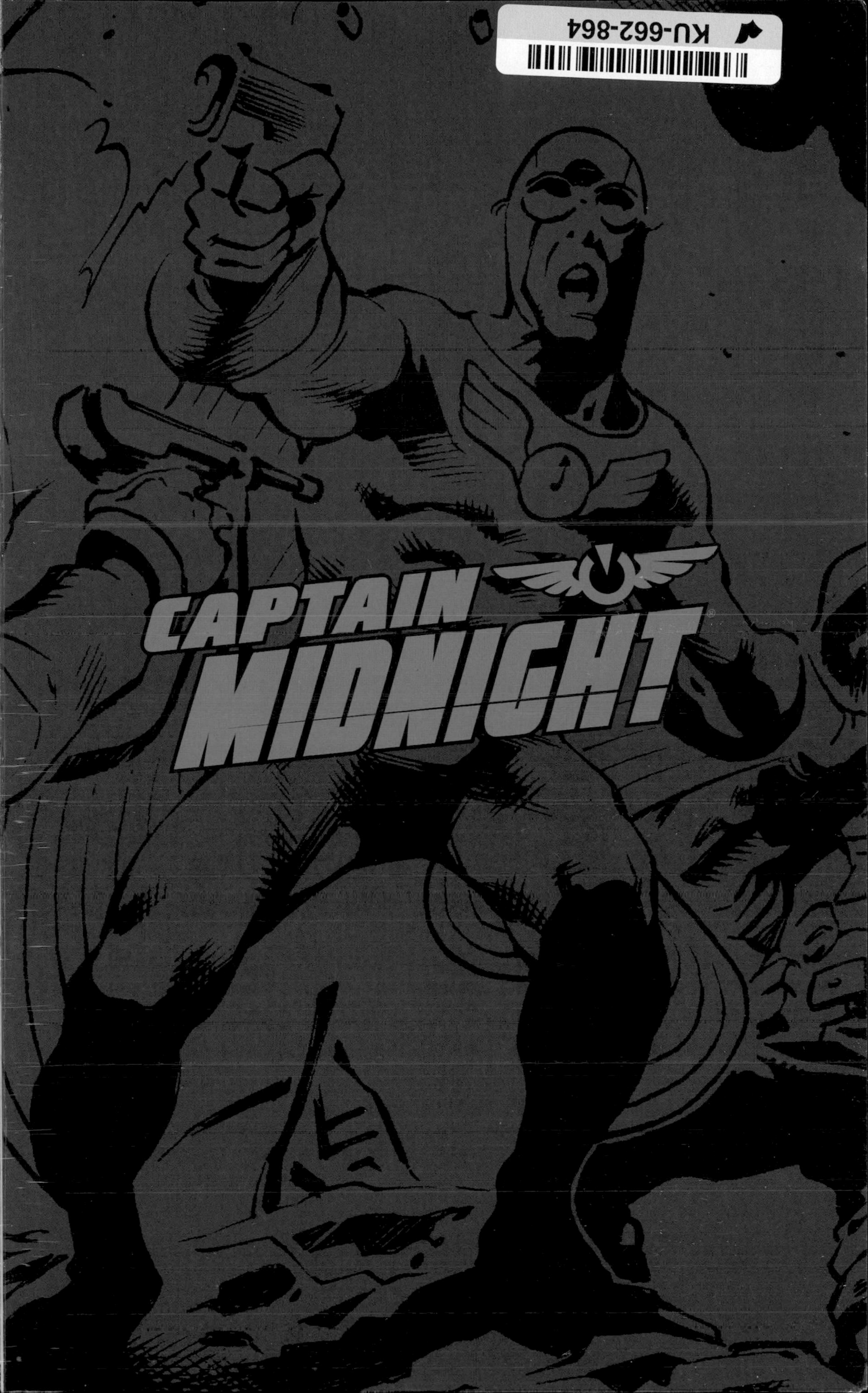
CAPTAIN
MIDNIGHT

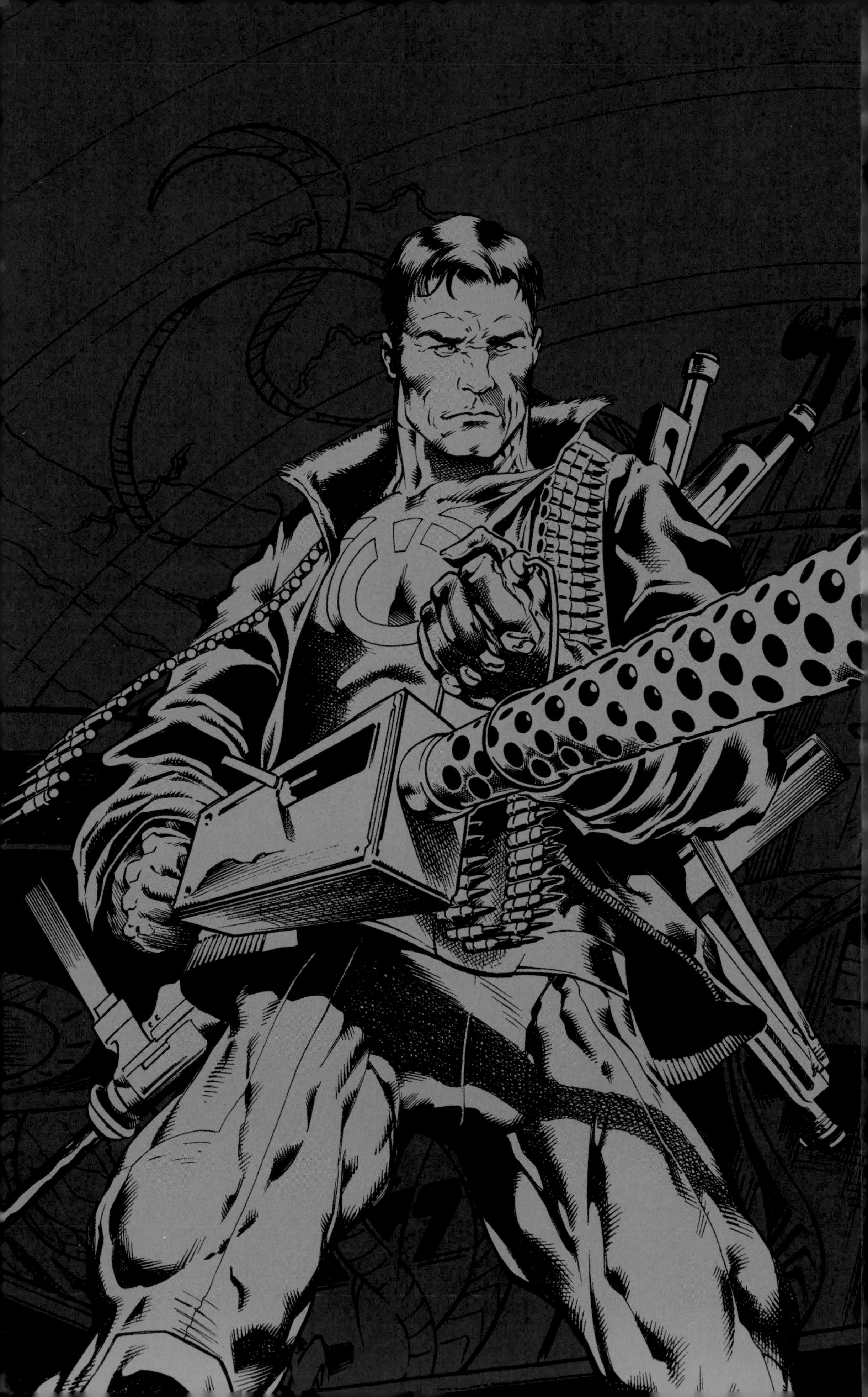

CAPTAIN MIDNIGHT®

VOLUME 4 CRASH AND BURN

STORY BY

JOSHUA WILLIAMSON

PENCILS BY

MANUEL GARCIA

INKS BY

BIT

COLORS BY

MARTA MARTÍNEZ

LETTERS BY

NATE PIEKOS OF BLAMBOT®

COVER BY

FREDDIE WILLIAMS II AND JEREMY ROBERTS

CHAPTER BREAK ART BY

FREDDIE WILLIAMS II AND JEREMY ROBERTS
(CHAPTER 1)

DUSTIN NGUYEN
(CHAPTER 2)

DECLAN SHALVEY AND JORDIE BELLAIRE
(CHAPTER 3)

VICTOR IBÁÑEZ
(CHAPTER 4)

DARK HORSE BOOKS

PUBLISHER.....................**MIKE RICHARDSON**

EDITOR.............................**JIM GIBBONS**

ASSISTANT EDITOR.........**SPENCER CUSHING**

DIGITAL PRODUCTION........**ALLYSON HALLER**

COLLECTION DESIGNER.................**NICK JAMES**

Special thanks to Mike Richardson, Randy Stradley, Scott Allie, and David Macho Gómez and Spanish Inq.

Mike Richardson, President and Publisher | Neil Hankerson, Executive Vice President | Tom Weddle, Chief Financial Officer | Randy Stradley, Vice President of Publishing | Michael Martens, Vice President of Book Trade Sales | Scott Allie, Editor in Chief | Matt Parkinson, Vice President of Marketing | David Scroggy, Vice President of Product Development | Dale LaFountain, Vice President of Information Technology | Darlene Vogel, Senior Director of Print, Design, and Production | Ken Lizzi, General Counsel | Davey Estrada, Editorial Director | Chris Warner, Senior Books Editor | Diana Schutz, Executive Editor | Cary Grazzini, Director of Print and Development | Lia Ribacchi, Art Director | Cara Niece, Director of Scheduling | Mark Bernardi, Director of Digital Publishing

Published by Dark Horse Books
A division of Dark Horse Comics, Inc.
10956 SE Main Street
Milwaukie, OR 97222

First edition: January 2015
ISBN 978-1-61655-518-4

1 3 5 7 9 10 8 6 4 2
Printed in China

International Licensing: (503) 905-2377
Comic Shop Locator Service: (888) 266-4226

CAPTAIN MIDNIGHT VOLUME 4: CRASH AND BURN

This volume collects Captain Midnight #12–#15, from the ongoing series from Dark Horse Comics, as well as Project Black Sky: Secret Files—The Archon, originally published on ProjectBlackSky.net.

Library of Congress Cataloging-in-Publication Data

Williamson, Joshua.
 Captain Midnight : crash and burn / story by Joshua Williamson ; pencils by Manuel Garcia ; inks by Bit ; colors by Marta Martínez ; letters by Nate Piekos of BLAMBOT ; cover by Freddie Williams II and Jeremy Roberts ; chapter break art by Freddie Williams II and Jeremy Roberts (Chapter 1), Dustin Nguyen (Chapter 2), Declan Shalvey and Jordie Bellaire (Chapter 3), Victor Ibanez (Chapter 4) -- First edition.
    pages cm
 "This volume collects Captain Midnight #12-#15, from the ongoing series from Dark Horse Comics, as well as Project Black Sky: Secret Files-The Archon, originally published on ProjectBlackSky.net"--T.p. verso.
 Summary: "Captain Midnight must protect himself and those around him from a techno terrorist who is trying to steal his brain!"-- Provided by publisher.
 ISBN 978-1-61655-518-4 (pbk.)
 1. Graphic novels. [1. Graphic novels. 2. Superheroes--Fiction.] I. Garcia, Manuel (Cartoonist) II. Title.
 PZ7.7.W558Cap 2015
 741.5'973--dc23
                                        2014034085

CHAPTER 1

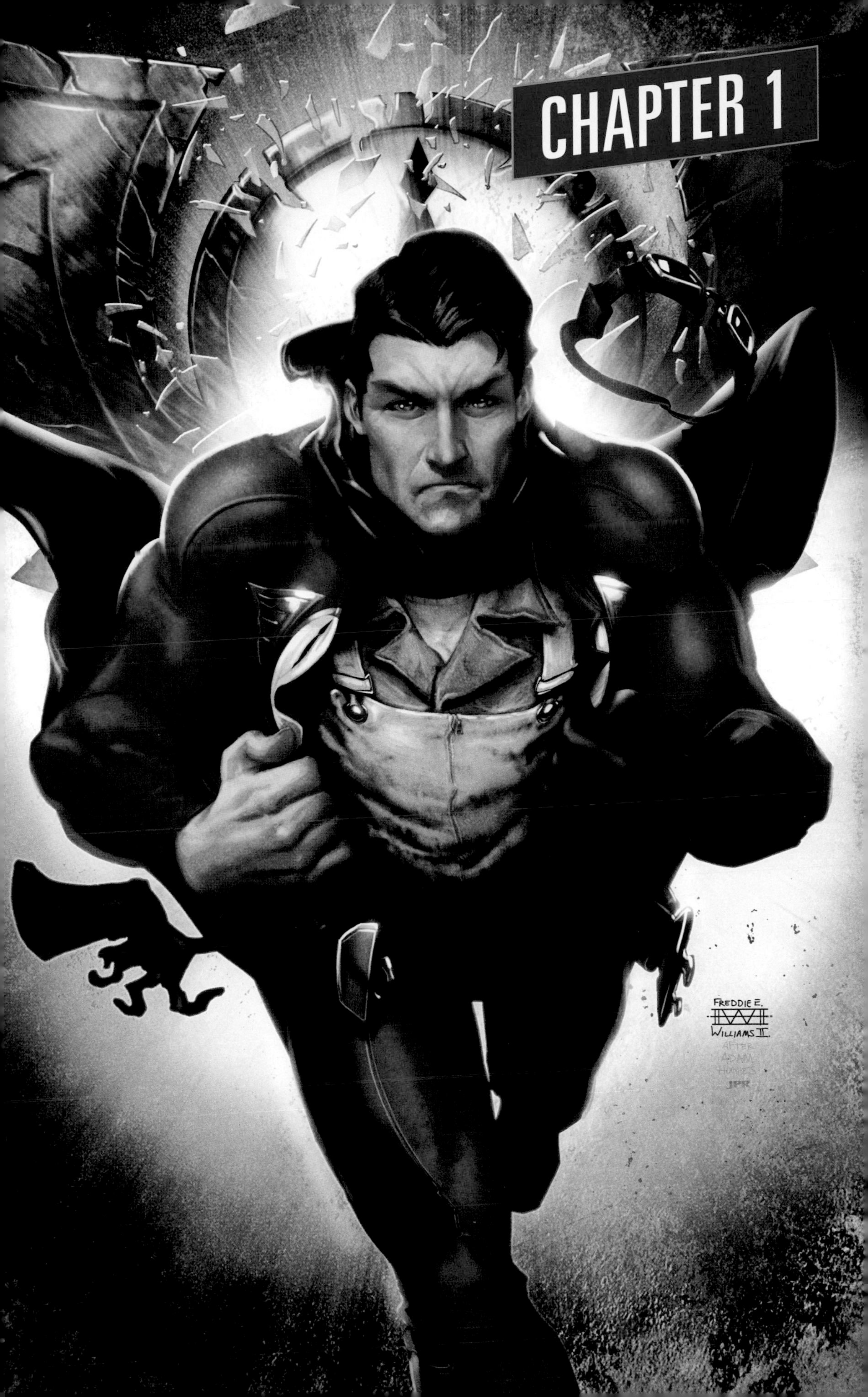

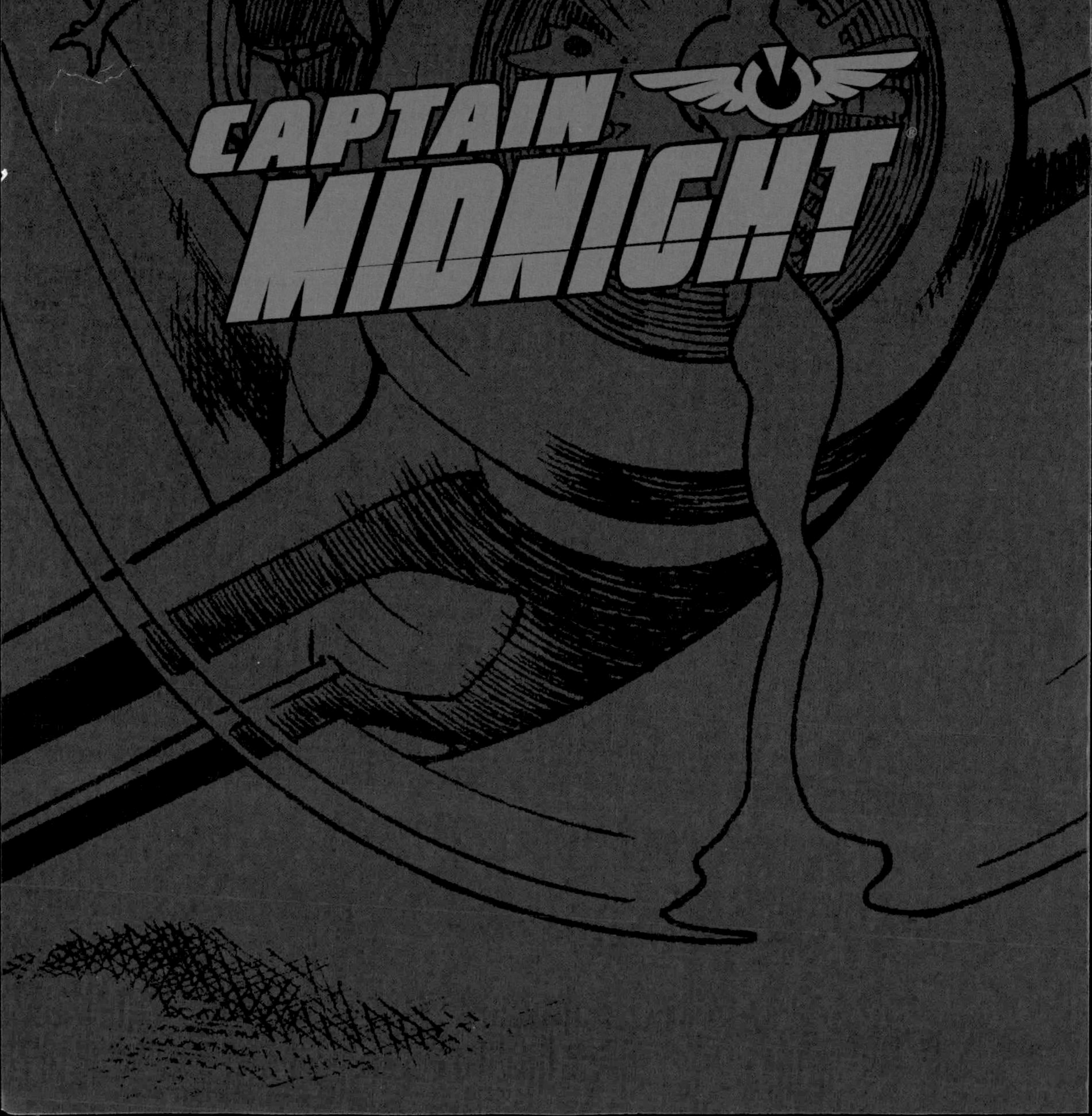
CAPTAIN
MIDNIGHT

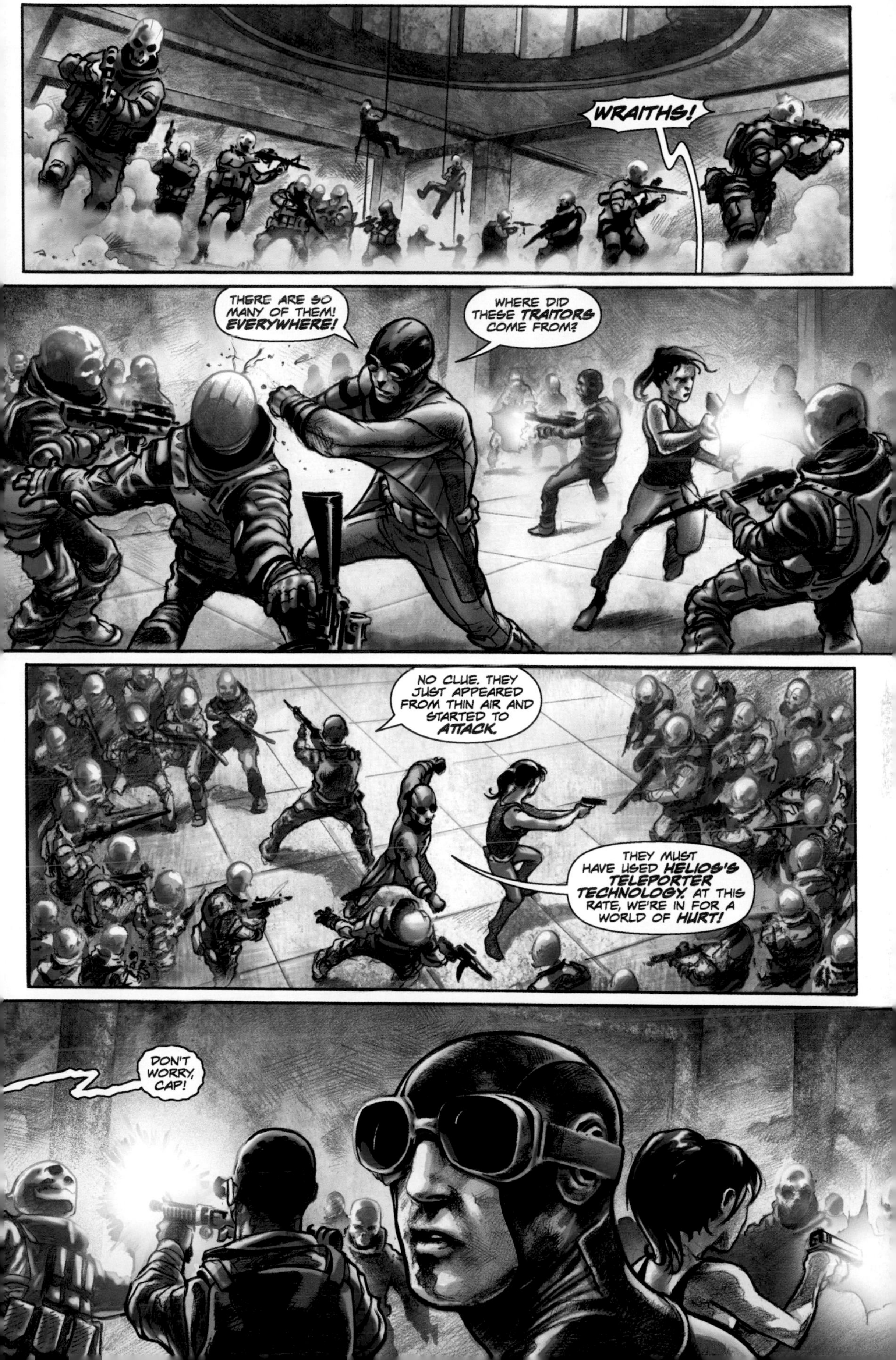
WRAITHS!
THERE ARE SO MANY OF THEM! EVERYWHERE!
WHERE DID THESE TRAITORS COME FROM?
NO CLUE. THEY JUST APPEARED FROM THIN AIR AND STARTED TO ATTACK.
THEY MUST HAVE USED HELIOS'S TELEPORTER TECHNOLOGY. AT THIS RATE, WE'RE IN FOR A WORLD OF HURT!
DON'T WORRY, CAP!

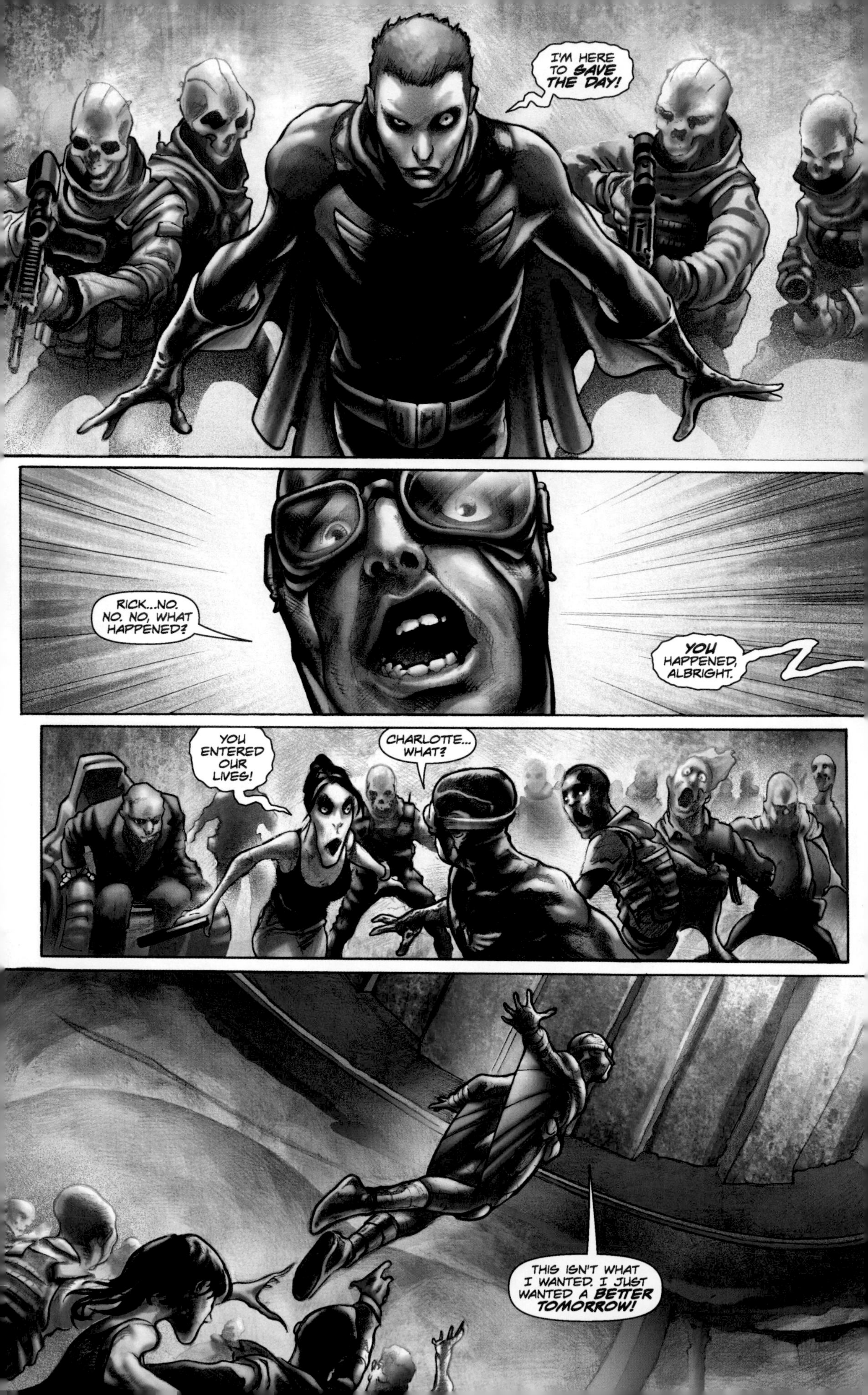
I'M HERE TO SAVE THE DAY!
RICK...NO. NO. NO, WHAT HAPPENED?
YOU HAPPENED, ALBRIGHT.
YOU ENTERED OUR LIVES!
CHARLOTTE... WHAT?
THIS ISN'T WHAT I WANTED. I JUST WANTED A BETTER TOMORROW!

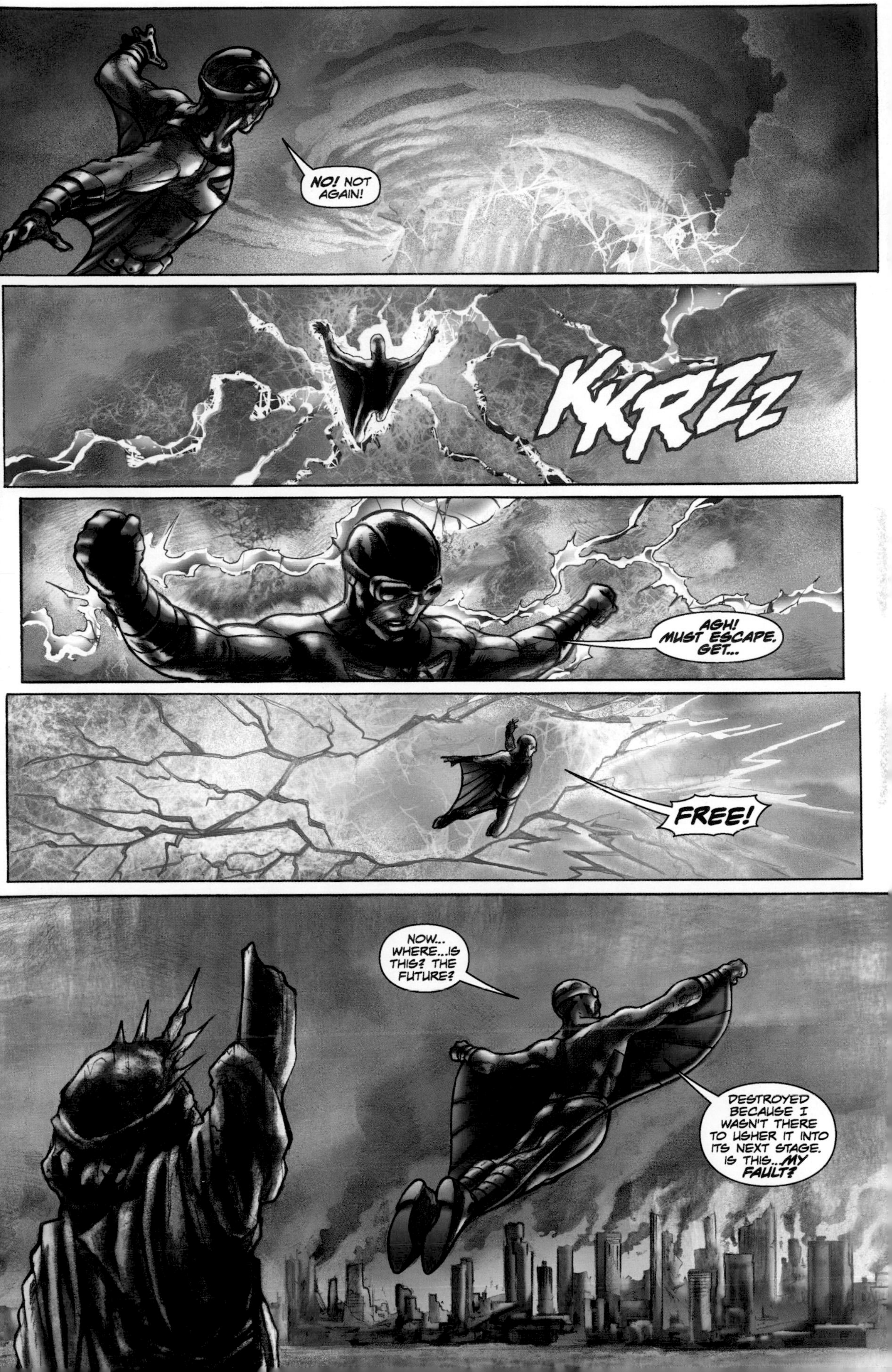
NO! NOT AGAIN!
KKRZZ
AGH! MUST ESCAPE. GET...
FREE!
NOW... WHERE...IS THIS? THE FUTURE?
DESTROYED BECAUSE I WASN'T THERE TO USHER IT INTO ITS NEXT STAGE. IS THIS...MY FAULT?

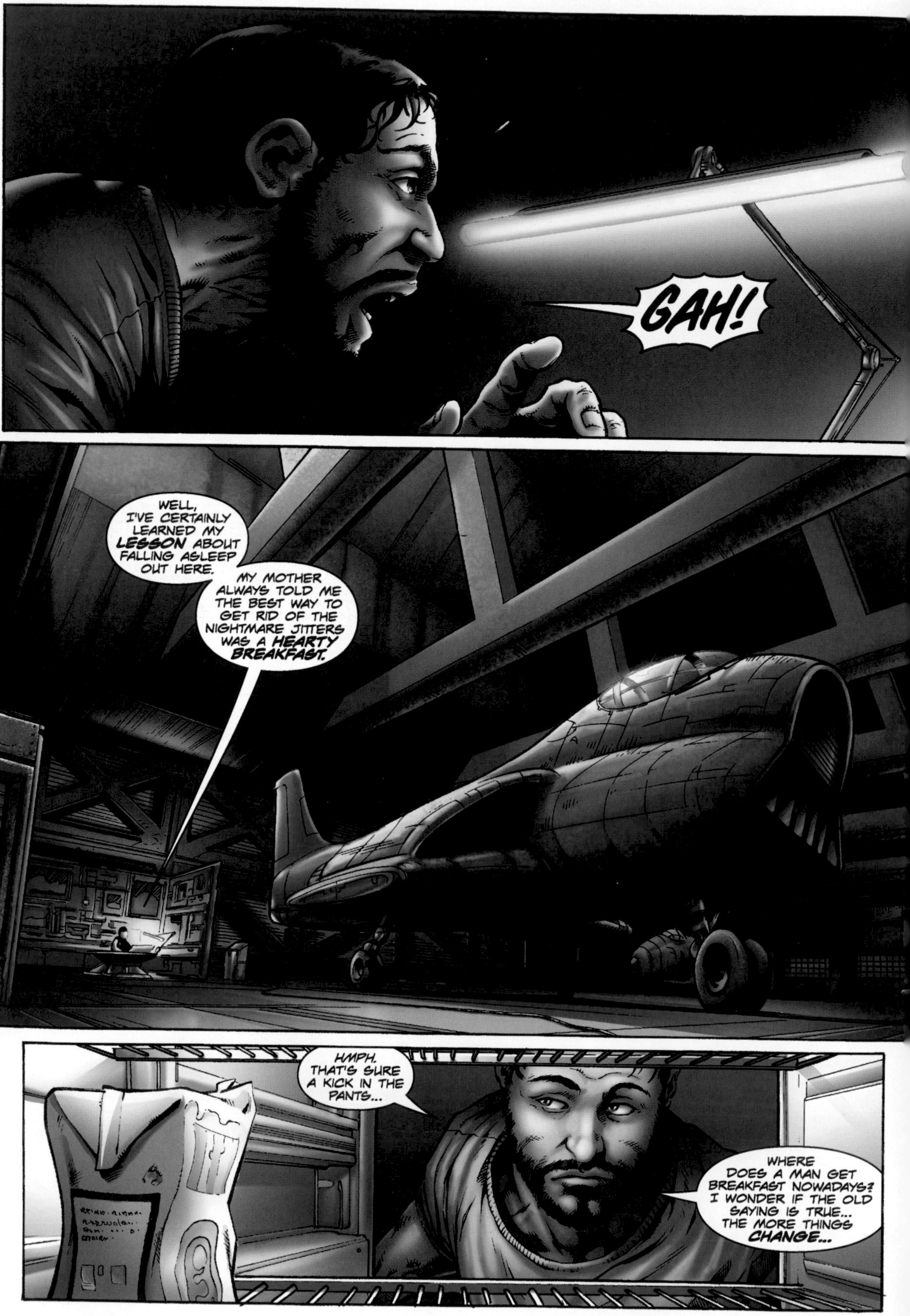
GAH!
WELL, I'VE CERTAINLY LEARNED MY LESSON ABOUT FALLING ASLEEP OUT HERE.
MY MOTHER ALWAYS TOLD ME THE BEST WAY TO GET RID OF THE NIGHTMARE JITTERS WAS A HEARTY BREAKFAST.
HMPH. THAT'S SURE A KICK IN THE PANTS...
WHERE DOES A MAN GET BREAKFAST NOWADAYS? I WONDER IF THE OLD SAYING IS TRUE... THE MORE THINGS CHANGE...

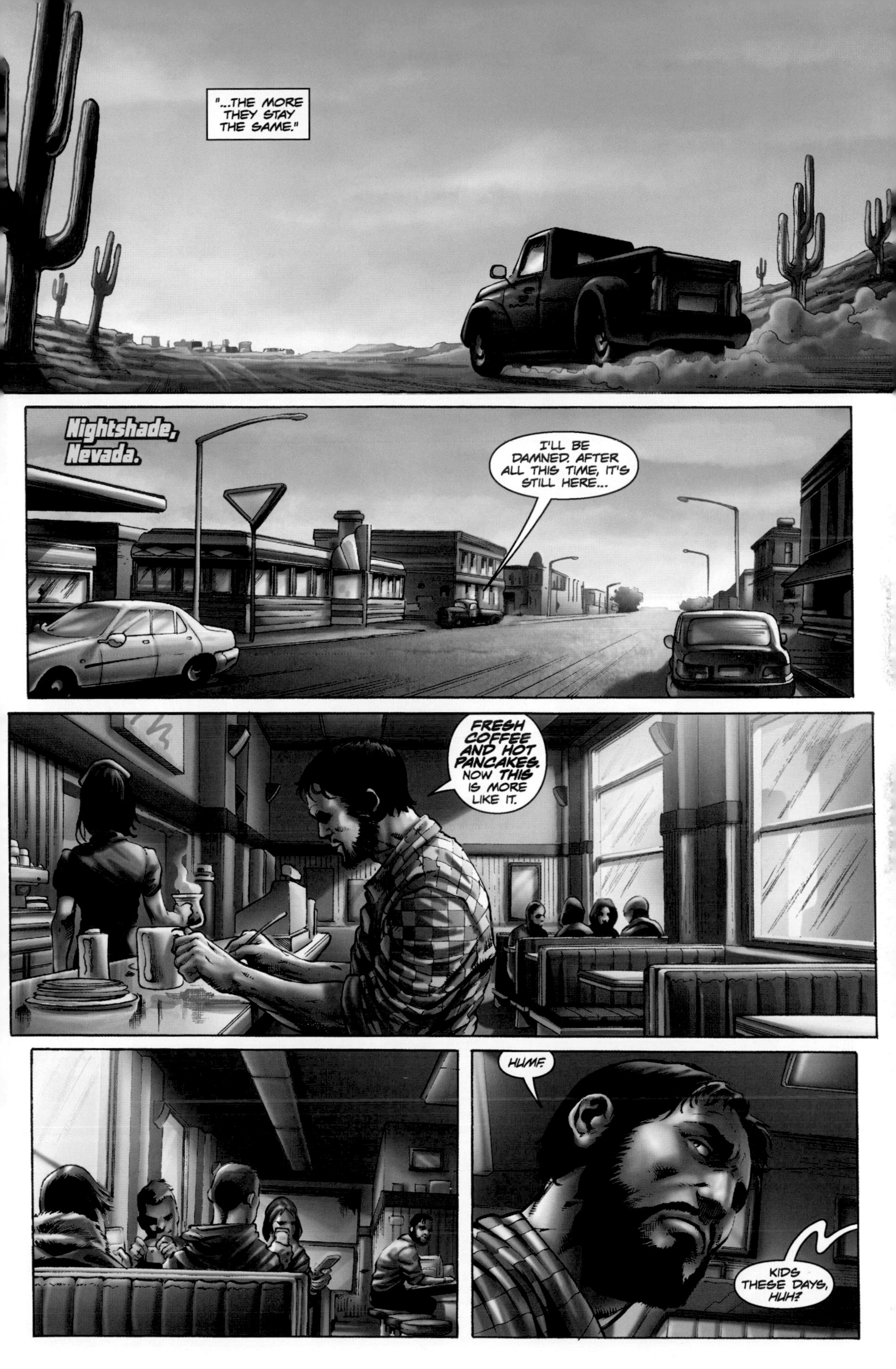
"...THE MORE THEY STAY THE SAME."
Nightshade, Nevada.
I'LL BE DAMNED. AFTER ALL THIS TIME, IT'S STILL HERE...
FRESH COFFEE AND HOT PANCAKES. NOW THIS IS MORE LIKE IT.
HUMF.
KIDS THESE DAYS, HUH?

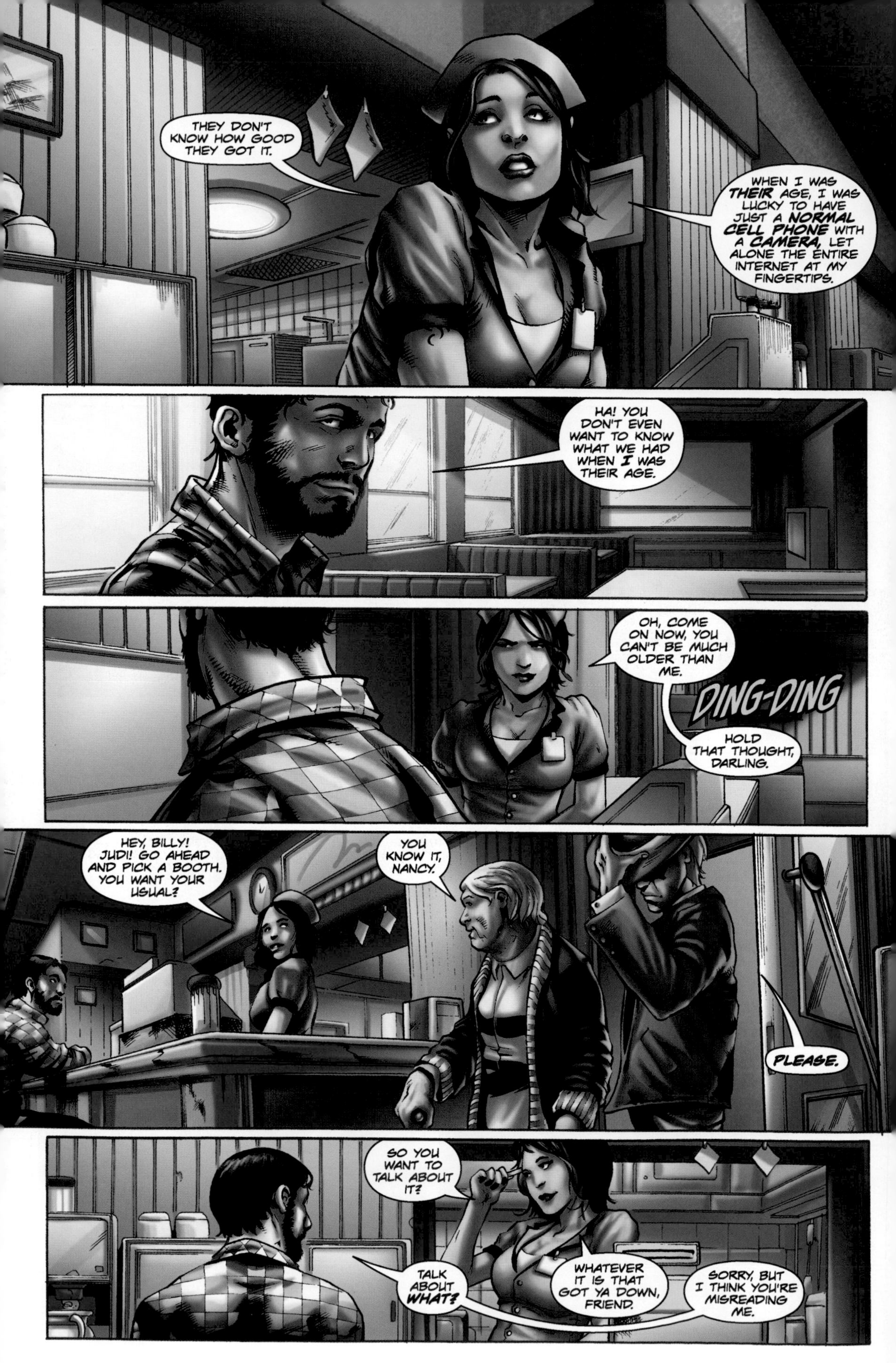
THEY DON'T KNOW HOW GOOD THEY GOT IT.
WHEN I WAS THEIR AGE, I WAS LUCKY TO HAVE JUST A NORMAL CELL PHONE WITH A CAMERA, LET ALONE THE ENTIRE INTERNET AT MY FINGERTIPS.
HA! YOU DON'T EVEN WANT TO KNOW WHAT WE HAD WHEN I WAS THEIR AGE.
OH, COME ON NOW, YOU CAN'T BE MUCH OLDER THAN ME.
DING-DING
HOLD THAT THOUGHT, DARLING.
HEY, BILLY! JUDI! GO AHEAD AND PICK A BOOTH. YOU WANT YOUR USUAL?
YOU KNOW IT, NANCY.
PLEASE.
SO YOU WANT TO TALK ABOUT IT?
TALK ABOUT WHAT?
WHATEVER IT IS THAT GOT YA DOWN, FRIEND.
SORRY, BUT I THINK YOU'RE MISREADING ME.

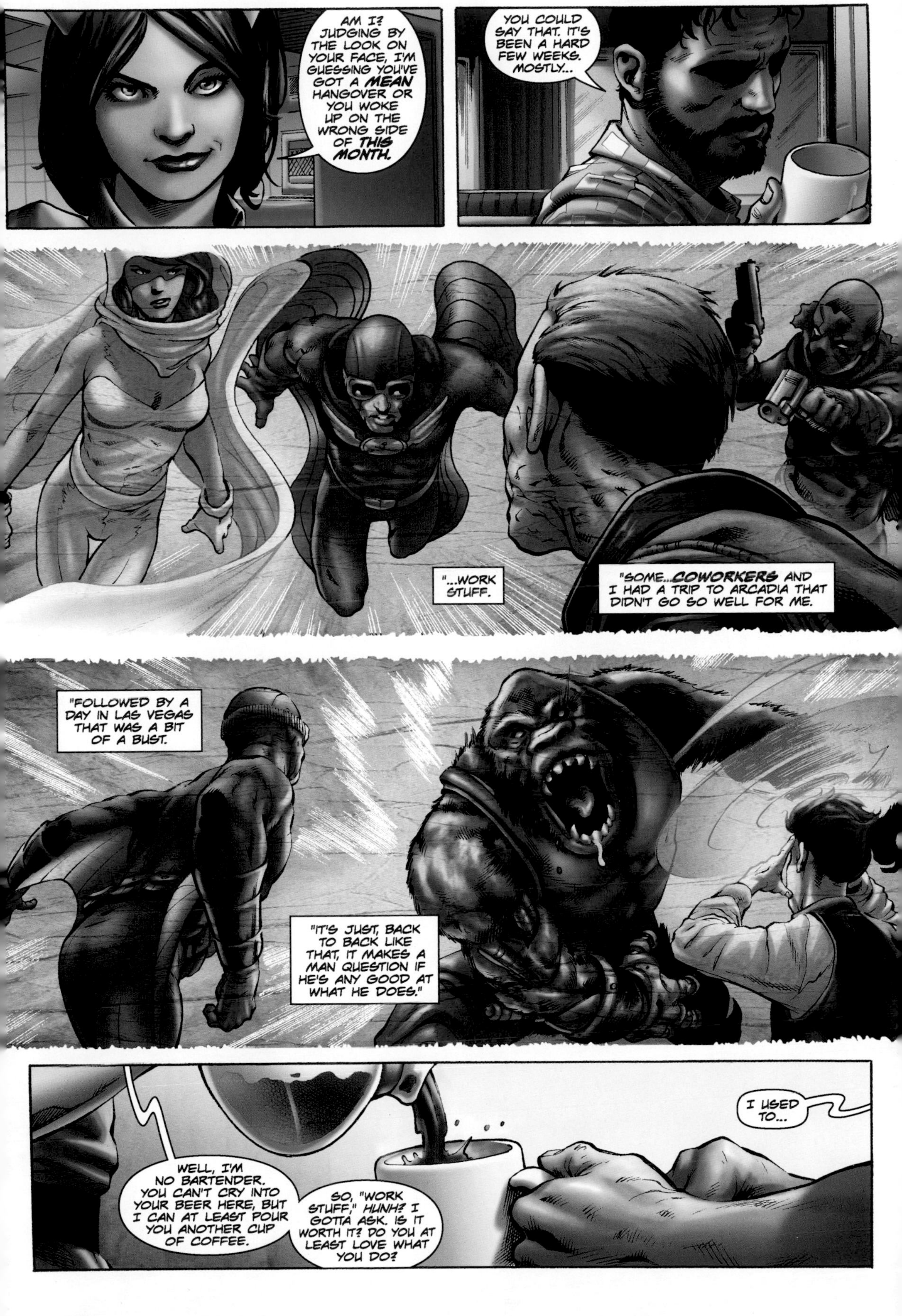
AM I? JUDGING BY THE LOOK ON YOUR FACE, I'M GUESSING YOU'VE GOT A MEAN HANGOVER OR YOU WOKE UP ON THE WRONG SIDE OF THIS MONTH.
YOU COULD SAY THAT. IT'S BEEN A HARD FEW WEEKS. MOSTLY...
"...WORK STUFF.
"SOME...COWORKERS AND I HAD A TRIP TO ARCADIA THAT DIDN'T GO SO WELL FOR ME.
"FOLLOWED BY A DAY IN LAS VEGAS THAT WAS A BIT OF A BUST.
"IT'S JUST, BACK TO BACK LIKE THAT, IT MAKES A MAN QUESTION IF HE'S ANY GOOD AT WHAT HE DOES."
WELL, I'M NO BARTENDER. YOU CAN'T CRY INTO YOUR BEER HERE, BUT I CAN AT LEAST POUR YOU ANOTHER CUP OF COFFEE.
SO, "WORK STUFF," HUNH? I GOTTA ASK. IS IT WORTH IT? DO YOU AT LEAST LOVE WHAT YOU DO?
I USED TO...

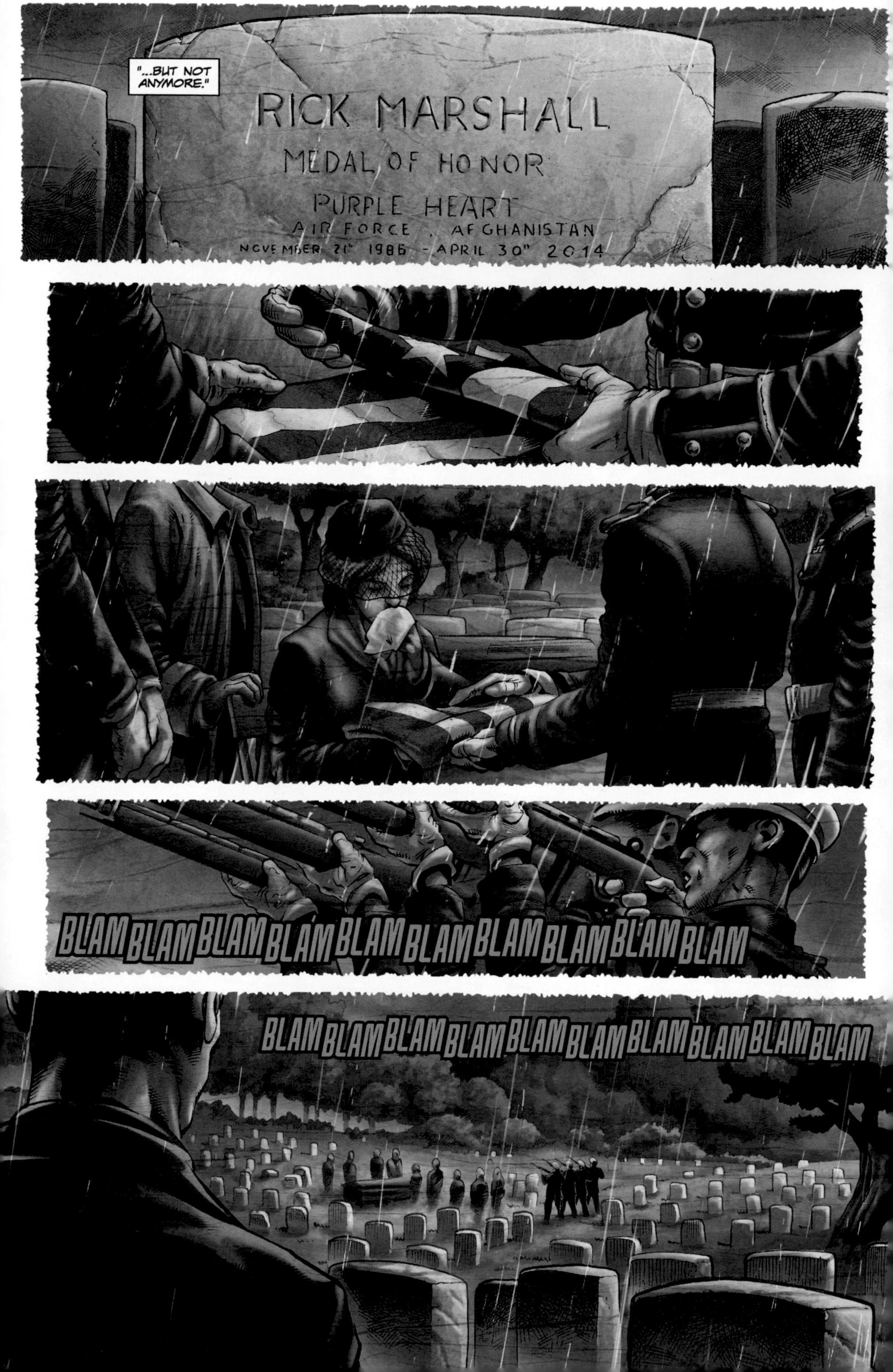
"...BUT NOT ANYMORE."
RICK MARSHALL
MEDAL OF HONOR
PURPLE HEART
AIR FORCE , AFGHANISTAN
NOVEMBER 21st 1986 - APRIL 30th 2014
BLAM BLAM BLAM BLAM BLAM BLAM BLAM BLAM BLAM BLAM
BLAM BLAM BLAM BLAM BLAM BLAM BLAM BLAM BLAM BLAM

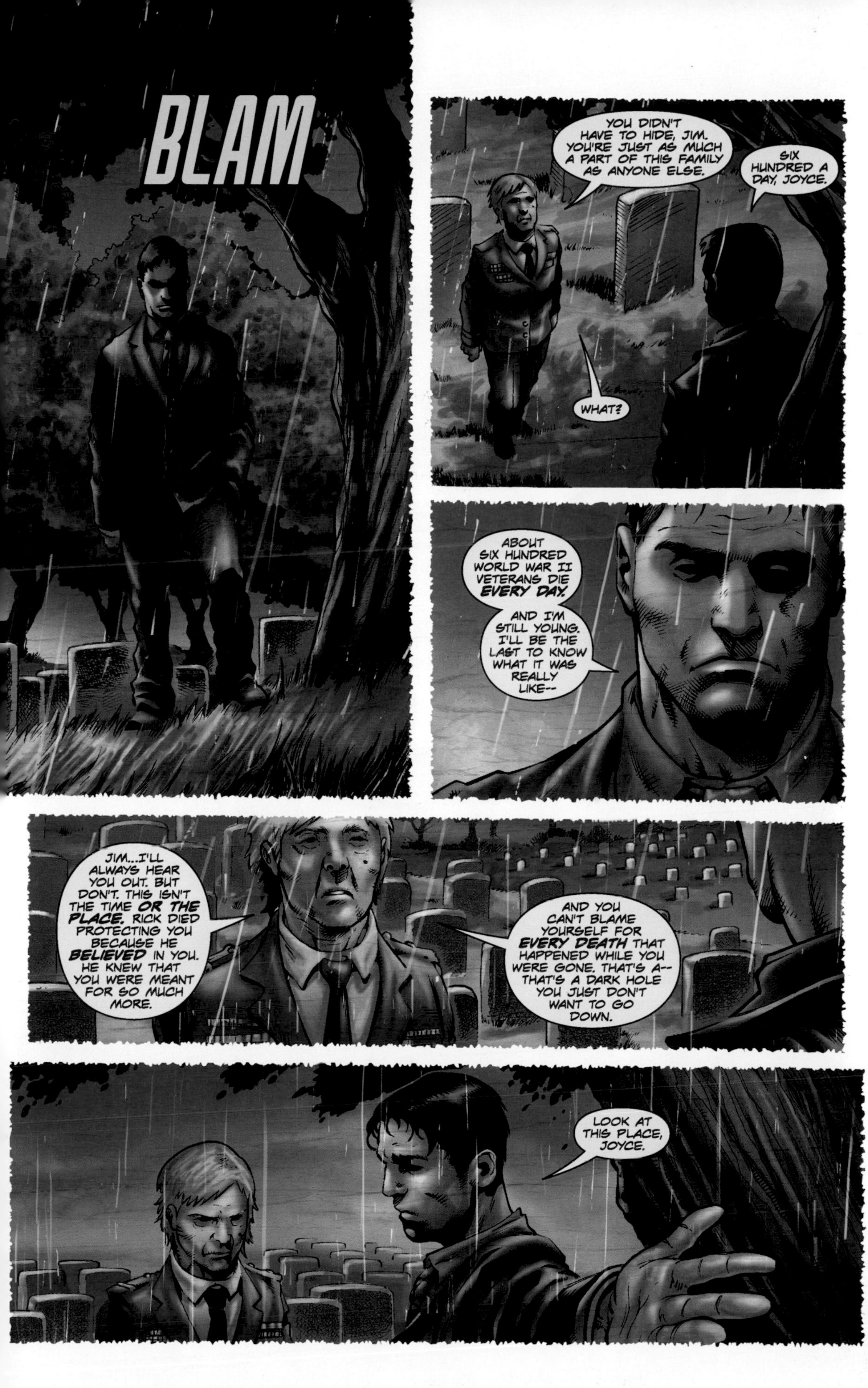
BLAM
YOU DIDN'T HAVE TO HIDE, JIM. YOU'RE JUST AS MUCH A PART OF THIS FAMILY AS ANYONE ELSE.
SIX HUNDRED A DAY, JOYCE.
WHAT?
ABOUT SIX HUNDRED WORLD WAR II VETERANS DIE EVERY DAY.
AND I'M STILL YOUNG. I'LL BE THE LAST TO KNOW WHAT IT WAS REALLY LIKE--
JIM...I'LL ALWAYS HEAR YOU OUT. BUT DON'T. THIS ISN'T THE TIME OR THE PLACE. RICK DIED PROTECTING YOU BECAUSE HE BELIEVED IN YOU. HE KNEW THAT YOU WERE MEANT FOR SO MUCH MORE.
AND YOU CAN'T BLAME YOURSELF FOR EVERY DEATH THAT HAPPENED WHILE YOU WERE GONE. THAT'S A-- THAT'S A DARK HOLE YOU JUST DON'T WANT TO GO DOWN.
LOOK AT THIS PLACE, JOYCE.

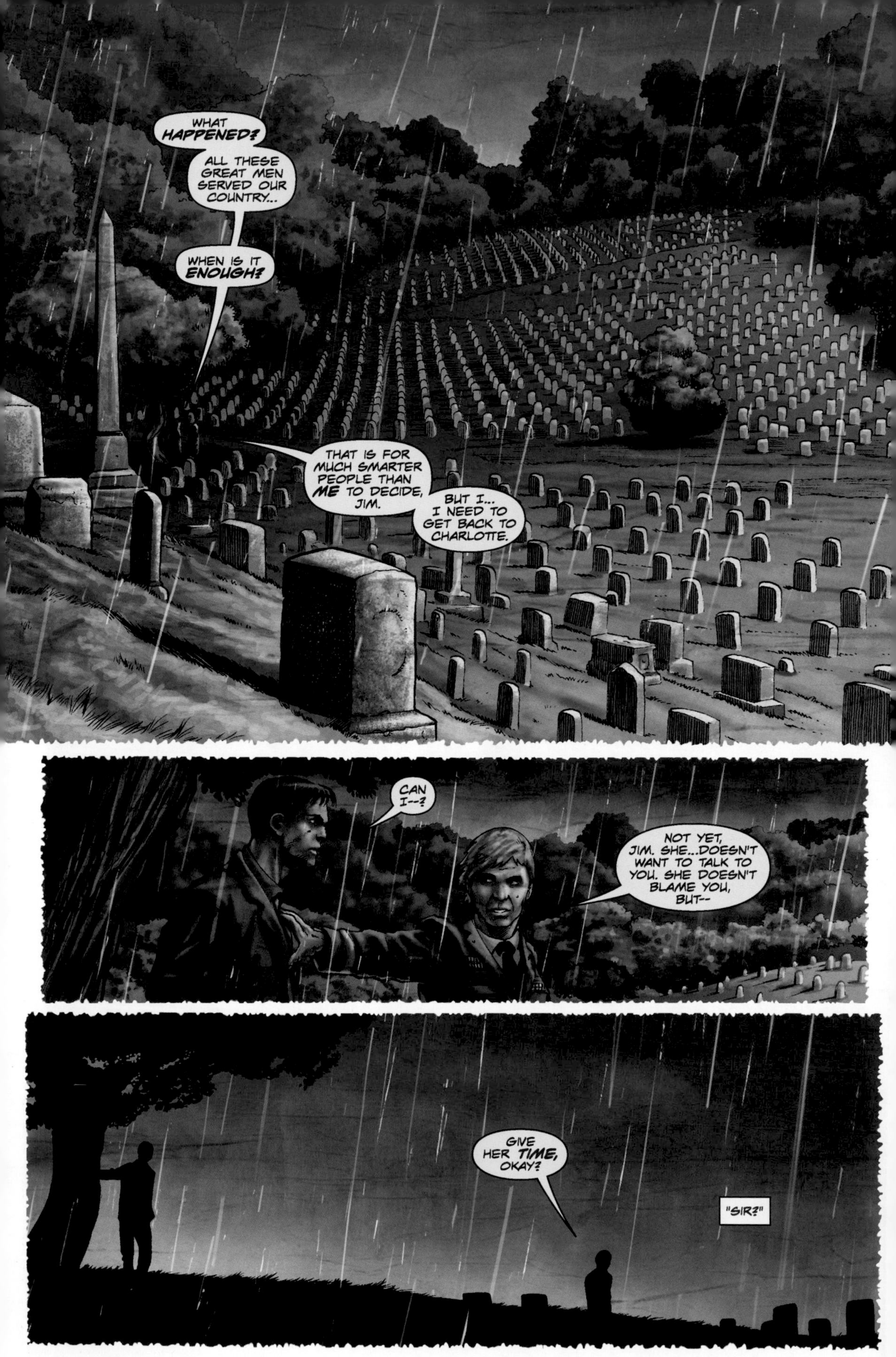
WHAT HAPPENED?
ALL THESE GREAT MEN SERVED OUR COUNTRY...
WHEN IS IT ENOUGH?
THAT IS FOR MUCH SMARTER PEOPLE THAN ME TO DECIDE, JIM.
BUT I... I NEED TO GET BACK TO CHARLOTTE.
CAN I--?
NOT YET, JIM. SHE...DOESN'T WANT TO TALK TO YOU. SHE DOESN'T BLAME YOU, BUT--
GIVE HER TIME, OKAY?
"SIR?"

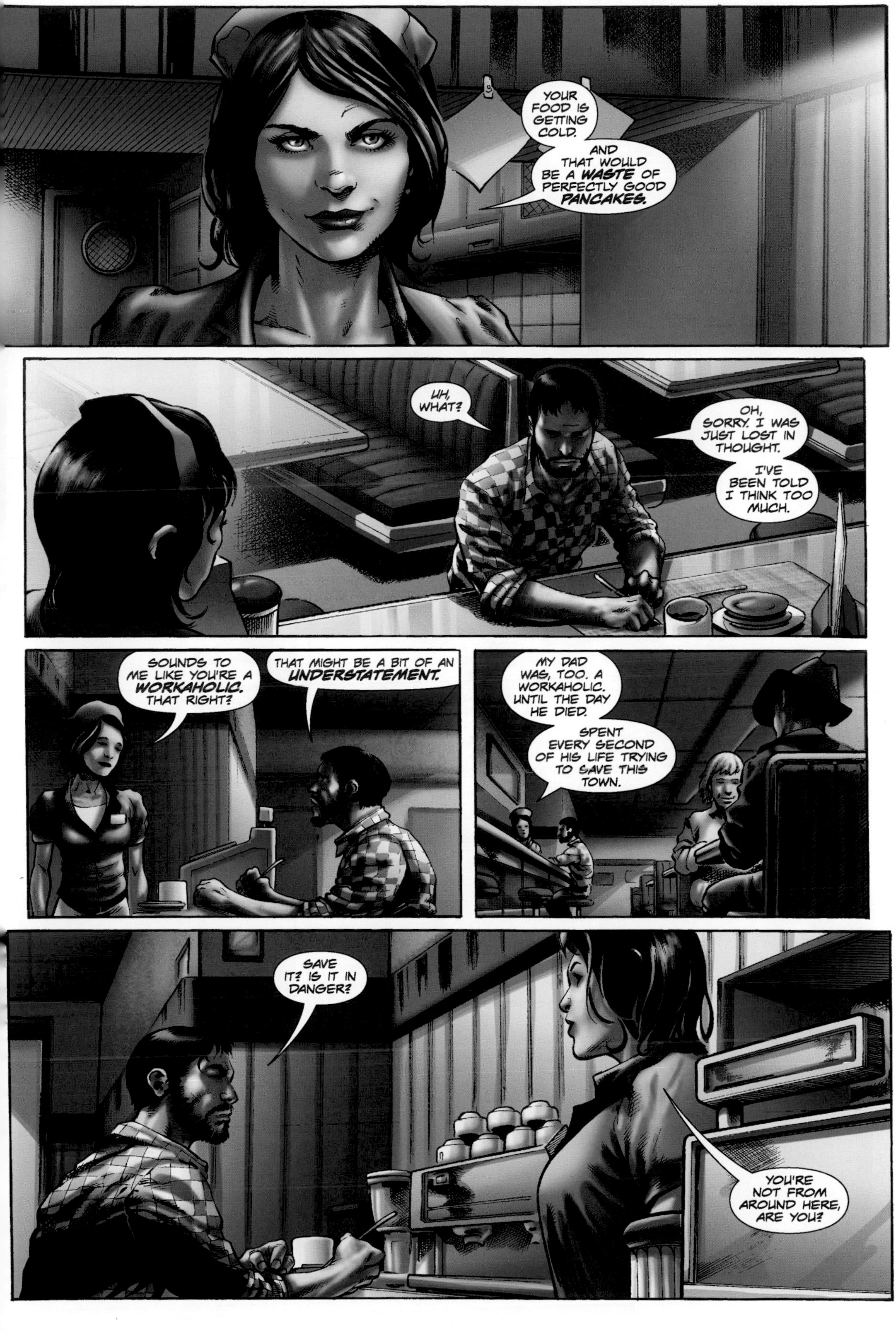
YOUR FOOD IS GETTING COLD.
AND THAT WOULD BE A WASTE OF PERFECTLY GOOD PANCAKES.
UH, WHAT?
OH, SORRY. I WAS JUST LOST IN THOUGHT.
I'VE BEEN TOLD I THINK TOO MUCH.
SOUNDS TO ME LIKE YOU'RE A WORKAHOLIC. THAT RIGHT?
THAT MIGHT BE A BIT OF AN UNDERSTATEMENT.
MY DAD WAS, TOO. A WORKAHOLIC. UNTIL THE DAY HE DIED.
SPENT EVERY SECOND OF HIS LIFE TRYING TO SAVE THIS TOWN.
SAVE IT? IS IT IN DANGER?
YOU'RE NOT FROM AROUND HERE, ARE YOU?

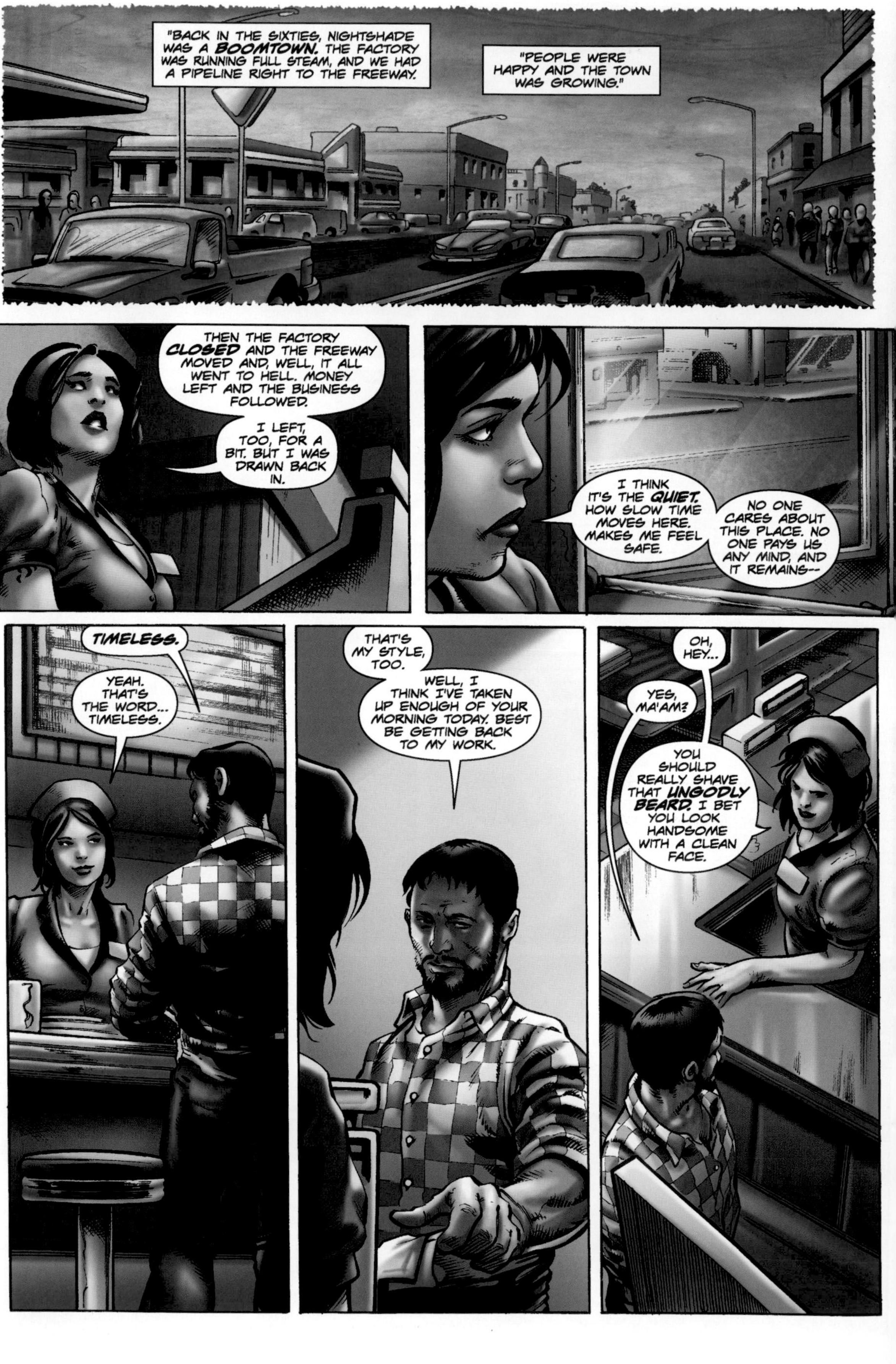
"BACK IN THE SIXTIES, NIGHTSHADE WAS A BOOMTOWN. THE FACTORY WAS RUNNING FULL STEAM, AND WE HAD A PIPELINE RIGHT TO THE FREEWAY.
"PEOPLE WERE HAPPY AND THE TOWN WAS GROWING."
THEN THE FACTORY CLOSED AND THE FREEWAY MOVED AND, WELL, IT ALL WENT TO HELL. MONEY LEFT AND THE BUSINESS FOLLOWED.
I LEFT, TOO, FOR A BIT. BUT I WAS DRAWN BACK IN.
I THINK IT'S THE QUIET. HOW SLOW TIME MOVES HERE. MAKES ME FEEL SAFE.
NO ONE CARES ABOUT THIS PLACE. NO ONE PAYS US ANY MIND, AND IT REMAINS--
TIMELESS.
YEAH. THAT'S THE WORD... TIMELESS.
THAT'S MY STYLE, TOO.
WELL, I THINK I'VE TAKEN UP ENOUGH OF YOUR MORNING TODAY. BEST BE GETTING BACK TO MY WORK.
OH, HEY...
YES, MA'AM?
YOU SHOULD REALLY SHAVE THAT UNGODLY BEARD. I BET YOU LOOK HANDSOME WITH A CLEAN FACE.

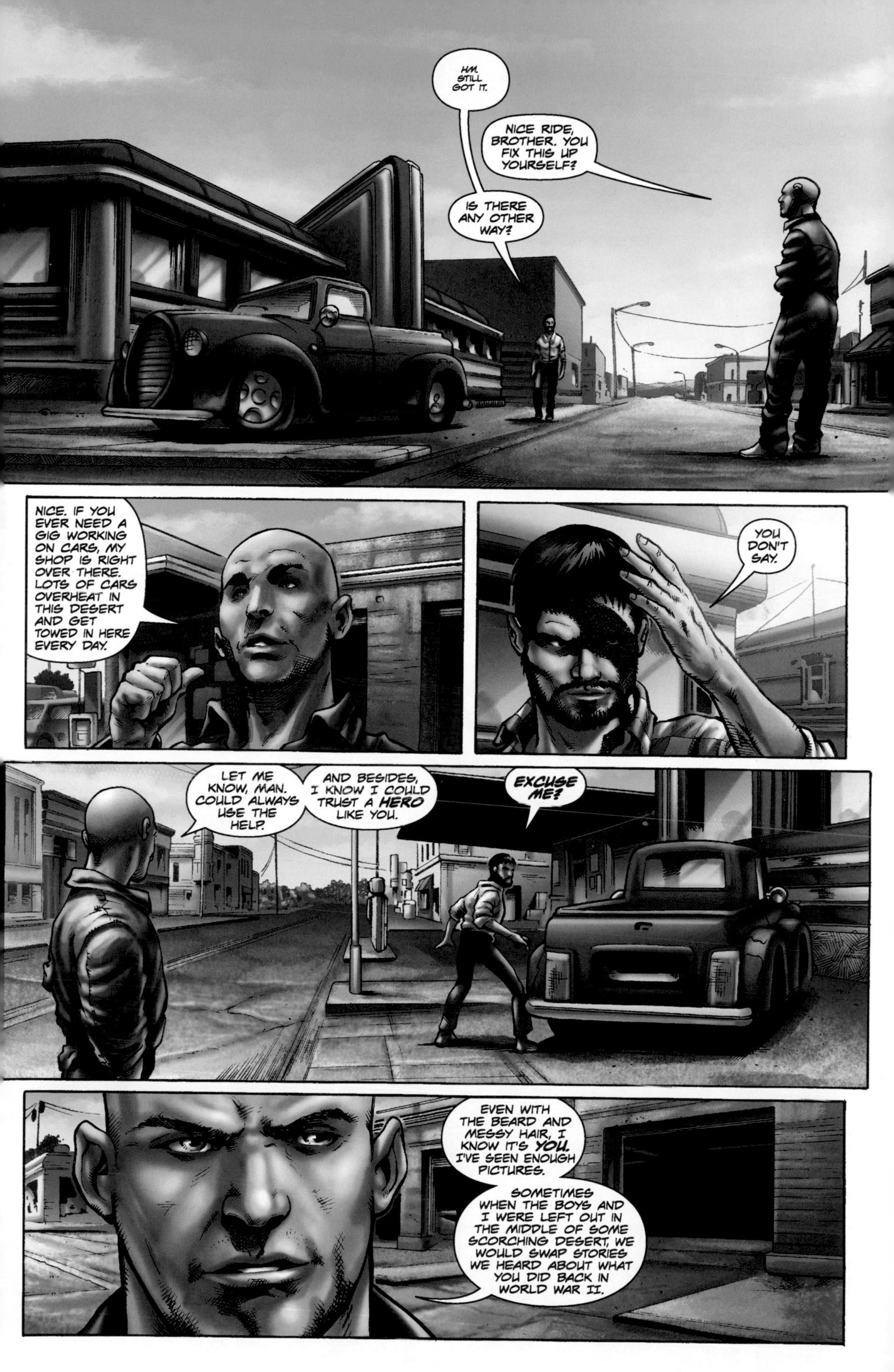
HM. STILL GOT IT.
NICE RIDE, BROTHER. YOU FIX THIS UP YOURSELF?
IS THERE ANY OTHER WAY?
NICE. IF YOU EVER NEED A GIG WORKING ON CARS, MY SHOP IS RIGHT OVER THERE. LOTS OF CARS OVERHEAT IN THIS DESERT AND GET TOWED IN HERE EVERY DAY.
YOU DON'T SAY.
LET ME KNOW, MAN. COULD ALWAYS USE THE HELP.
AND BESIDES, I KNOW I COULD TRUST A HERO LIKE YOU.
EXCUSE ME?
EVEN WITH THE BEARD AND MESSY HAIR, I KNOW IT'S YOU. I'VE SEEN ENOUGH PICTURES.
SOMETIMES WHEN THE BOYS AND I WERE LEFT OUT IN THE MIDDLE OF SOME SCORCHING DESERT, WE WOULD SWAP STORIES WE HEARD ABOUT WHAT YOU DID BACK IN WORLD WAR II.

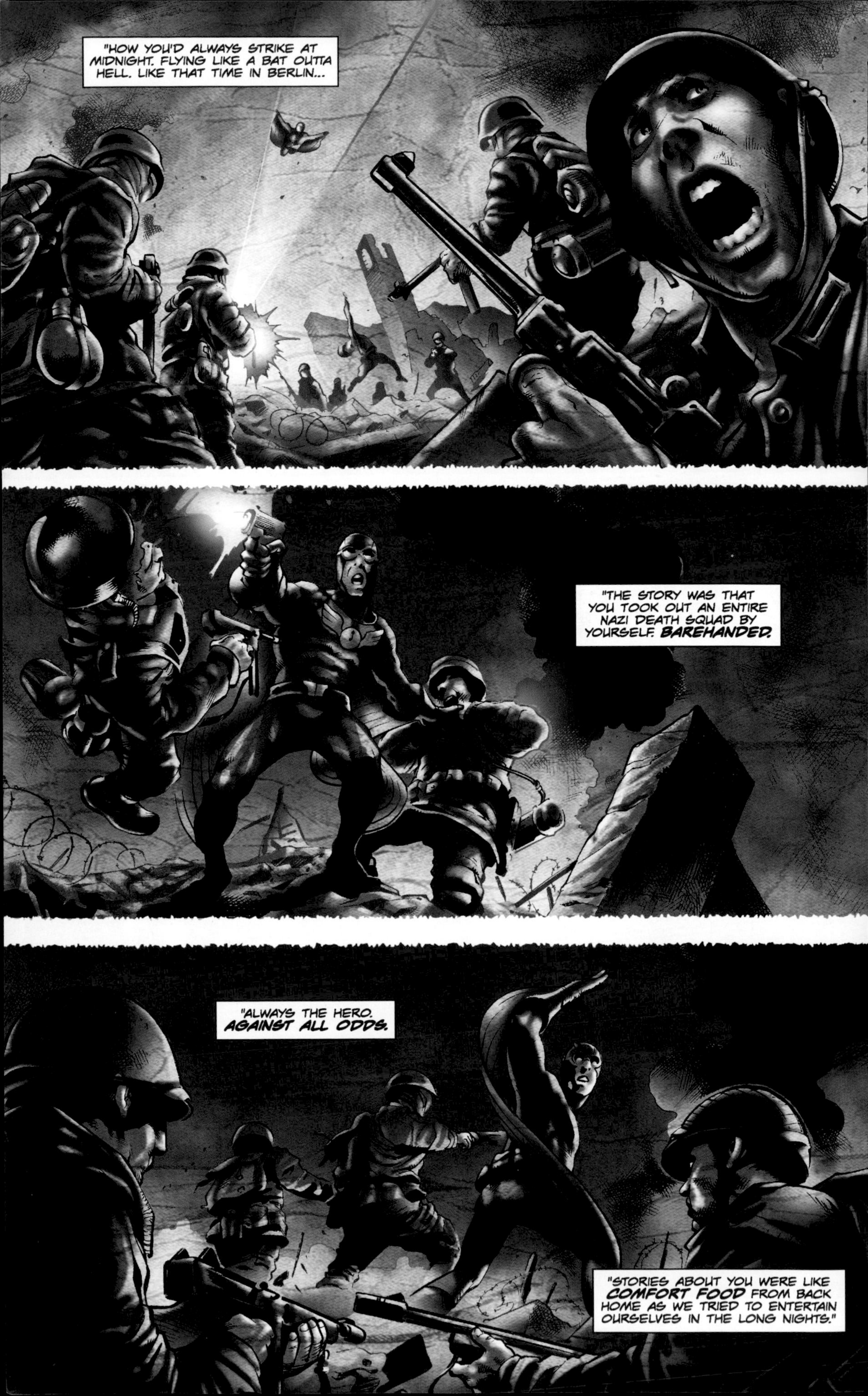
"HOW YOU'D ALWAYS STRIKE AT MIDNIGHT. FLYING LIKE A BAT OUTTA HELL. LIKE THAT TIME IN BERLIN...
"THE STORY WAS THAT YOU TOOK OUT AN ENTIRE NAZI DEATH SQUAD BY YOURSELF. BAREHANDED.
"ALWAYS THE HERO. AGAINST ALL ODDS.
"STORIES ABOUT YOU WERE LIKE COMFORT FOOD FROM BACK HOME AS WE TRIED TO ENTERTAIN OURSELVES IN THE LONG NIGHTS."

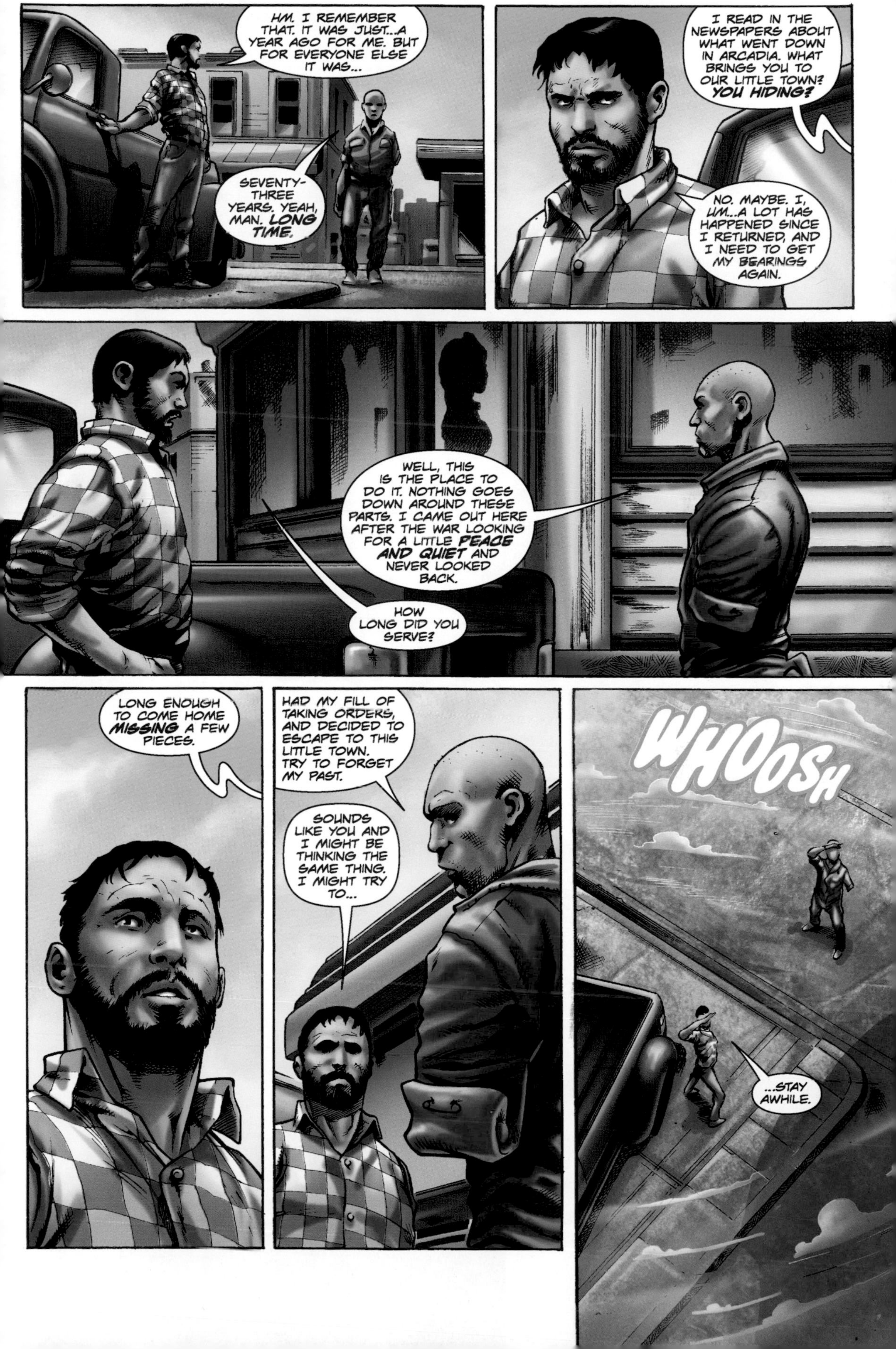
HM. I REMEMBER THAT. IT WAS JUST...A YEAR AGO FOR ME. BUT FOR EVERYONE ELSE IT WAS...
SEVENTY-THREE YEARS. YEAH, MAN. LONG TIME.
I READ IN THE NEWSPAPERS ABOUT WHAT WENT DOWN IN ARCADIA. WHAT BRINGS YOU TO OUR LITTLE TOWN? YOU HIDING?
NO. MAYBE. I, UM...A LOT HAS HAPPENED SINCE I RETURNED, AND I NEED TO GET MY BEARINGS AGAIN.
WELL, THIS IS THE PLACE TO DO IT. NOTHING GOES DOWN AROUND THESE PARTS. I CAME OUT HERE AFTER THE WAR LOOKING FOR A LITTLE PEACE AND QUIET AND NEVER LOOKED BACK.
HOW LONG DID YOU SERVE?
LONG ENOUGH TO COME HOME MISSING A FEW PIECES.
HAD MY FILL OF TAKING ORDERS, AND DECIDED TO ESCAPE TO THIS LITTLE TOWN. TRY TO FORGET MY PAST.
SOUNDS LIKE YOU AND I MIGHT BE THINKING THE SAME THING. I MIGHT TRY TO...
WHOOSH
...STAY AWHILE.

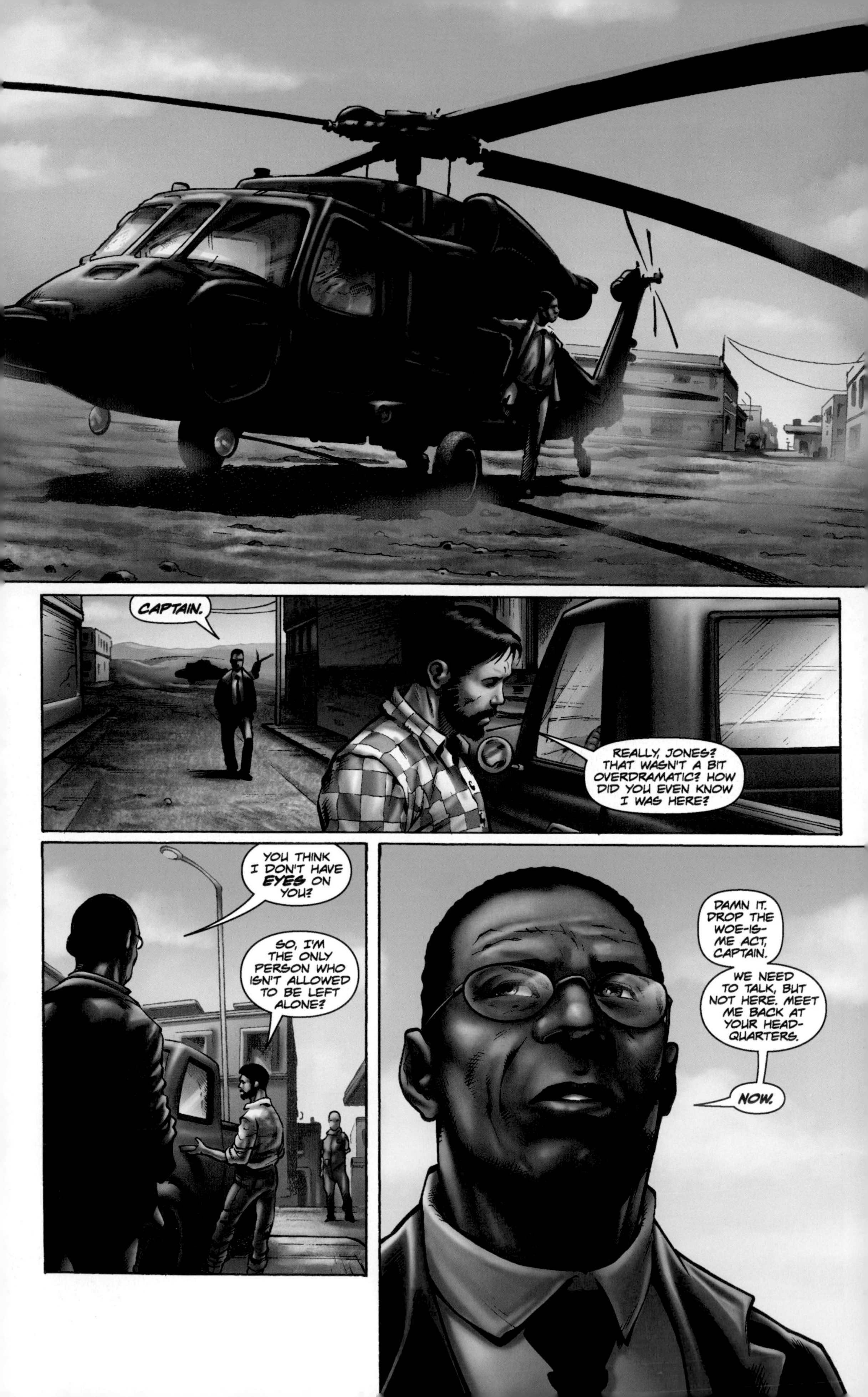
CAPTAIN.
REALLY, JONES? THAT WASN'T A BIT OVERDRAMATIC? HOW DID YOU EVEN KNOW I WAS HERE?
YOU THINK I DON'T HAVE EYES ON YOU?
SO, I'M THE ONLY PERSON WHO ISN'T ALLOWED TO BE LEFT ALONE?
DAMN IT. DROP THE WOE-IS-ME ACT, CAPTAIN.
WE NEED TO TALK, BUT NOT HERE. MEET ME BACK AT YOUR HEAD-QUARTERS.
NOW.

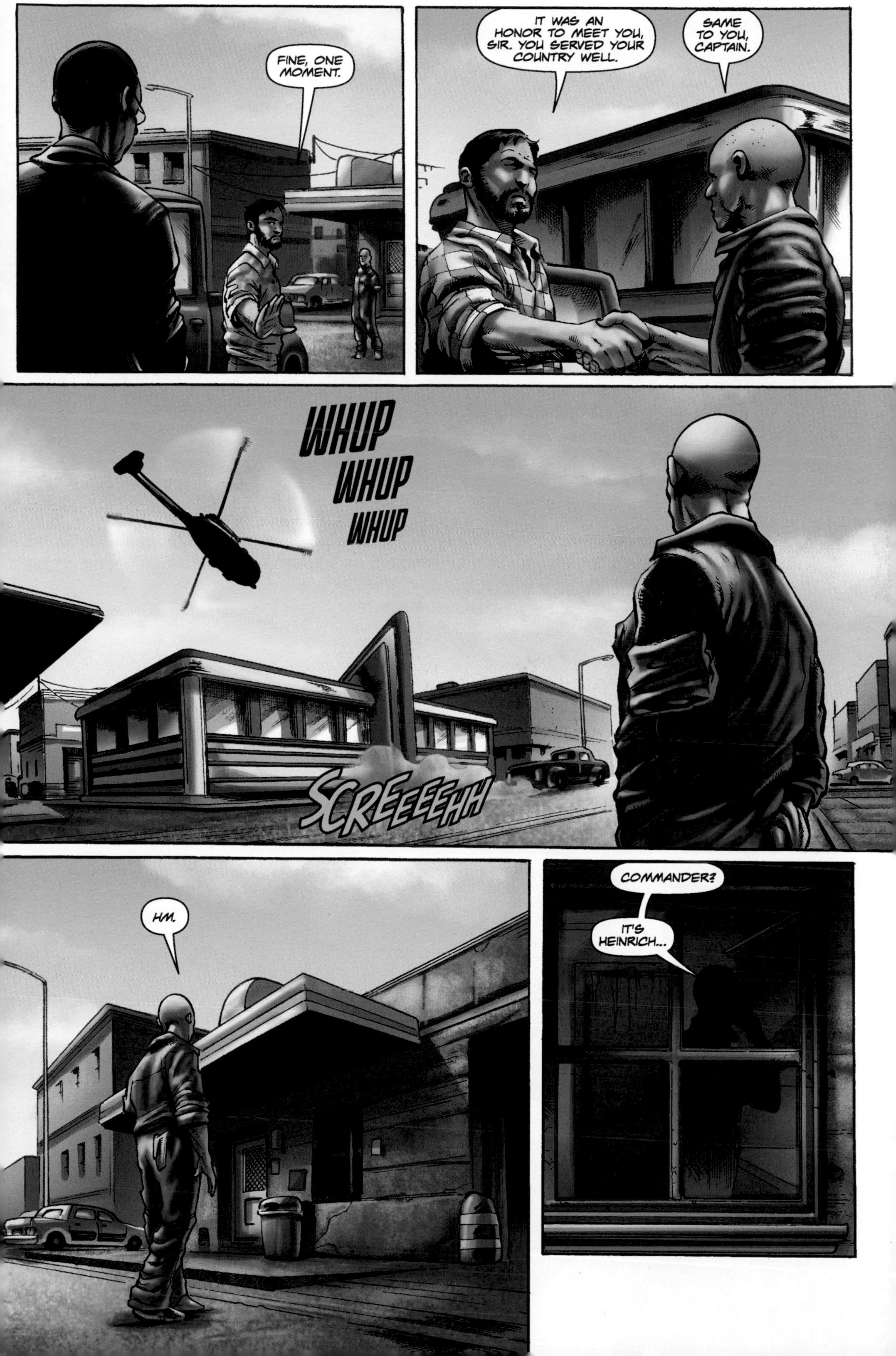
FINE, ONE MOMENT.
IT WAS AN HONOR TO MEET YOU, SIR. YOU SERVED YOUR COUNTRY WELL.
SAME TO YOU, CAPTAIN.
WHUP WHUP WHUP
SCREEEEHH
HM.
COMMANDER?
IT'S HEINRICH...

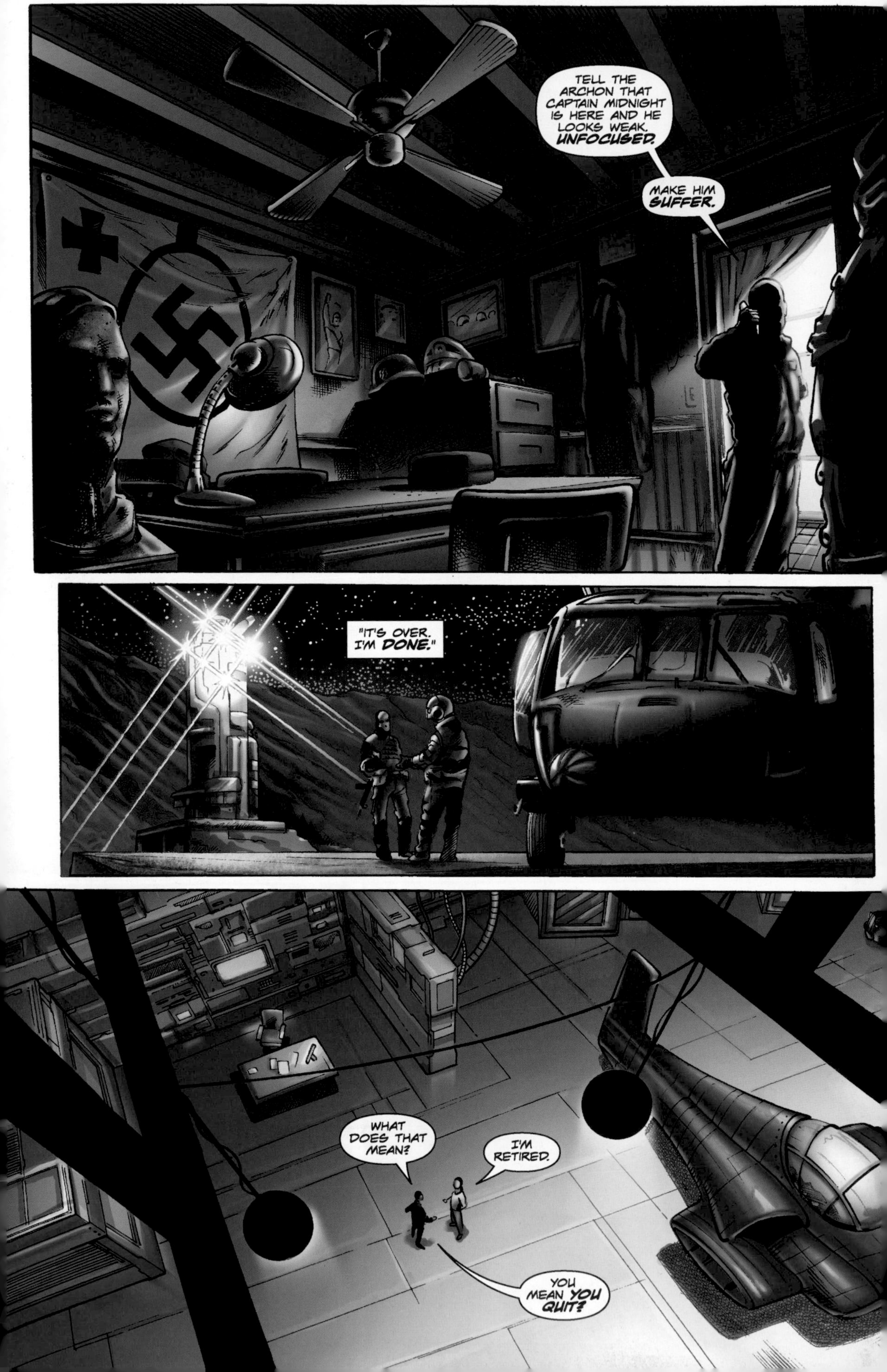
TELL THE ARCHON THAT CAPTAIN MIDNIGHT IS HERE AND HE LOOKS WEAK. UNFOCUSED.
MAKE HIM SUFFER.
"IT'S OVER. I'M DONE."
WHAT DOES THAT MEAN?
I'M RETIRED.
YOU MEAN YOU QUIT?

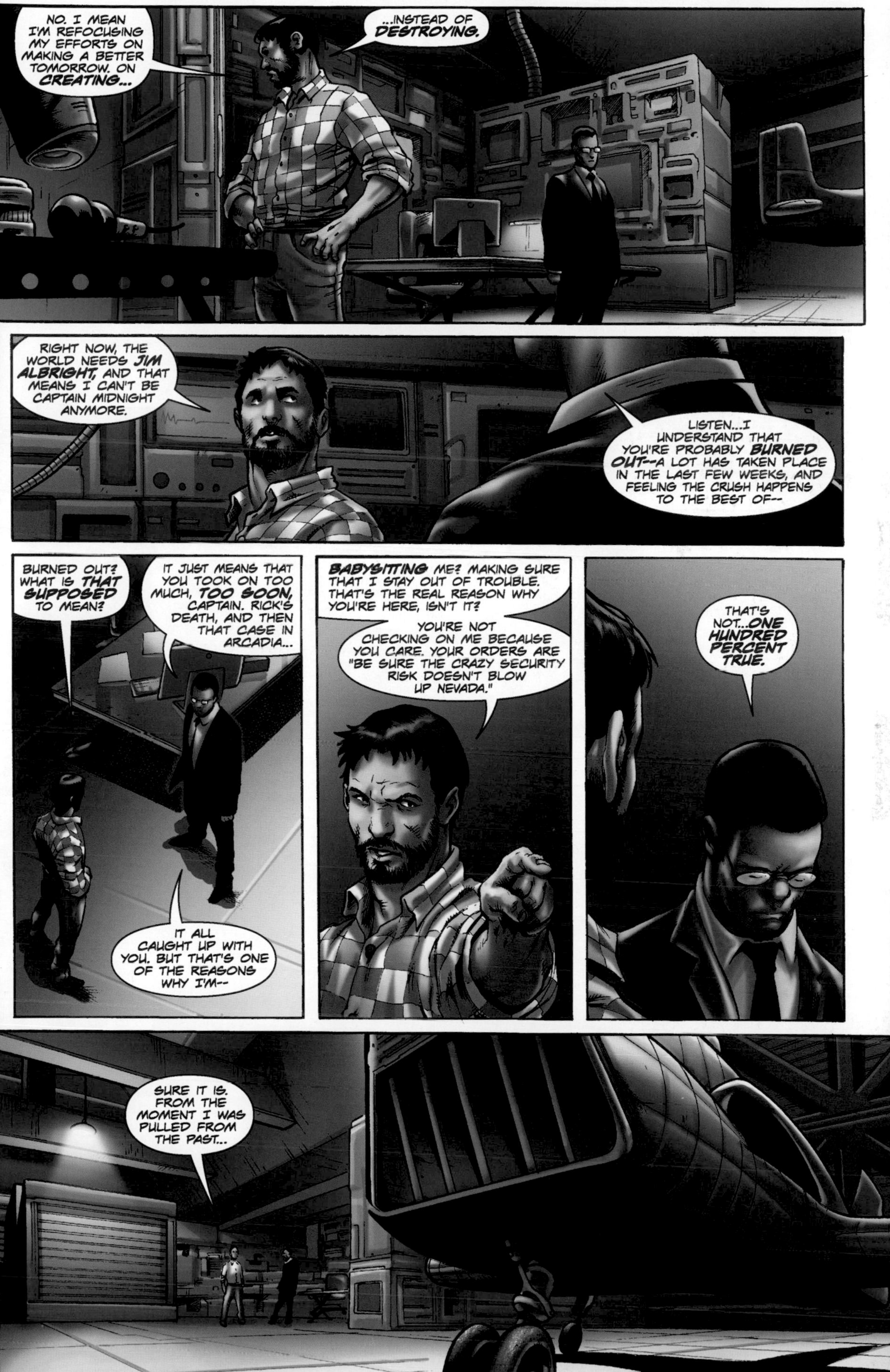
NO. I MEAN I'M REFOCUSING MY EFFORTS ON MAKING A BETTER TOMORROW. ON CREATING...
...INSTEAD OF DESTROYING.
RIGHT NOW, THE WORLD NEEDS JIM ALBRIGHT, AND THAT MEANS I CAN'T BE CAPTAIN MIDNIGHT ANYMORE.
LISTEN...I UNDERSTAND THAT YOU'RE PROBABLY BURNED OUT--A LOT HAS TAKEN PLACE IN THE LAST FEW WEEKS, AND FEELING THE CRUSH HAPPENS TO THE BEST OF--
BURNED OUT? WHAT IS THAT SUPPOSED TO MEAN?
IT JUST MEANS THAT YOU TOOK ON TOO MUCH, TOO SOON, CAPTAIN. RICK'S DEATH, AND THEN THAT CASE IN ARCADIA...
IT ALL CAUGHT UP WITH YOU. BUT THAT'S ONE OF THE REASONS WHY I'M--
BABYSITTING ME? MAKING SURE THAT I STAY OUT OF TROUBLE. THAT'S THE REAL REASON WHY YOU'RE HERE, ISN'T IT?
YOU'RE NOT CHECKING ON ME BECAUSE YOU CARE. YOUR ORDERS ARE "BE SURE THE CRAZY SECURITY RISK DOESN'T BLOW UP NEVADA."
THAT'S NOT...ONE HUNDRED PERCENT TRUE.
SURE IT IS. FROM THE MOMENT I WAS PULLED FROM THE PAST...

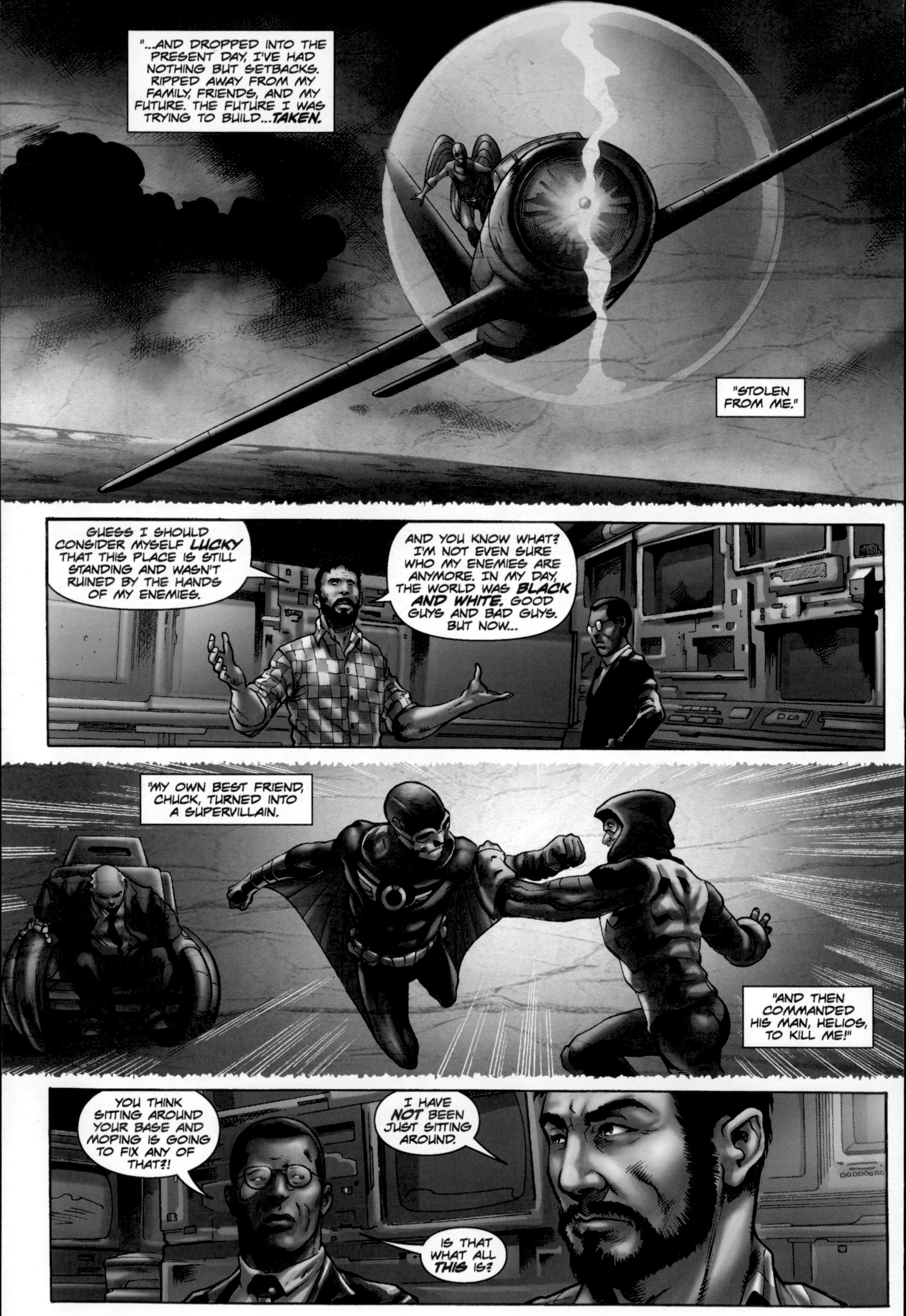
"...AND DROPPED INTO THE PRESENT DAY, I'VE HAD NOTHING BUT SETBACKS. RIPPED AWAY FROM MY FAMILY, FRIENDS, AND MY FUTURE. THE FUTURE I WAS TRYING TO BUILD...**TAKEN.**
"STOLEN FROM ME."
GUESS I SHOULD CONSIDER MYSELF **LUCKY** THAT THIS PLACE IS STILL STANDING AND WASN'T RUINED BY THE HANDS OF MY ENEMIES.
AND YOU KNOW WHAT? I'M NOT EVEN SURE WHO MY ENEMIES ARE ANYMORE. IN MY DAY, THE WORLD WAS **BLACK AND WHITE.** GOOD GUYS AND BAD GUYS. BUT NOW...
"MY OWN BEST FRIEND, CHUCK, TURNED INTO A SUPERVILLAIN.
"AND THEN COMMANDED HIS MAN, HELIOS, TO KILL ME!"
YOU THINK SITTING AROUND YOUR BASE AND MOPING IS GOING TO FIX ANY OF THAT?!
I HAVE **NOT** BEEN JUST SITTING AROUND.
IS THAT WHAT ALL **THIS** IS?

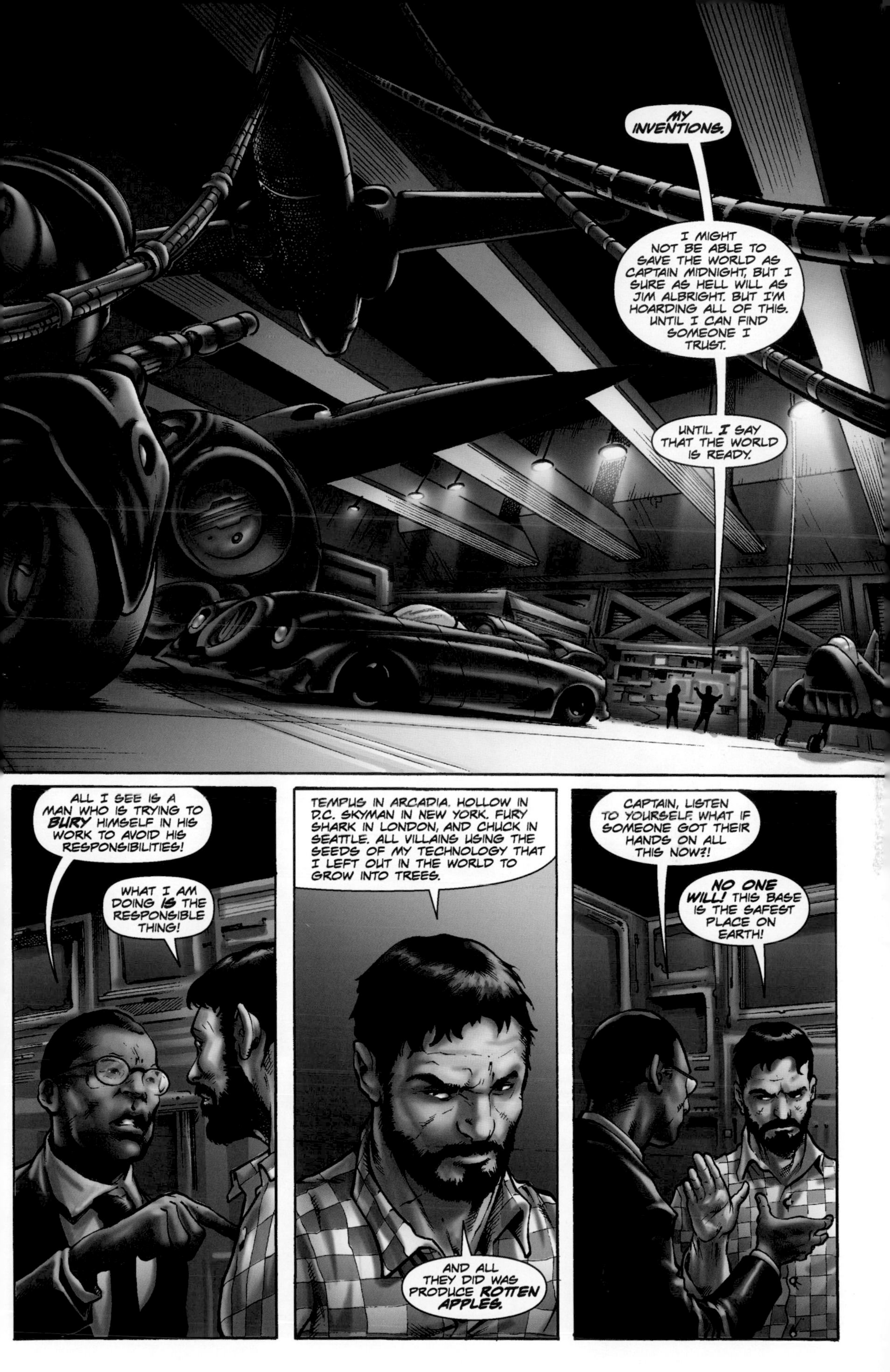
MY INVENTIONS.
I MIGHT NOT BE ABLE TO SAVE THE WORLD AS CAPTAIN MIDNIGHT, BUT I SURE AS HELL WILL AS JIM ALBRIGHT. BUT I'M HOARDING ALL OF THIS. UNTIL I CAN FIND SOMEONE I TRUST.
UNTIL I SAY THAT THE WORLD IS READY.
ALL I SEE IS A MAN WHO IS TRYING TO BURY HIMSELF IN HIS WORK TO AVOID HIS RESPONSIBILITIES!
WHAT I AM DOING IS THE RESPONSIBLE THING!
TEMPUS IN ARCADIA. HOLLOW IN D.C. SKYMAN IN NEW YORK. FURY SHARK IN LONDON, AND CHUCK IN SEATTLE. ALL VILLAINS USING THE SEEDS OF MY TECHNOLOGY THAT I LEFT OUT IN THE WORLD TO GROW INTO TREES.
AND ALL THEY DID WAS PRODUCE ROTTEN APPLES.
CAPTAIN, LISTEN TO YOURSELF. WHAT IF SOMEONE GOT THEIR HANDS ON ALL THIS NOW?!
NO ONE WILL! THIS BASE IS THE SAFEST PLACE ON EARTH!

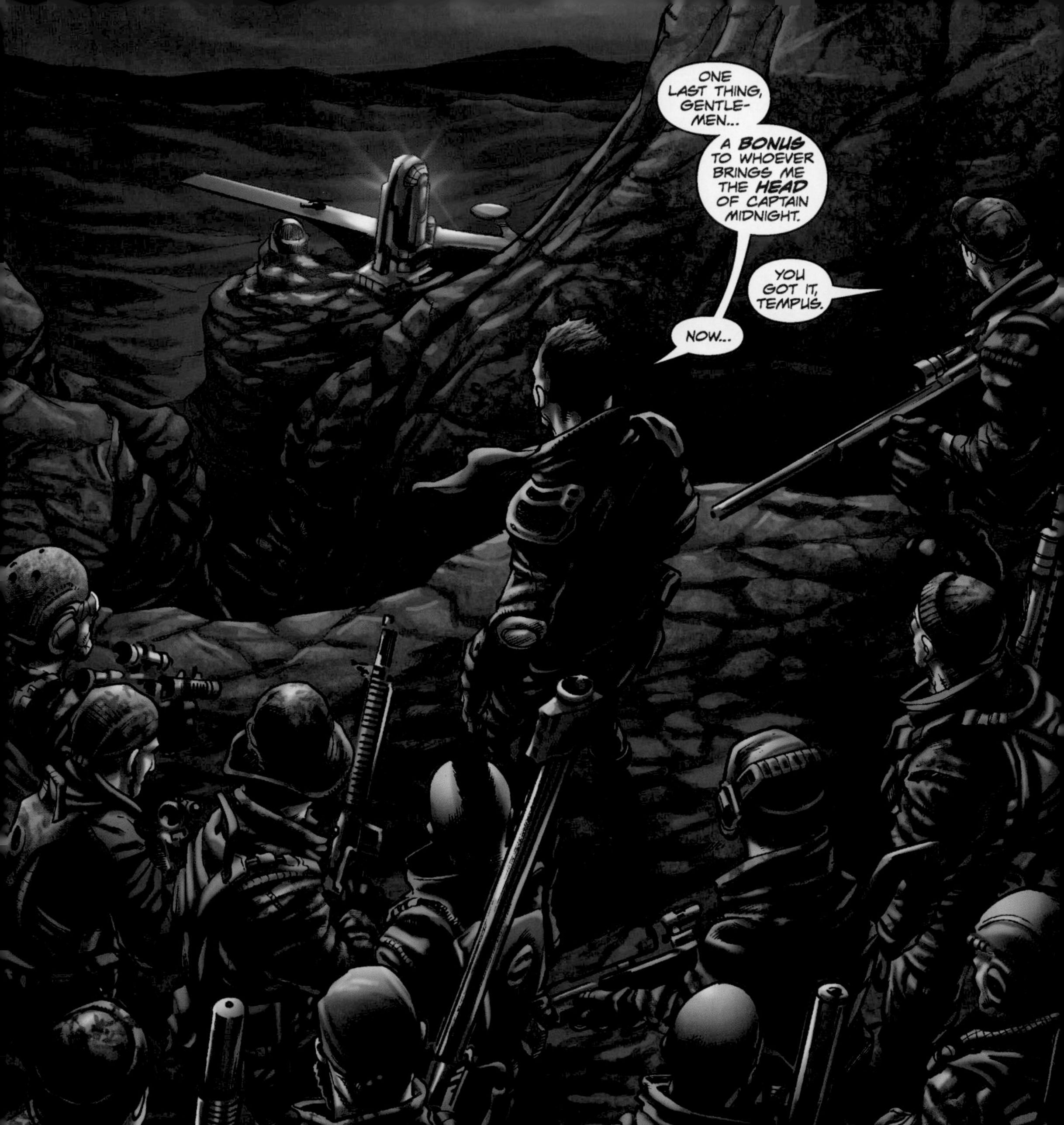
ONE LAST THING, GENTLE-MEN...
A BONUS TO WHOEVER BRINGS ME THE HEAD OF CAPTAIN MIDNIGHT.
YOU GOT IT, TEMPUS.
NOW...
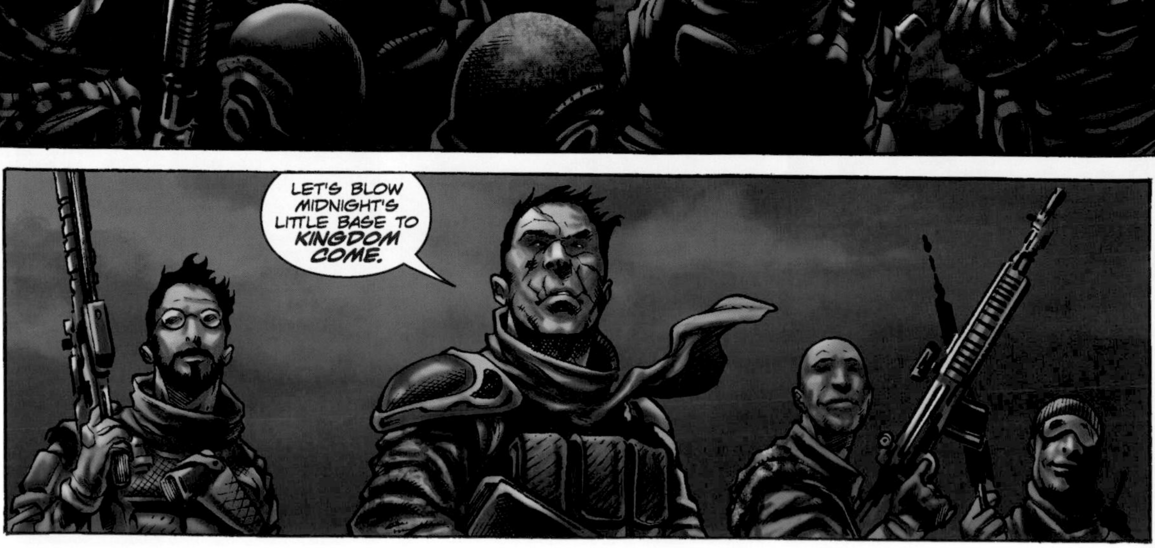
LET'S BLOW MIDNIGHT'S LITTLE BASE TO KINGDOM COME.

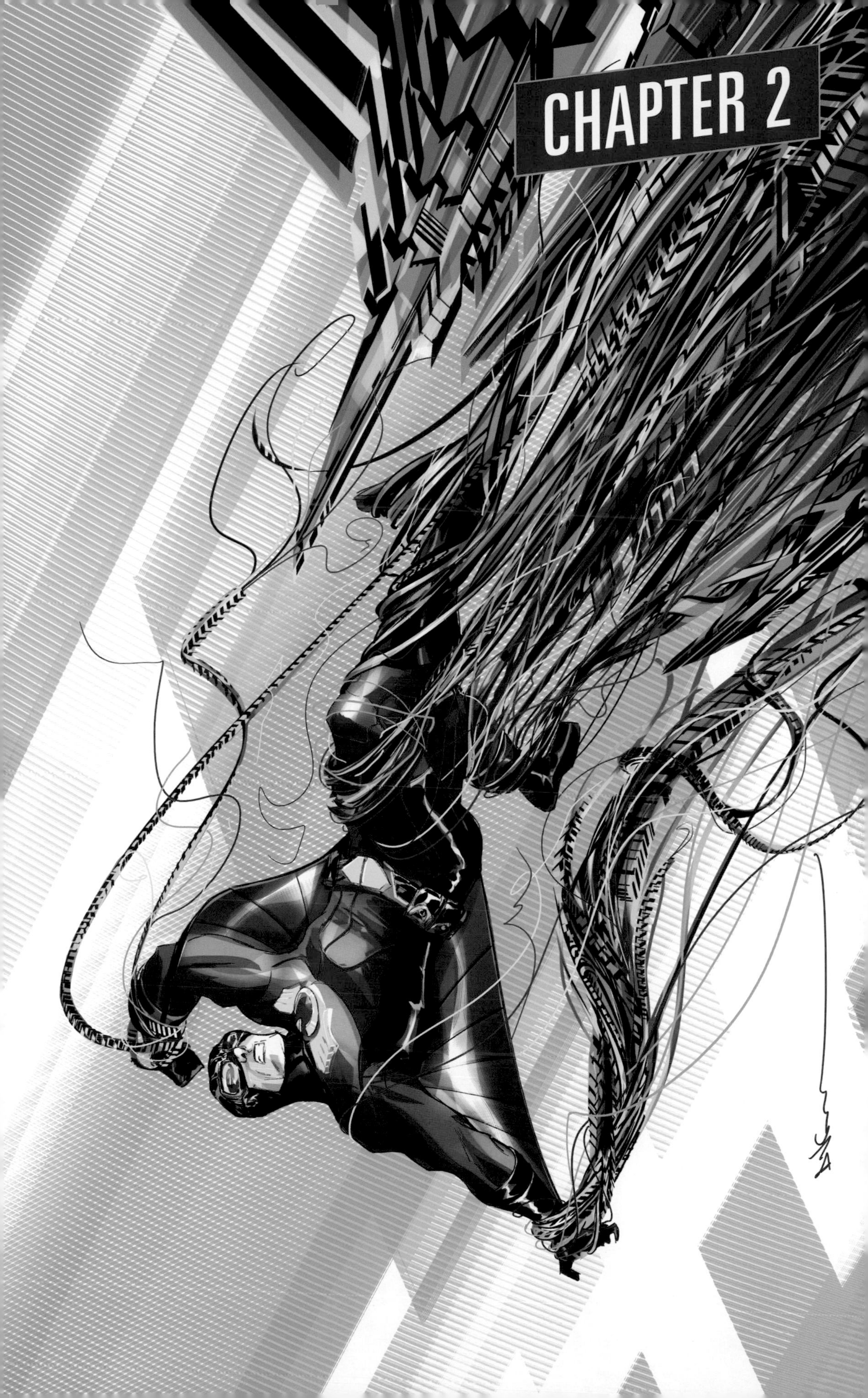
CHAPTER 2

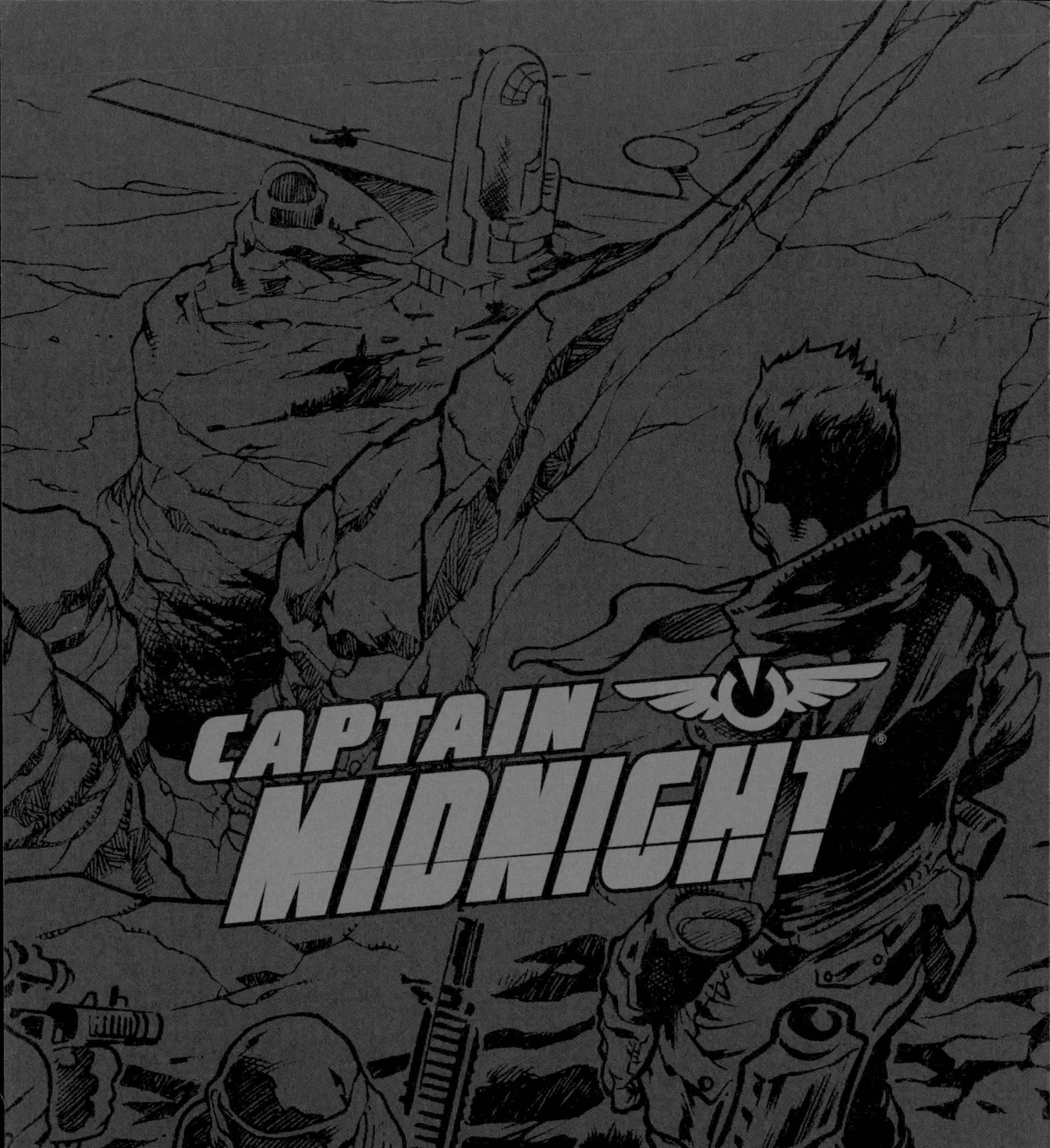
CAPTAIN
MIDNIGHT®

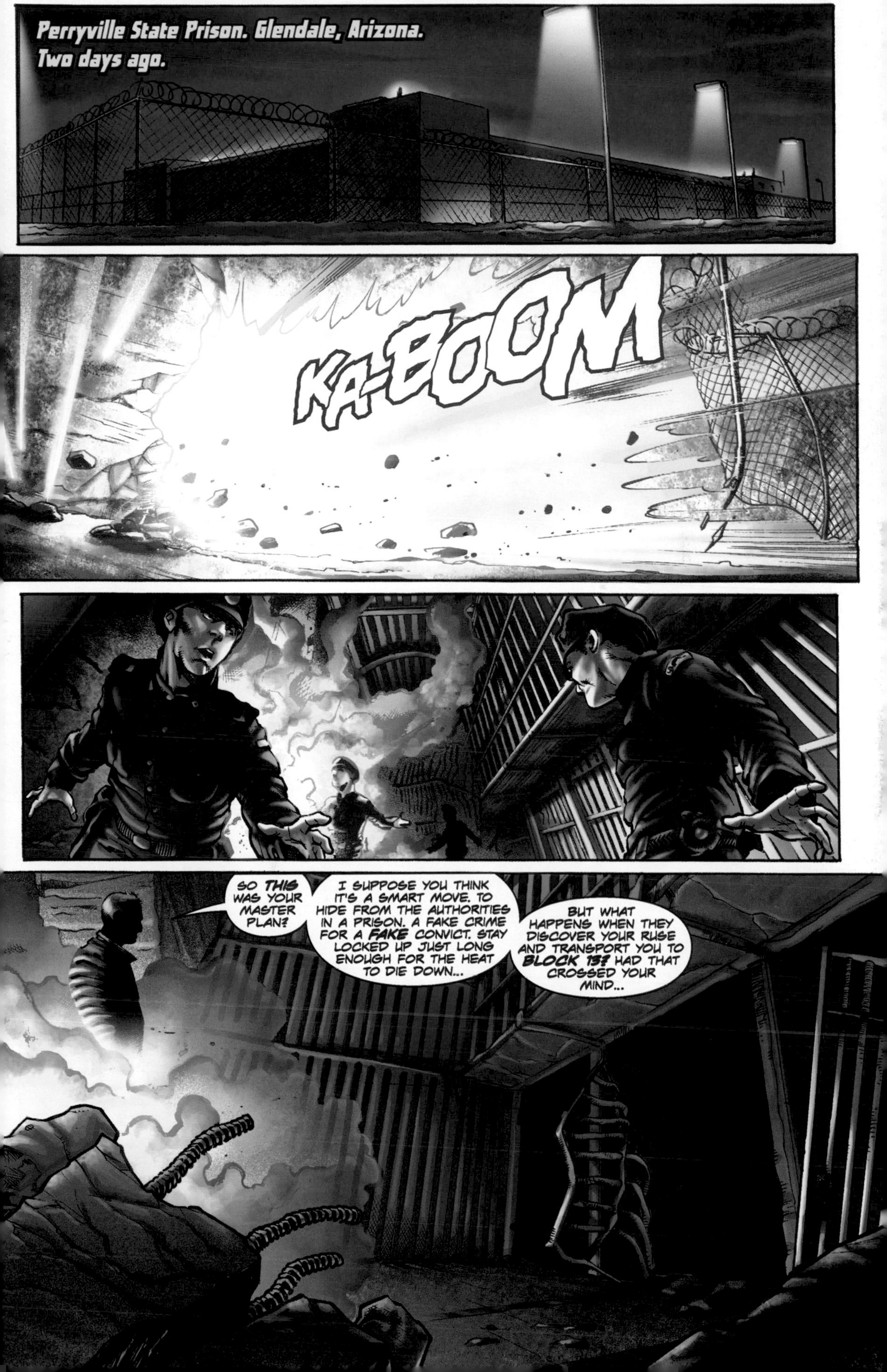
Perryville State Prison. Glendale, Arizona.
Two days ago.
KA-BOOM
SO THIS WAS YOUR MASTER PLAN?
I SUPPOSE YOU THINK IT'S A SMART MOVE. TO HIDE FROM THE AUTHORITIES IN A PRISON. A FAKE CRIME FOR A FAKE CONVICT. STAY LOCKED UP JUST LONG ENOUGH FOR THE HEAT TO DIE DOWN...
BUT WHAT HAPPENS WHEN THEY DISCOVER YOUR RUSE AND TRANSPORT YOU TO BLOCK 13? HAD THAT CROSSED YOUR MIND...

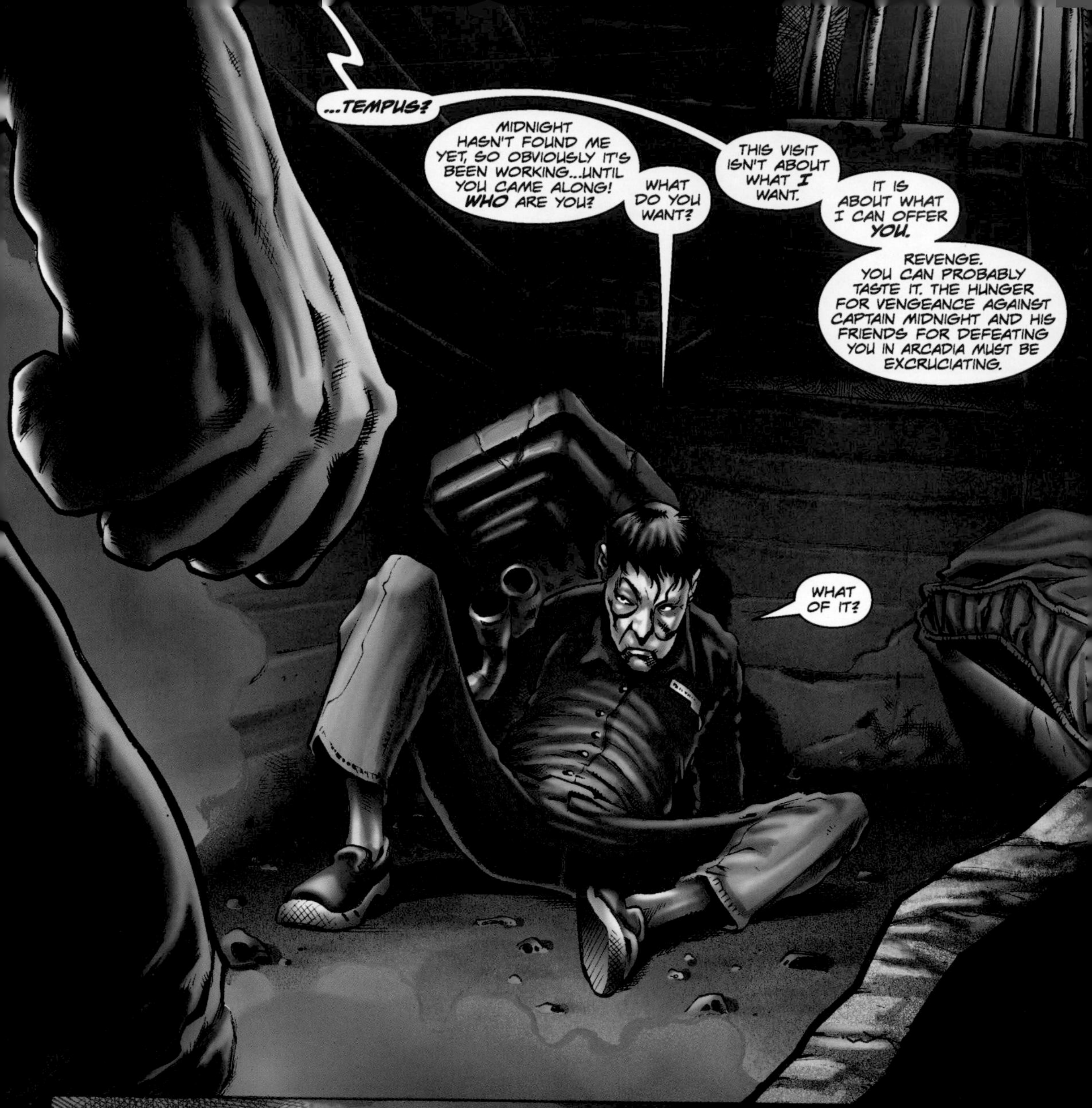
...TEMPUS?
MIDNIGHT HASN'T FOUND ME YET, SO OBVIOUSLY IT'S BEEN WORKING...UNTIL YOU CAME ALONG! WHO ARE YOU?
WHAT DO YOU WANT?
THIS VISIT ISN'T ABOUT WHAT I WANT.
IT IS ABOUT WHAT I CAN OFFER YOU.
REVENGE. YOU CAN PROBABLY TASTE IT. THE HUNGER FOR VENGEANCE AGAINST CAPTAIN MIDNIGHT AND HIS FRIENDS FOR DEFEATING YOU IN ARCADIA MUST BE EXCRUCIATING.
WHAT OF IT?

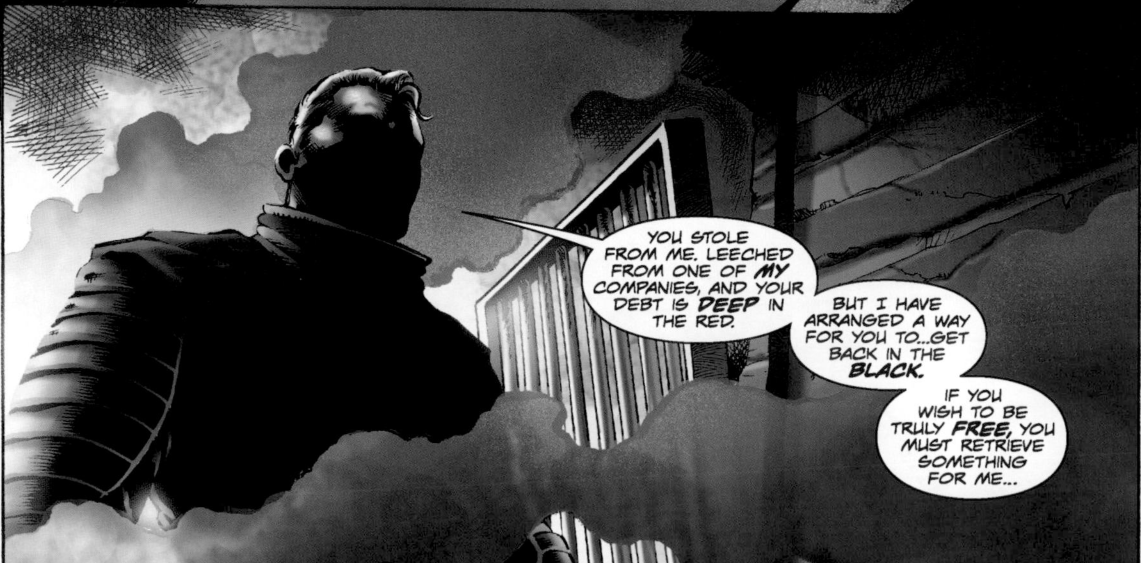
YOU STOLE FROM ME. LEECHED FROM ONE OF MY COMPANIES, AND YOUR DEBT IS DEEP IN THE RED.
BUT I HAVE ARRANGED A WAY FOR YOU TO...GET BACK IN THE BLACK.
IF YOU WISH TO BE TRULY FREE, YOU MUST RETRIEVE SOMETHING FOR ME...

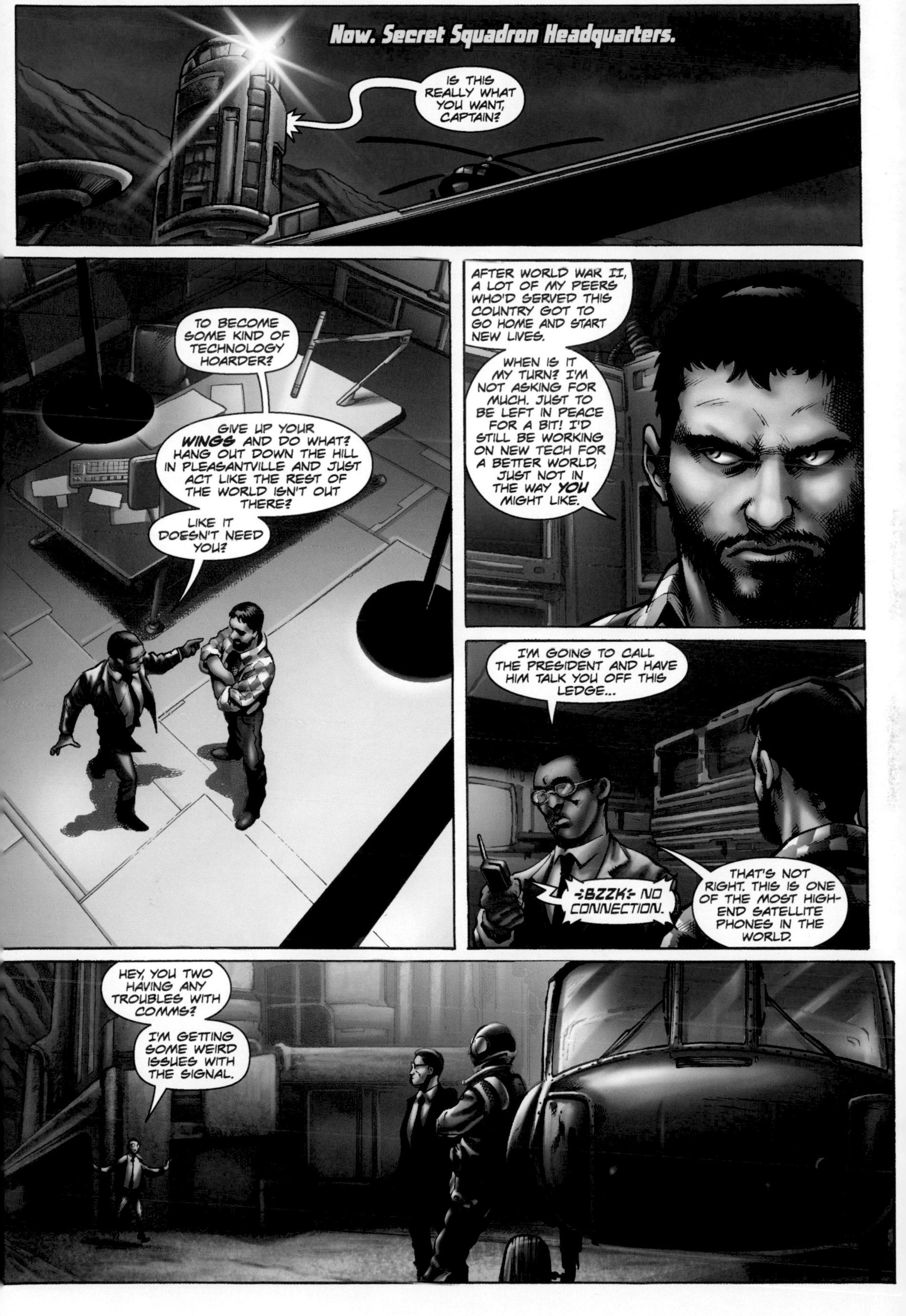
Now. Secret Squadron Headquarters.
IS THIS REALLY WHAT YOU WANT, CAPTAIN?
TO BECOME SOME KIND OF TECHNOLOGY HOARDER?
GIVE UP YOUR WINGS AND DO WHAT? HANG OUT DOWN THE HILL IN PLEASANTVILLE AND JUST ACT LIKE THE REST OF THE WORLD ISN'T OUT THERE?
LIKE IT DOESN'T NEED YOU?
AFTER WORLD WAR II, A LOT OF MY PEERS WHO'D SERVED THIS COUNTRY GOT TO GO HOME AND START NEW LIVES.
WHEN IS IT MY TURN? I'M NOT ASKING FOR MUCH. JUST TO BE LEFT IN PEACE FOR A BIT! I'D STILL BE WORKING ON NEW TECH FOR A BETTER WORLD, JUST NOT IN THE WAY YOU MIGHT LIKE.
I'M GOING TO CALL THE PRESIDENT AND HAVE HIM TALK YOU OFF THIS LEDGE...
-BZZK- NO CONNECTION.
THAT'S NOT RIGHT. THIS IS ONE OF THE MOST HIGH-END SATELLITE PHONES IN THE WORLD.
HEY, YOU TWO HAVING ANY TROUBLES WITH COMMS?
I'M GETTING SOME WEIRD ISSUES WITH THE SIGNAL.

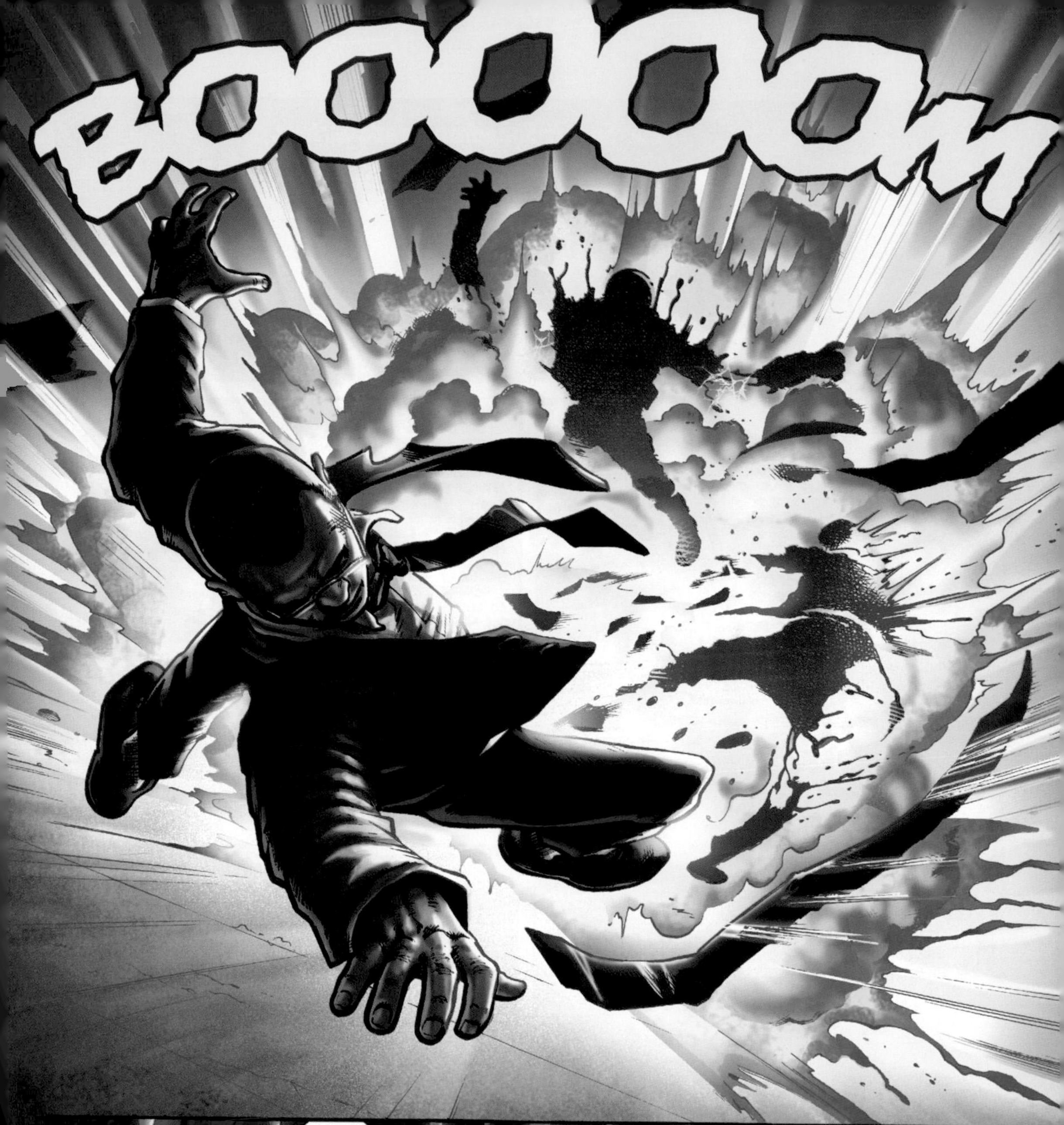
BOOOOOM

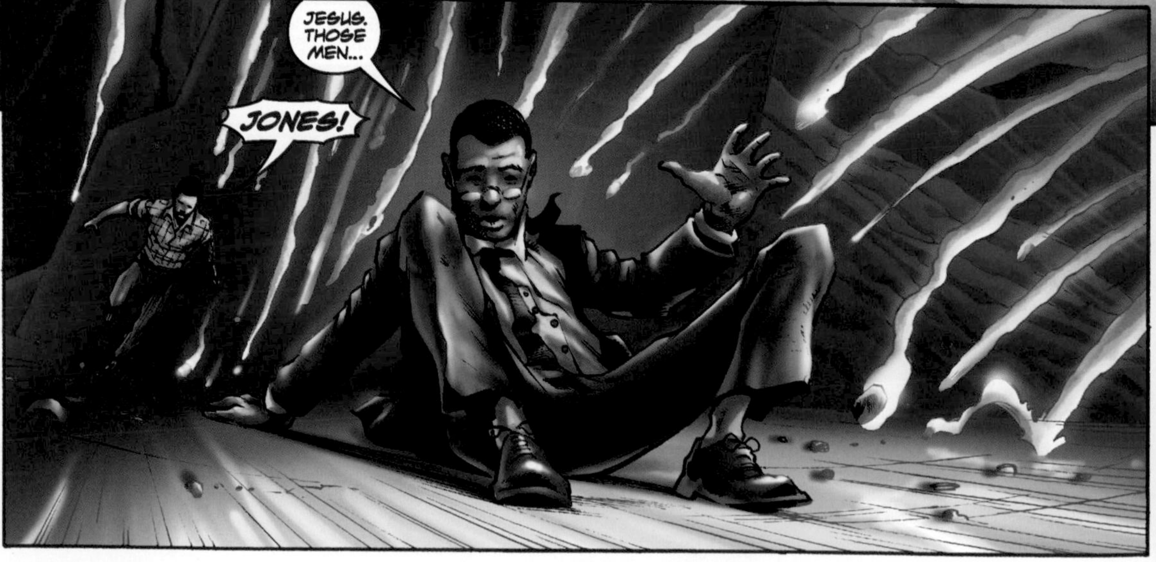
JESUS. THOSE MEN...
JONES!

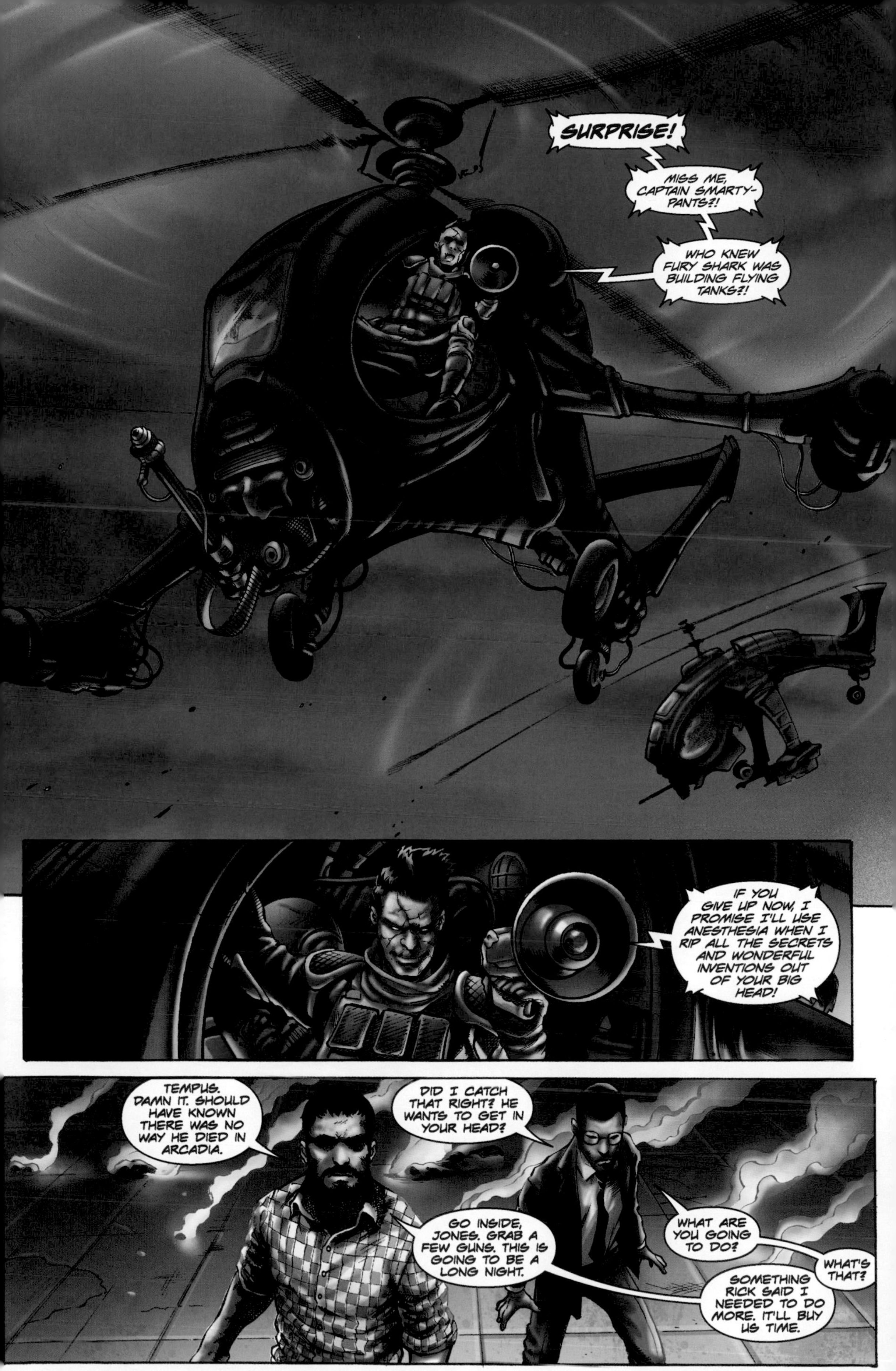
SURPRISE!
MISS ME, CAPTAIN SMARTY-PANTS?!
WHO KNEW FURY SHARK WAS BUILDING FLYING TANKS?!
IF YOU GIVE UP NOW, I PROMISE I'LL USE ANESTHESIA WHEN I RIP ALL THE SECRETS AND WONDERFUL INVENTIONS OUT OF YOUR BIG HEAD!
TEMPUS. DAMN IT. SHOULD HAVE KNOWN THERE WAS NO WAY HE DIED IN ARCADIA.
DID I CATCH THAT RIGHT? HE WANTS TO GET IN YOUR HEAD?
GO INSIDE, JONES. GRAB A FEW GUNS. THIS IS GOING TO BE A LONG NIGHT.
WHAT ARE YOU GOING TO DO?
SOMETHING RICK SAID I NEEDED TO DO MORE. IT'LL BUY US TIME.
WHAT'S THAT?

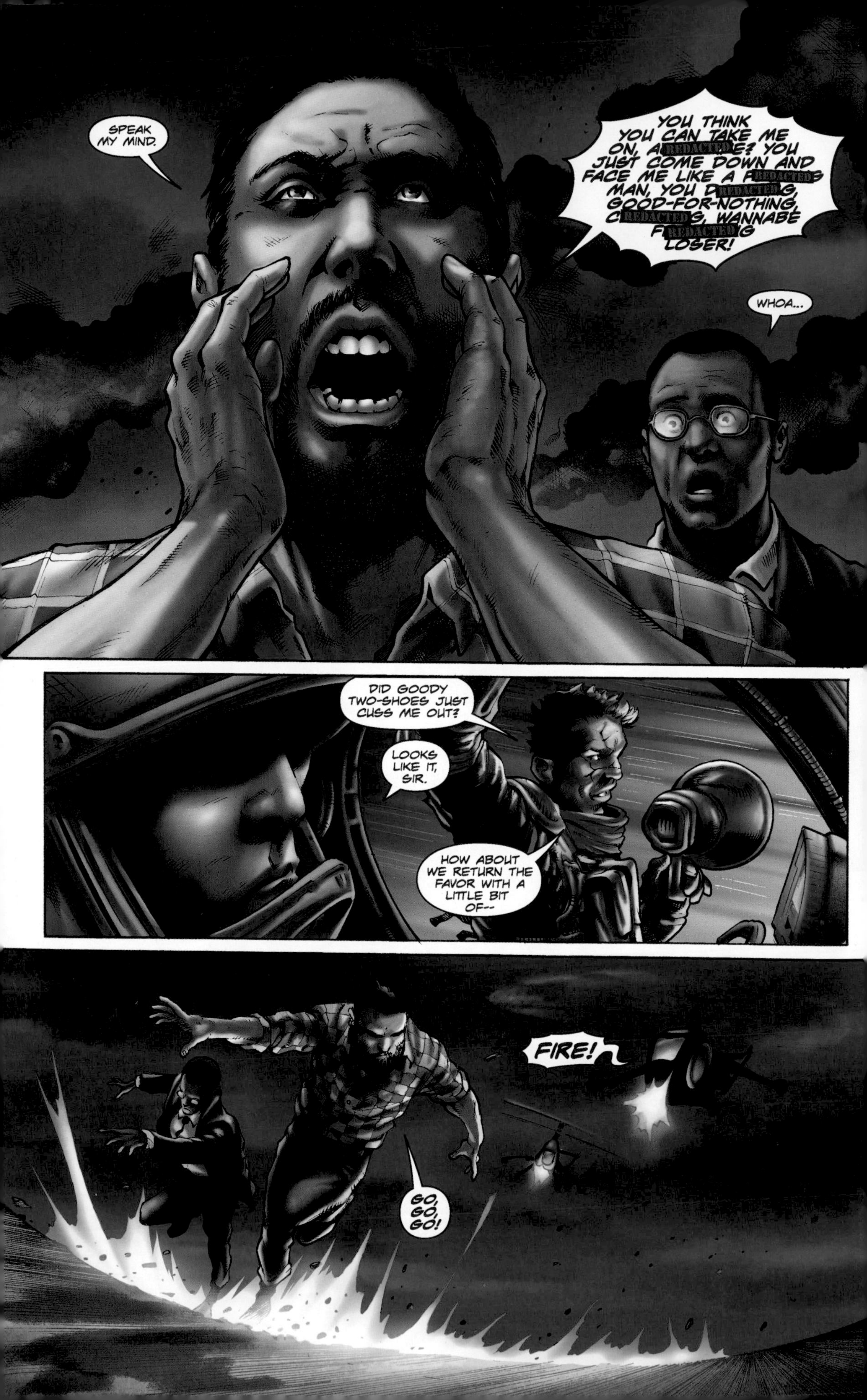
SPEAK MY MIND.
YOU THINK YOU CAN TAKE ME ON, A REDACTED E? YOU JUST COME DOWN AND FACE ME LIKE A F REDACTED G MAN, YOU D REDACTED G, GOOD-FOR-NOTHING, C REDACTED G, WANNABE F REDACTED G LOSER!
WHOA...
DID GOODY TWO-SHOES JUST CUSS ME OUT?
LOOKS LIKE IT, SIR.
HOW ABOUT WE RETURN THE FAVOR WITH A LITTLE BIT OF--
FIRE!
GO, GO, GO!

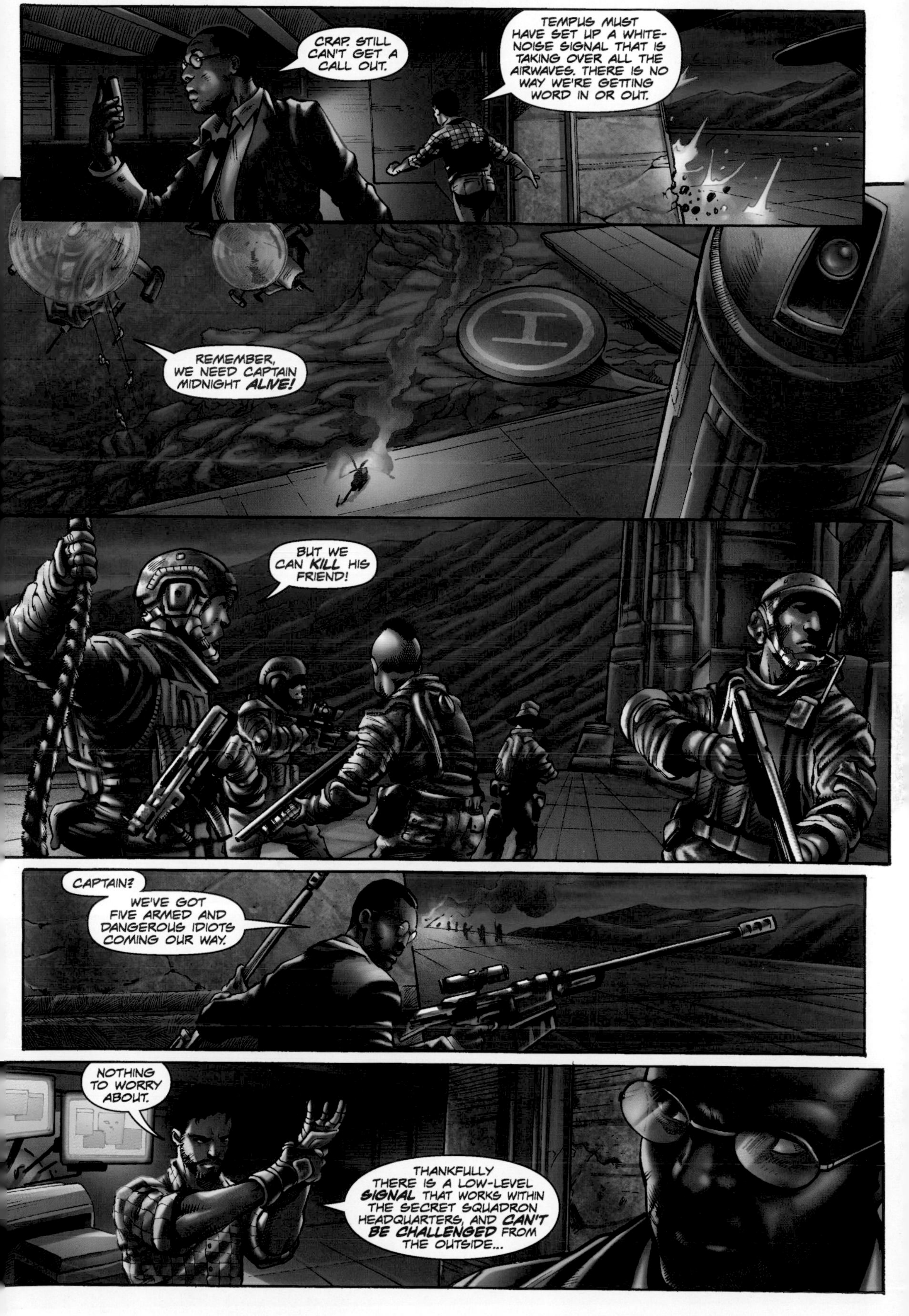
CRAP. STILL CAN'T GET A CALL OUT.
TEMPUS MUST HAVE SET UP A WHITE-NOISE SIGNAL THAT IS TAKING OVER ALL THE AIRWAVES. THERE IS NO WAY WE'RE GETTING WORD IN OR OUT.
REMEMBER, WE NEED CAPTAIN MIDNIGHT ALIVE!
BUT WE CAN KILL HIS FRIEND!
CAPTAIN?
WE'VE GOT FIVE ARMED AND DANGEROUS IDIOTS COMING OUR WAY.
NOTHING TO WORRY ABOUT.
THANKFULLY THERE IS A LOW-LEVEL SIGNAL THAT WORKS WITHIN THE SECRET SQUADRON HEADQUARTERS, AND CAN'T BE CHALLENGED FROM THE OUTSIDE...

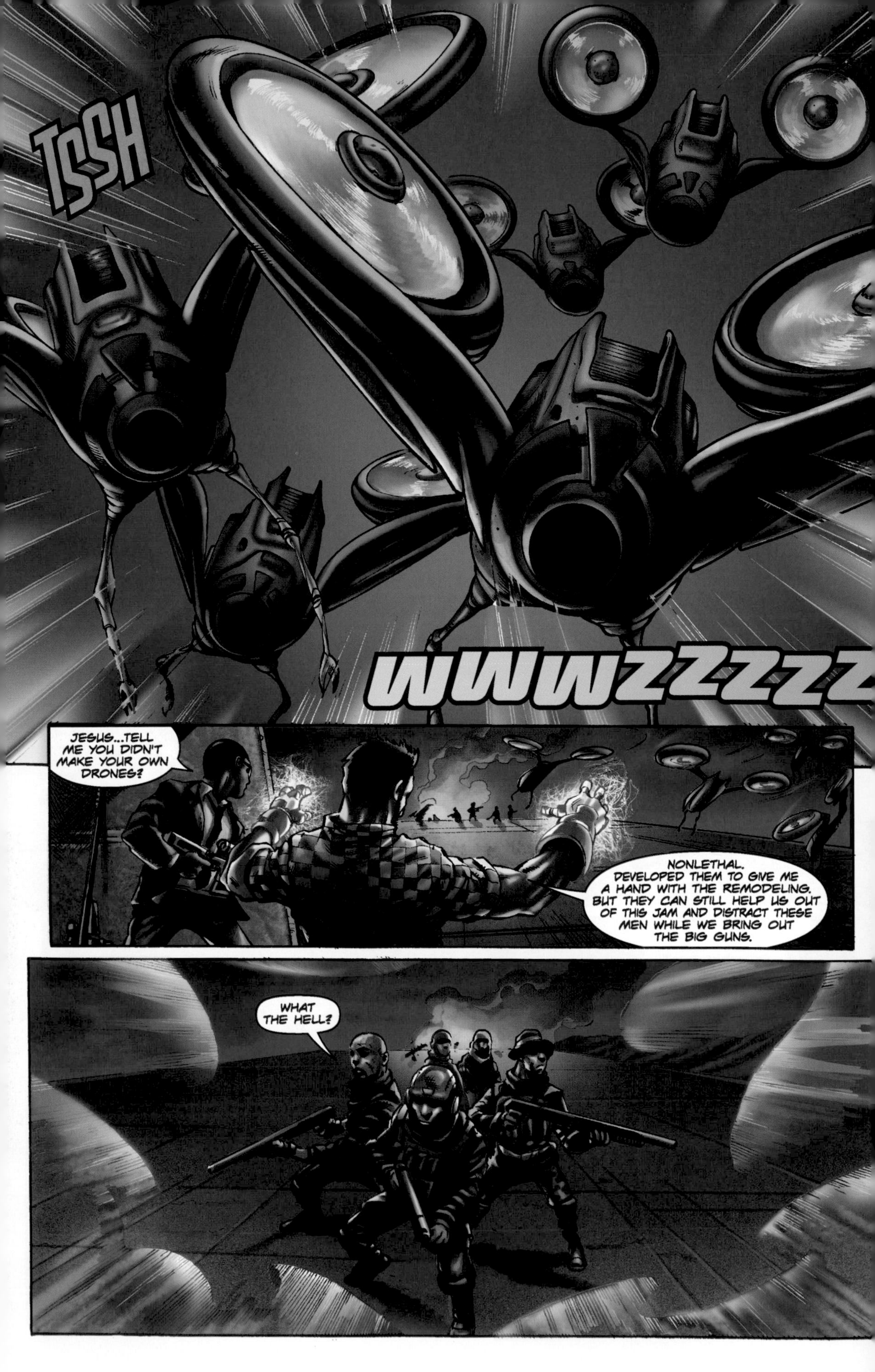
TSSH
WWWZZZZZ
JESUS...TELL ME YOU DIDN'T MAKE YOUR OWN DRONES?
NONLETHAL. DEVELOPED THEM TO GIVE ME A HAND WITH THE REMODELING. BUT THEY CAN STILL HELP US OUT OF THIS JAM AND DISTRACT THESE MEN WHILE WE BRING OUT THE BIG GUNS.
WHAT THE HELL?

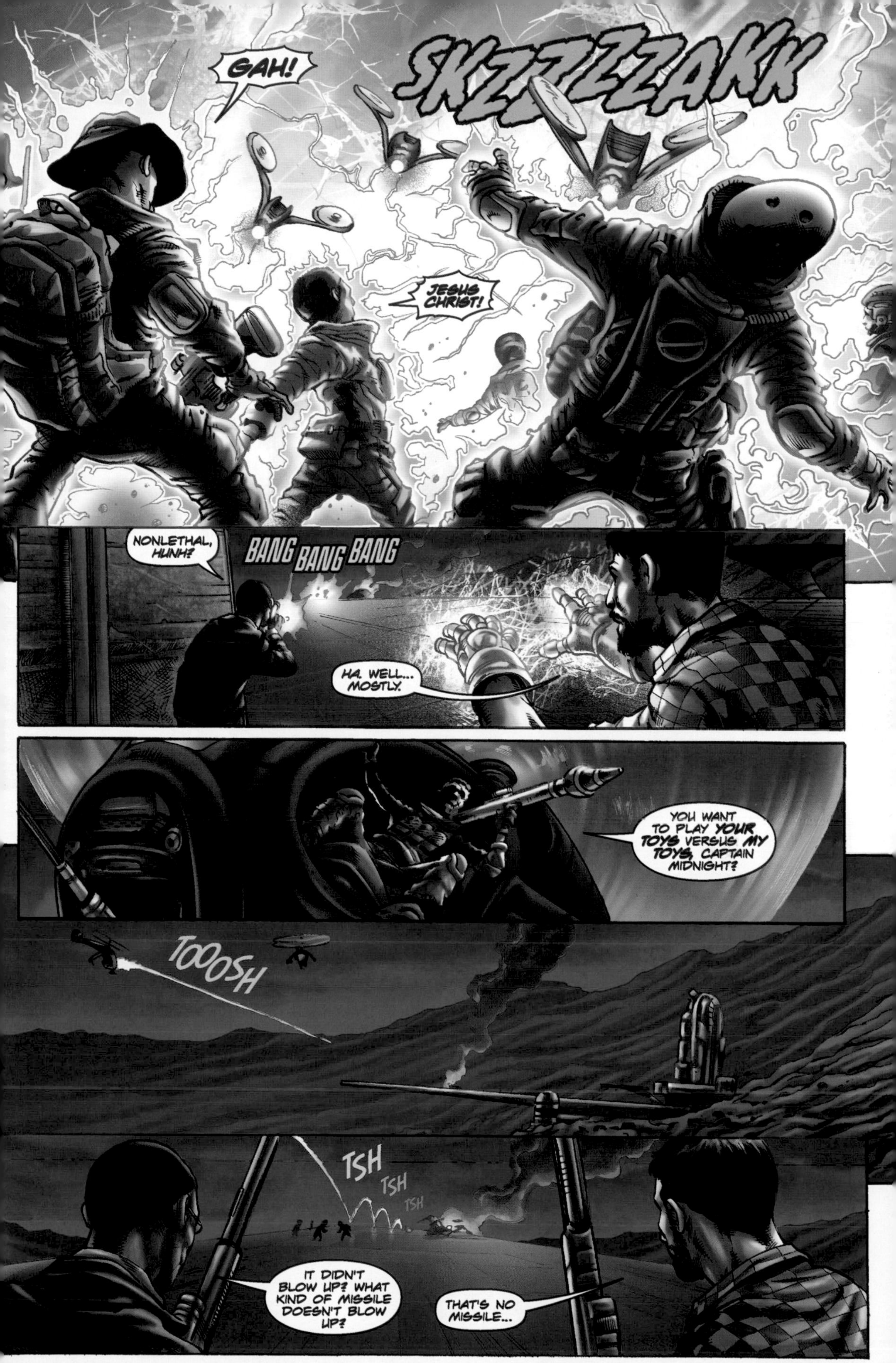
GAH!
SKZZZZZAKK
JESUS CHRIST!
NONLETHAL, HUNH?
BANG BANG BANG
HA. WELL... MOSTLY.
YOU WANT TO PLAY YOUR TOYS VERSUS MY TOYS, CAPTAIN MIDNIGHT?
TOOOSH
TSH TSH TSH
IT DIDN'T BLOW UP? WHAT KIND OF MISSILE DOESN'T BLOW UP?
THAT'S NO MISSILE...

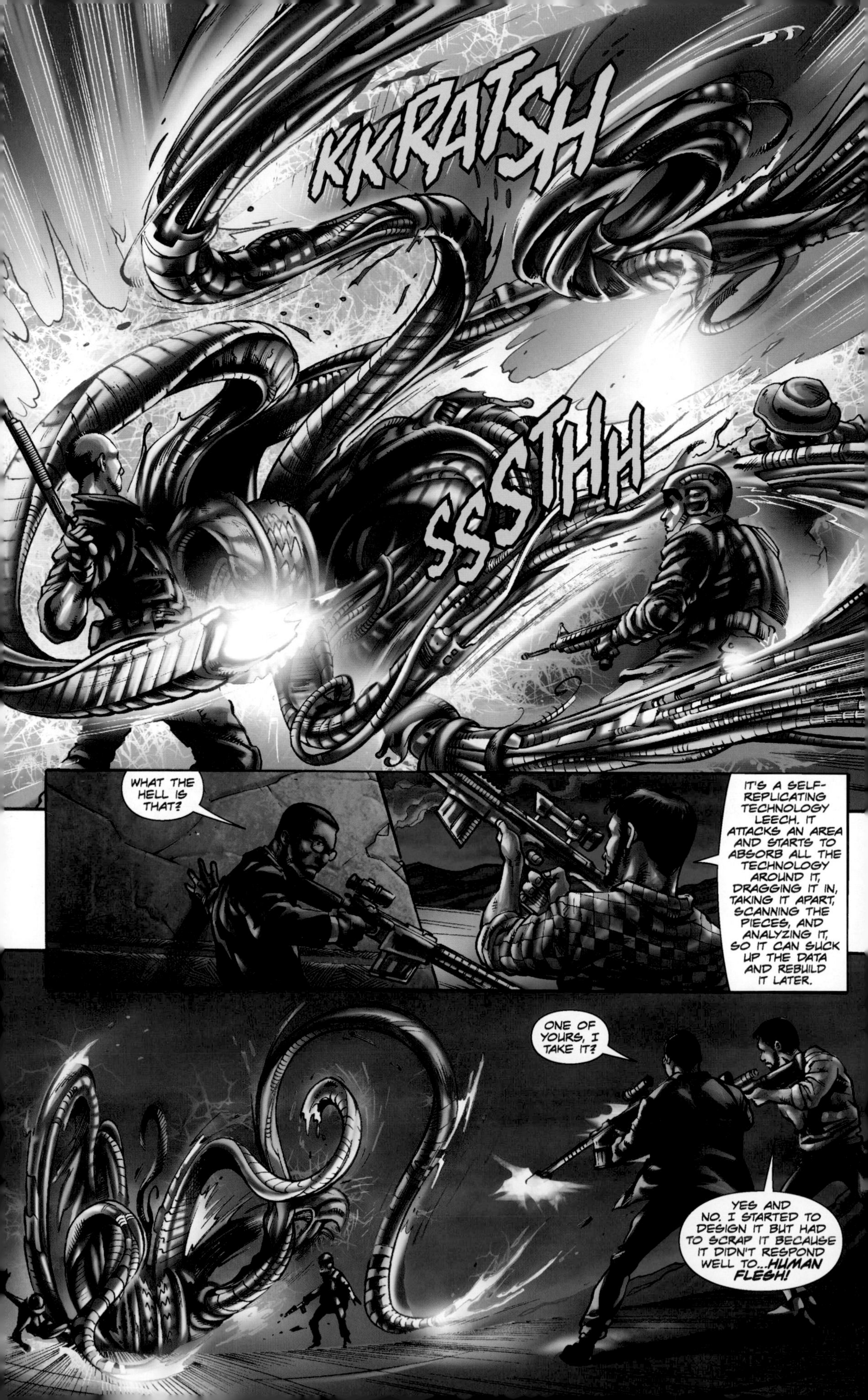
KKRATSH
SSSTHH
WHAT THE HELL IS THAT?
IT'S A SELF-REPLICATING TECHNOLOGY LEECH. IT ATTACKS AN AREA AND STARTS TO ABSORB ALL THE TECHNOLOGY AROUND IT, DRAGGING IT IN, TAKING IT APART, SCANNING THE PIECES, AND ANALYZING IT, SO IT CAN SUCK UP THE DATA AND REBUILD IT LATER.
ONE OF YOURS, I TAKE IT?
YES AND NO. I STARTED TO DESIGN IT BUT HAD TO SCRAP IT BECAUSE IT DIDN'T RESPOND WELL TO...HUMAN FLESH!

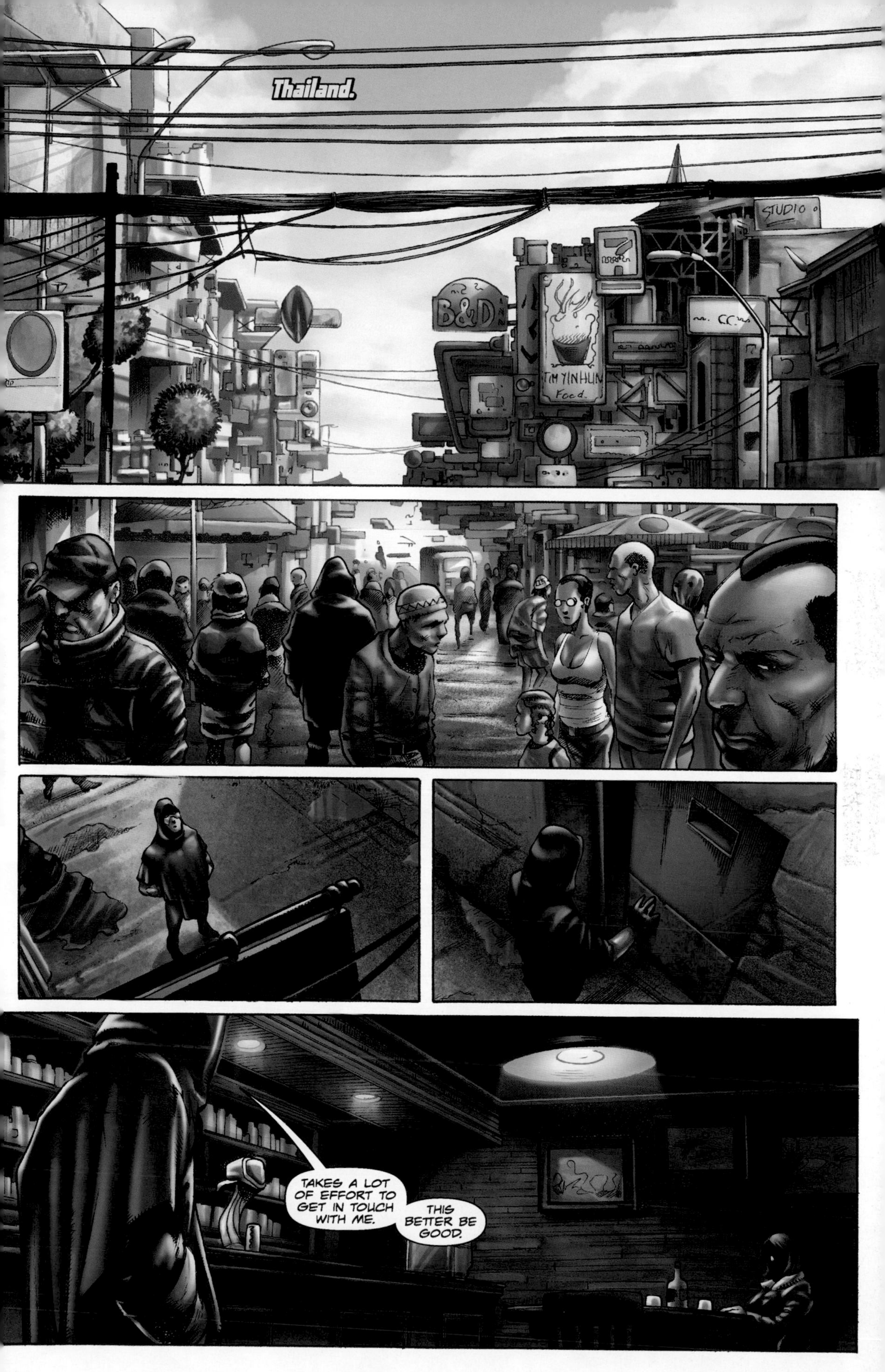
Thailand.
STUDIO
B&D
TIMYINHUN Food.
TAKES A LOT OF EFFORT TO GET IN TOUCH WITH ME.
THIS BETTER BE GOOD.

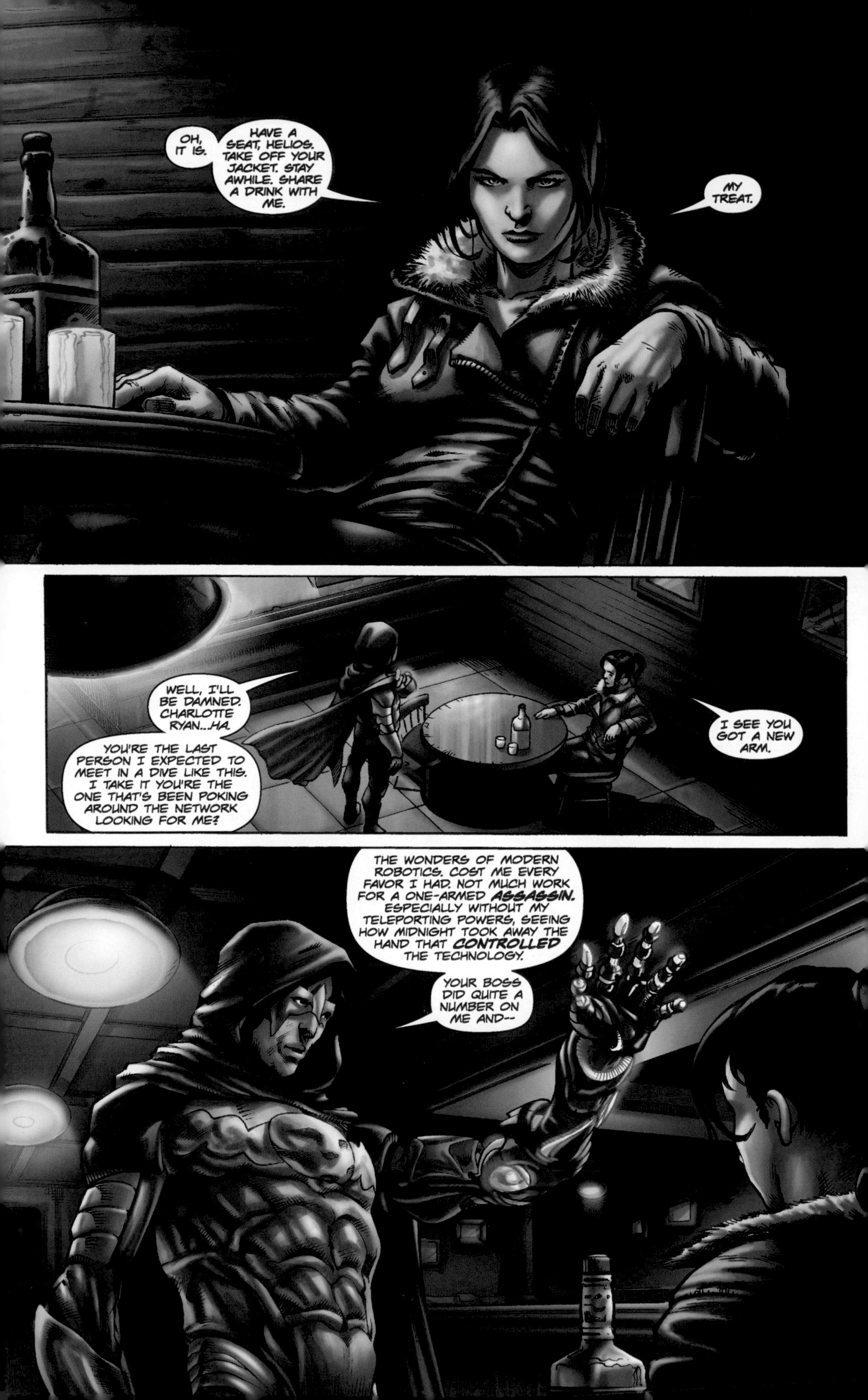
OH, IT IS.
HAVE A SEAT, HELIOS. TAKE OFF YOUR JACKET. STAY AWHILE. SHARE A DRINK WITH ME.
MY TREAT.
WELL, I'LL BE DAMNED. CHARLOTTE RYAN...HA.
YOU'RE THE LAST PERSON I EXPECTED TO MEET IN A DIVE LIKE THIS. I TAKE IT YOU'RE THE ONE THAT'S BEEN POKING AROUND THE NETWORK LOOKING FOR ME?
I SEE YOU GOT A NEW ARM.
THE WONDERS OF MODERN ROBOTICS. COST ME EVERY FAVOR I HAD. NOT MUCH WORK FOR A ONE-ARMED ASSASSIN. ESPECIALLY WITHOUT MY TELEPORTING POWERS, SEEING HOW MIDNIGHT TOOK AWAY THE HAND THAT CONTROLLED THE TECHNOLOGY.
YOUR BOSS DID QUITE A NUMBER ON ME AND--

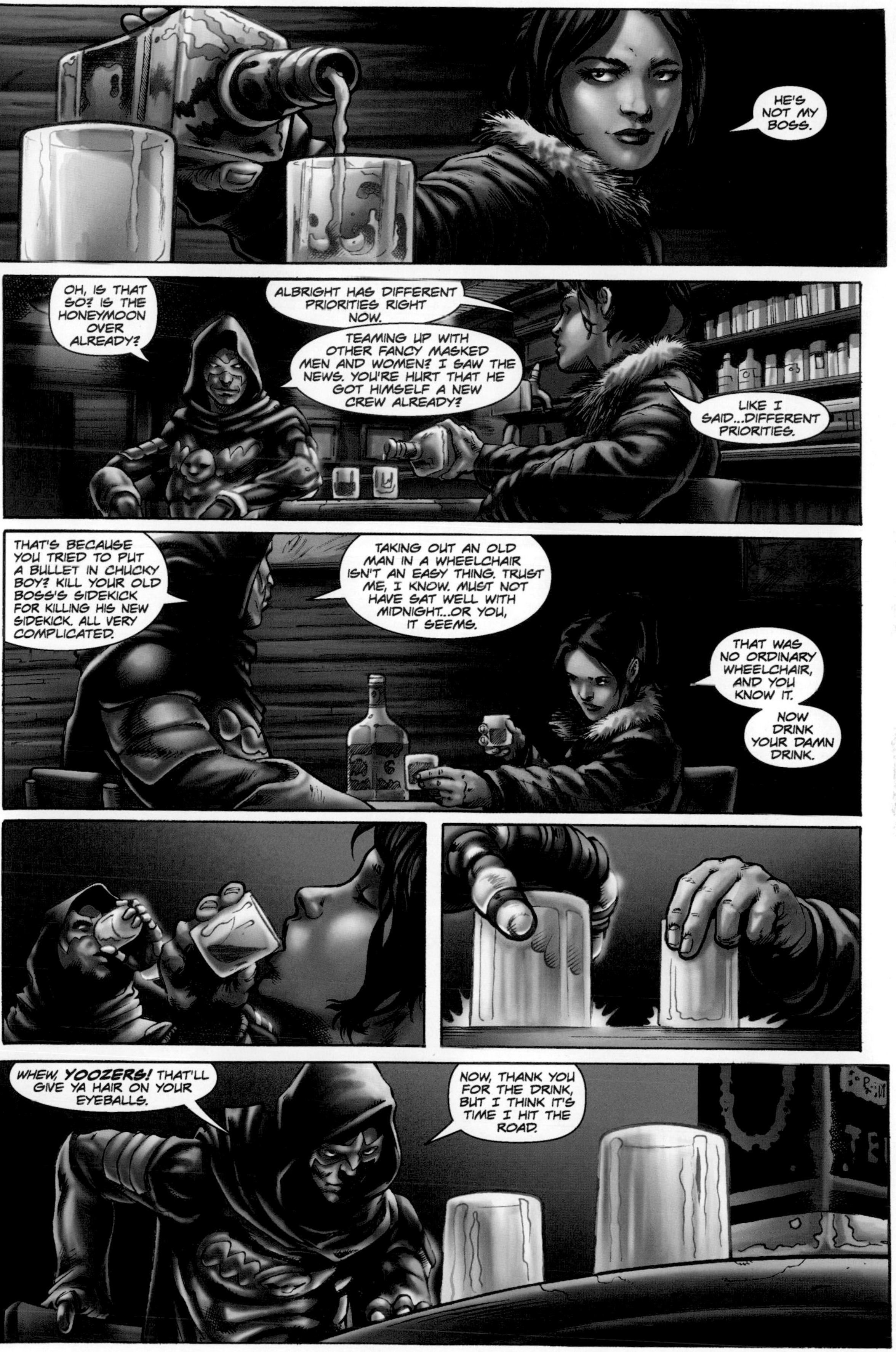
HE'S NOT MY BOSS.
OH, IS THAT SO? IS THE HONEYMOON OVER ALREADY?
ALBRIGHT HAS DIFFERENT PRIORITIES RIGHT NOW.
TEAMING UP WITH OTHER FANCY MASKED MEN AND WOMEN? I SAW THE NEWS. YOU'RE HURT THAT HE GOT HIMSELF A NEW CREW ALREADY?
LIKE I SAID...DIFFERENT PRIORITIES.
THAT'S BECAUSE YOU TRIED TO PUT A BULLET IN CHUCKY BOY? KILL YOUR OLD BOSS'S SIDEKICK FOR KILLING HIS NEW SIDEKICK. ALL VERY COMPLICATED.
TAKING OUT AN OLD MAN IN A WHEELCHAIR ISN'T AN EASY THING. TRUST ME, I KNOW. MUST NOT HAVE SAT WELL WITH MIDNIGHT...OR YOU, IT SEEMS.
THAT WAS NO ORDINARY WHEELCHAIR, AND YOU KNOW IT.
NOW DRINK YOUR DAMN DRINK.
WHEW, YOOZERS! THAT'LL GIVE YA HAIR ON YOUR EYEBALLS.
NOW, THANK YOU FOR THE DRINK, BUT I THINK IT'S TIME I HIT THE ROAD.

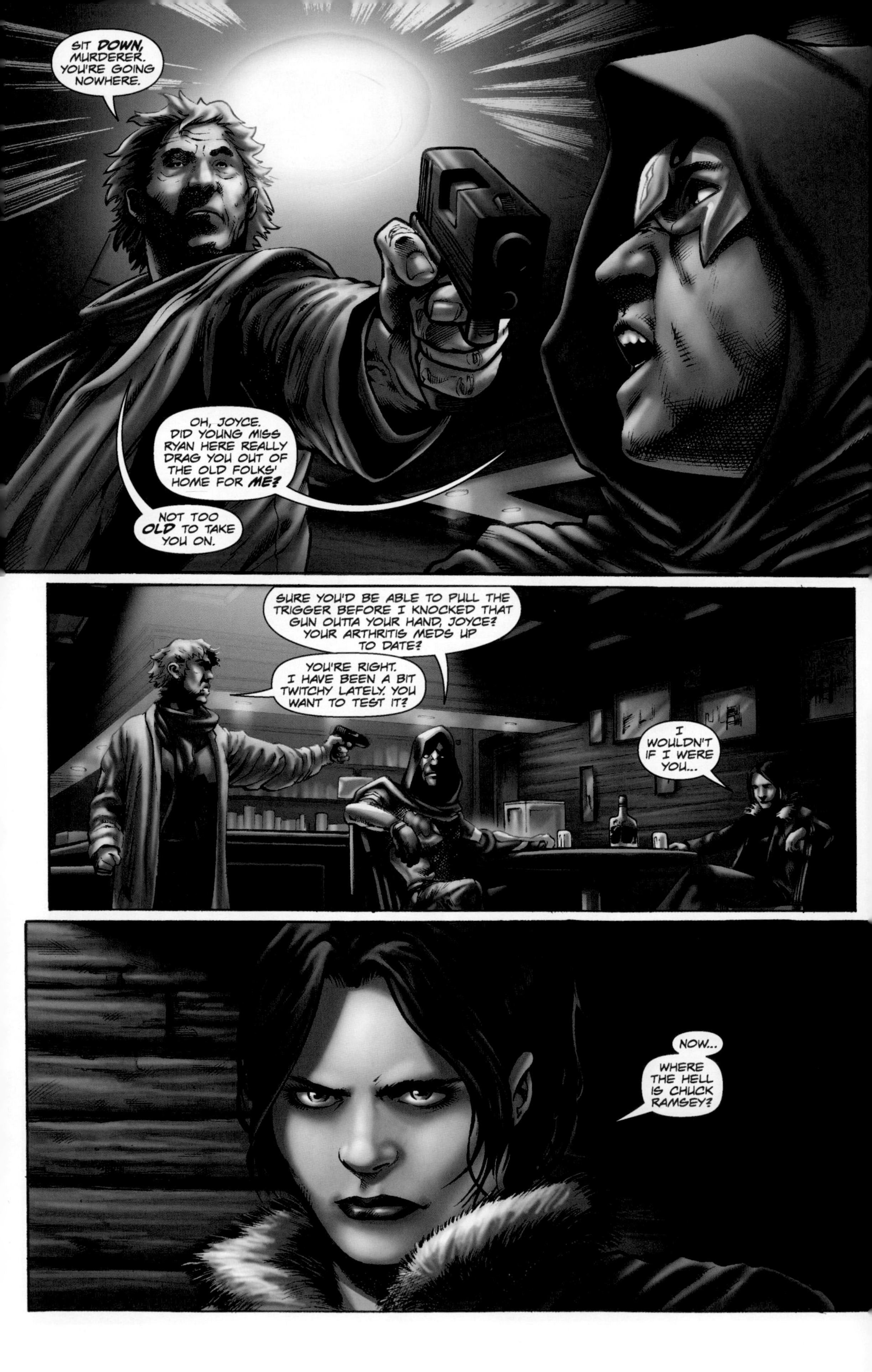
SIT DOWN, MURDERER. YOU'RE GOING NOWHERE.
OH, JOYCE. DID YOUNG MISS RYAN HERE REALLY DRAG YOU OUT OF THE OLD FOLKS' HOME FOR ME?
NOT TOO OLD TO TAKE YOU ON.
SURE YOU'D BE ABLE TO PULL THE TRIGGER BEFORE I KNOCKED THAT GUN OUTTA YOUR HAND, JOYCE? YOUR ARTHRITIS MEDS UP TO DATE?
YOU'RE RIGHT. I HAVE BEEN A BIT TWITCHY LATELY. YOU WANT TO TEST IT?
I WOULDN'T IF I WERE YOU...
NOW... WHERE THE HELL IS CHUCK RAMSEY?

BANG BANG BANG BANG BANG

BANG BANG BANG

CAP! WE'RE FIGHTING A LOSING BATTLE HERE!

I KNOW! THE ONLY WAY TO STOP THE LEECH IS TO ACTIVATE AN ELECTROMAGNETIC PULSE TO SHORT IT OUT. AFTER OUR BATTLE WITH CHUCK AND HIS IMPLOSION DEVICE, I GOT A FEW IDEAS. BUT IT WILL ONLY LAST A FEW MINUTES AND WILL MESS WITH ALL OUR TECH AS WELL.

THE E.M.P. IS STILL CHARGING UP, AND I NEED TO BE HERE TO TURN IT ON.

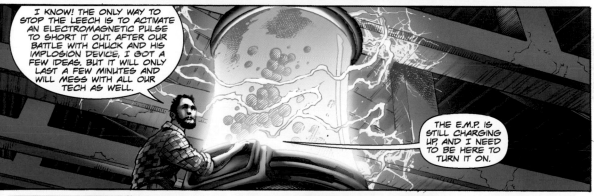

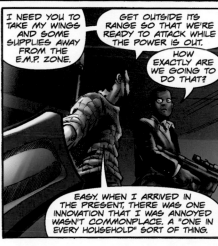

I NEED YOU TO TAKE MY WINGS AND SOME SUPPLIES AWAY FROM THE E.M.P. ZONE.

GET OUTSIDE ITS RANGE SO THAT WE'RE READY TO ATTACK WHILE THE POWER IS OUT.

HOW EXACTLY ARE WE GOING TO DO THAT?

EASY. WHEN I ARRIVED IN THE PRESENT, THERE WAS ONE INNOVATION THAT I WAS ANNOYED WASN'T COMMONPLACE. A "ONE IN EVERY HOUSEHOLD" SORT OF THING.

SO AS SOON AS I HAD SOME FREE TIME... I INVENTED IT. ACTUALLY, MORE LIKE PERFECTED IT.

BANG

YEAH? AND WHAT WOULD THAT BE?

HM.

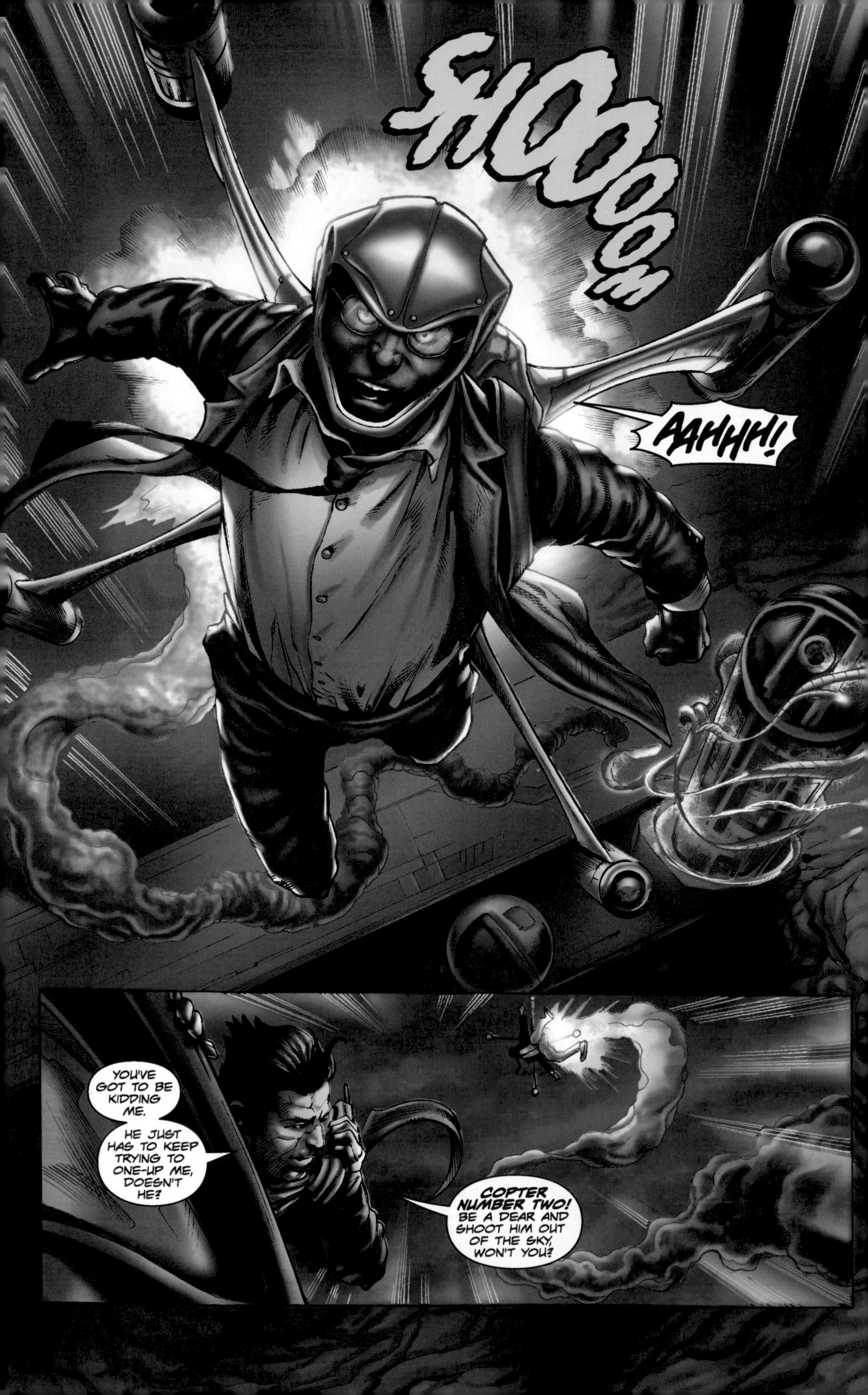
SHOOOOOM
AAHHH!
YOU'VE GOT TO BE KIDDING ME.
HE JUST HAS TO KEEP TRYING TO ONE-UP ME, DOESN'T HE?
COPTER NUMBER TWO! BE A DEAR AND SHOOT HIM OUT OF THE SKY, WON'T YOU?

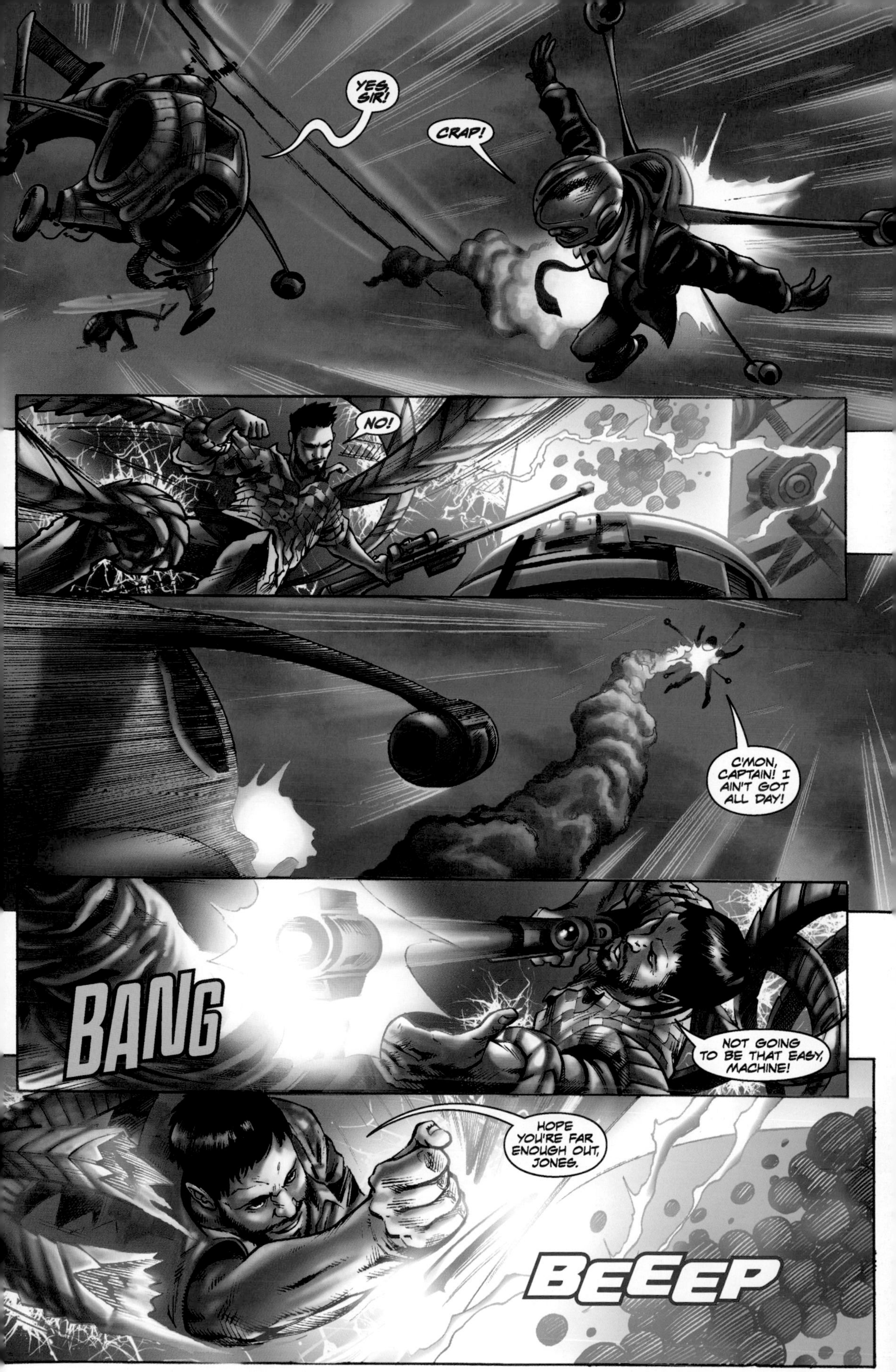
YES, SIR!
CRAP!
NO!
C'MON, CAPTAIN! I AIN'T GOT ALL DAY!
BANG
NOT GOING TO BE THAT EASY, MACHINE!
HOPE YOU'RE FAR ENOUGH OUT, JONES.
BEEEP

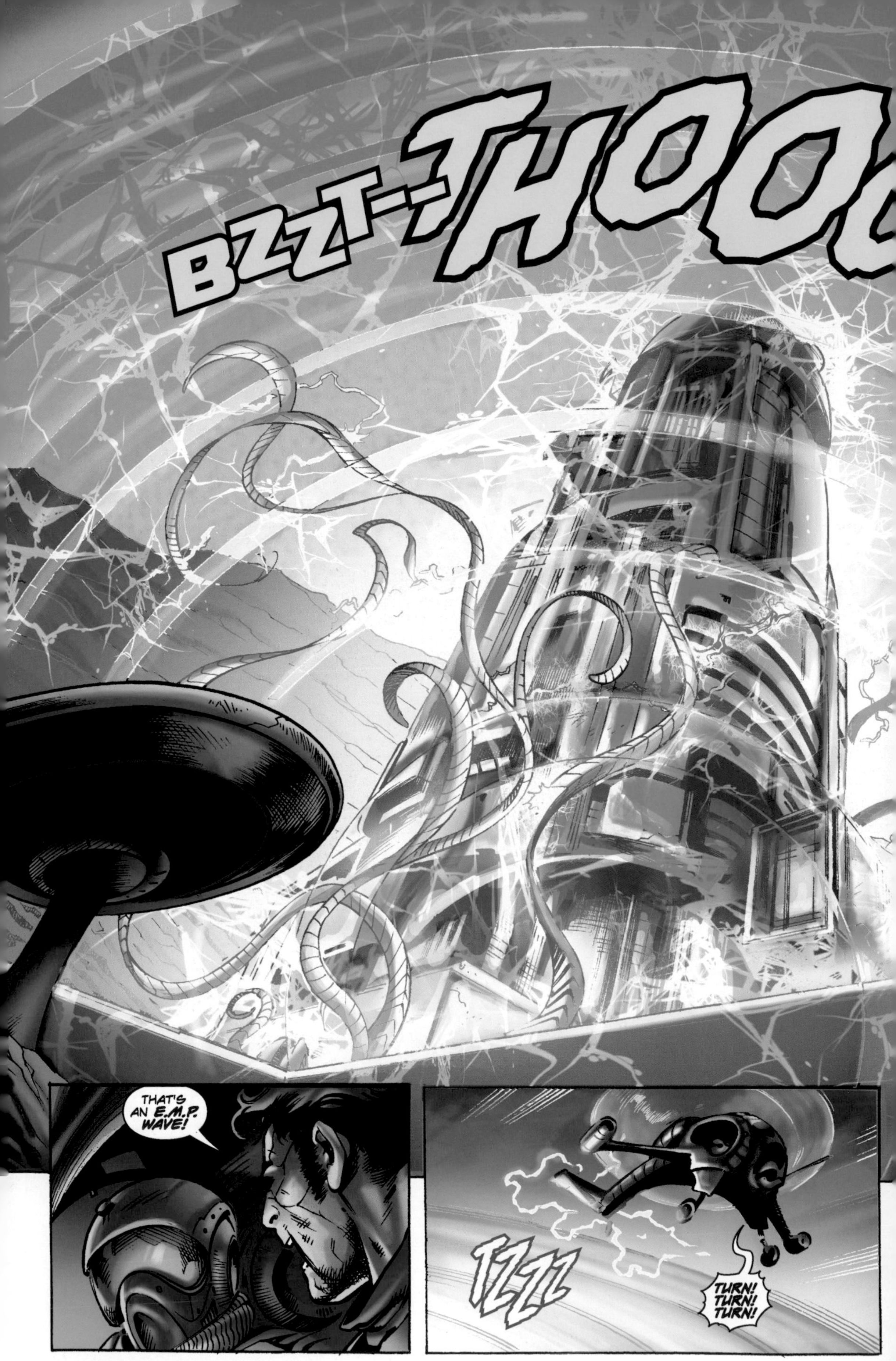
BZZT--THOO
THAT'S AN E.M.P. WAVE!
TZZZ
TURN! TURN! TURN!

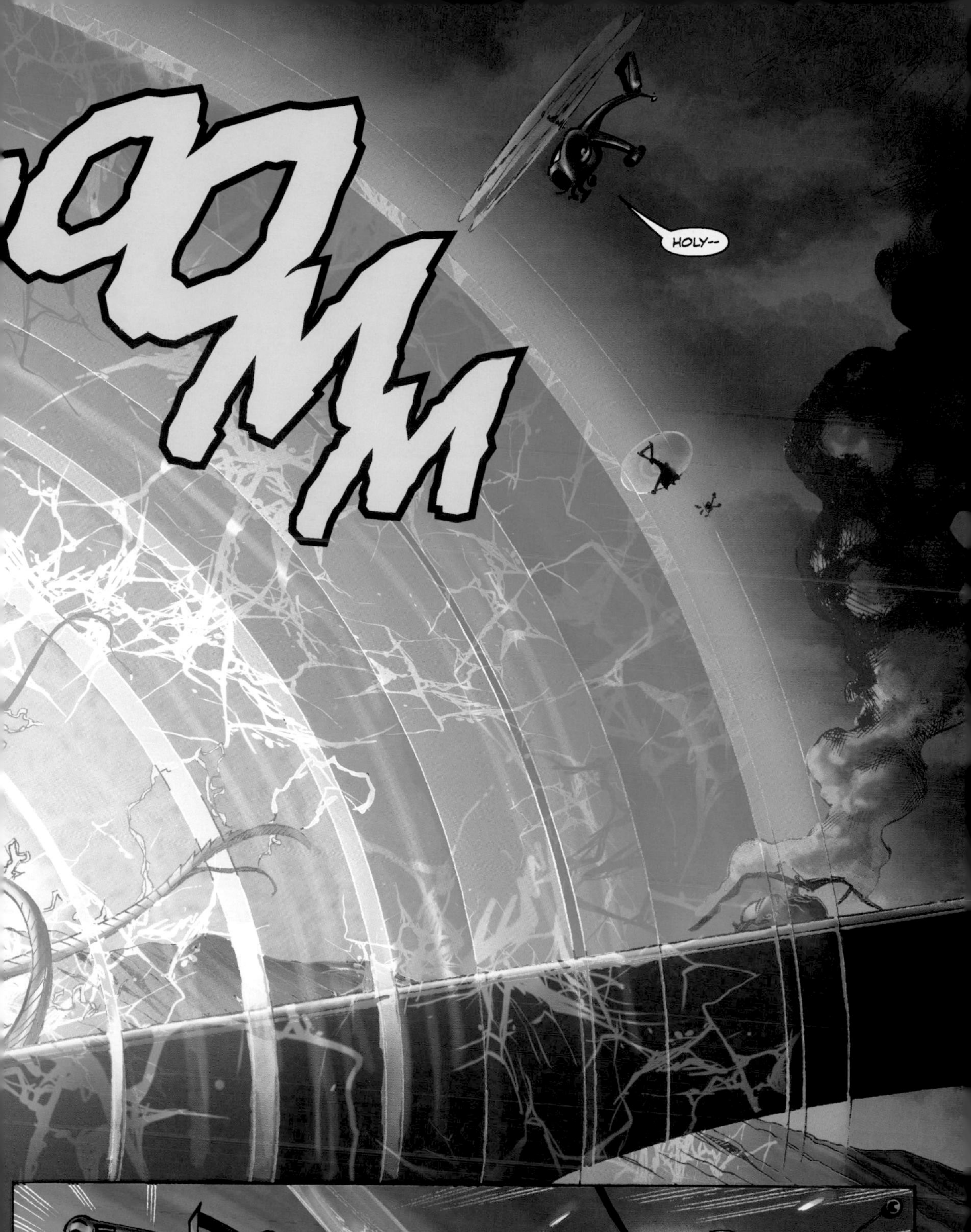
HOLY--

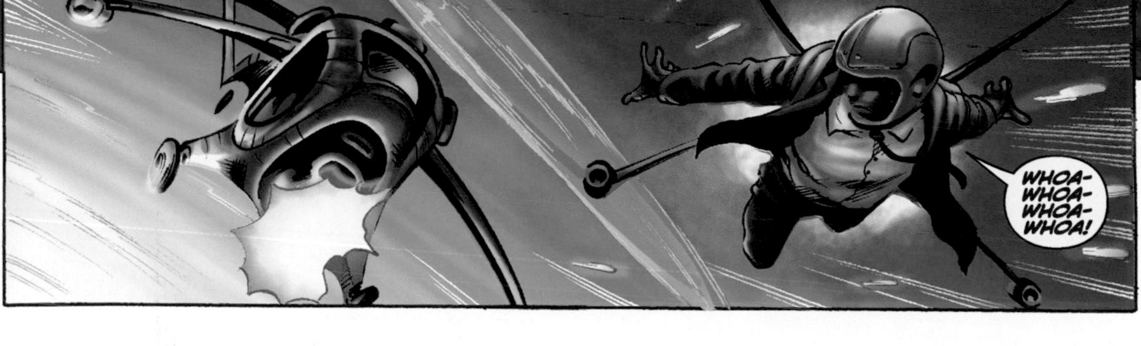
WHOA-WHOA-WHOA-WHOA!

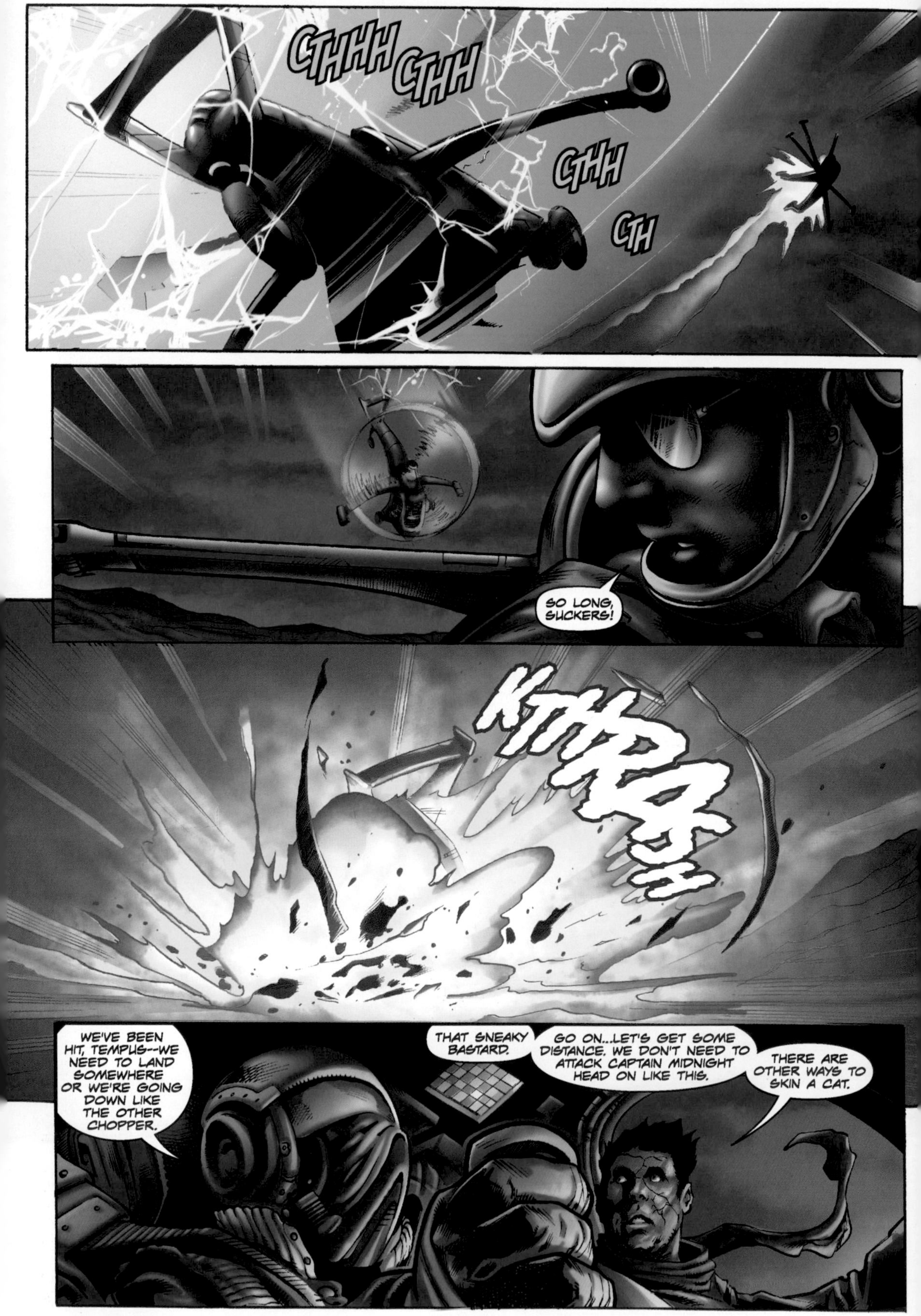
CTHHH CTHH
CTHH
CTH
SO LONG, SUCKERS!
KTHRASH
WE'VE BEEN HIT, TEMPUS--WE NEED TO LAND SOMEWHERE OR WE'RE GOING DOWN LIKE THE OTHER CHOPPER.
THAT SNEAKY BASTARD.
GO ON...LET'S GET SOME DISTANCE. WE DON'T NEED TO ATTACK CAPTAIN MIDNIGHT HEAD ON LIKE THIS.
THERE ARE OTHER WAYS TO SKIN A CAT.

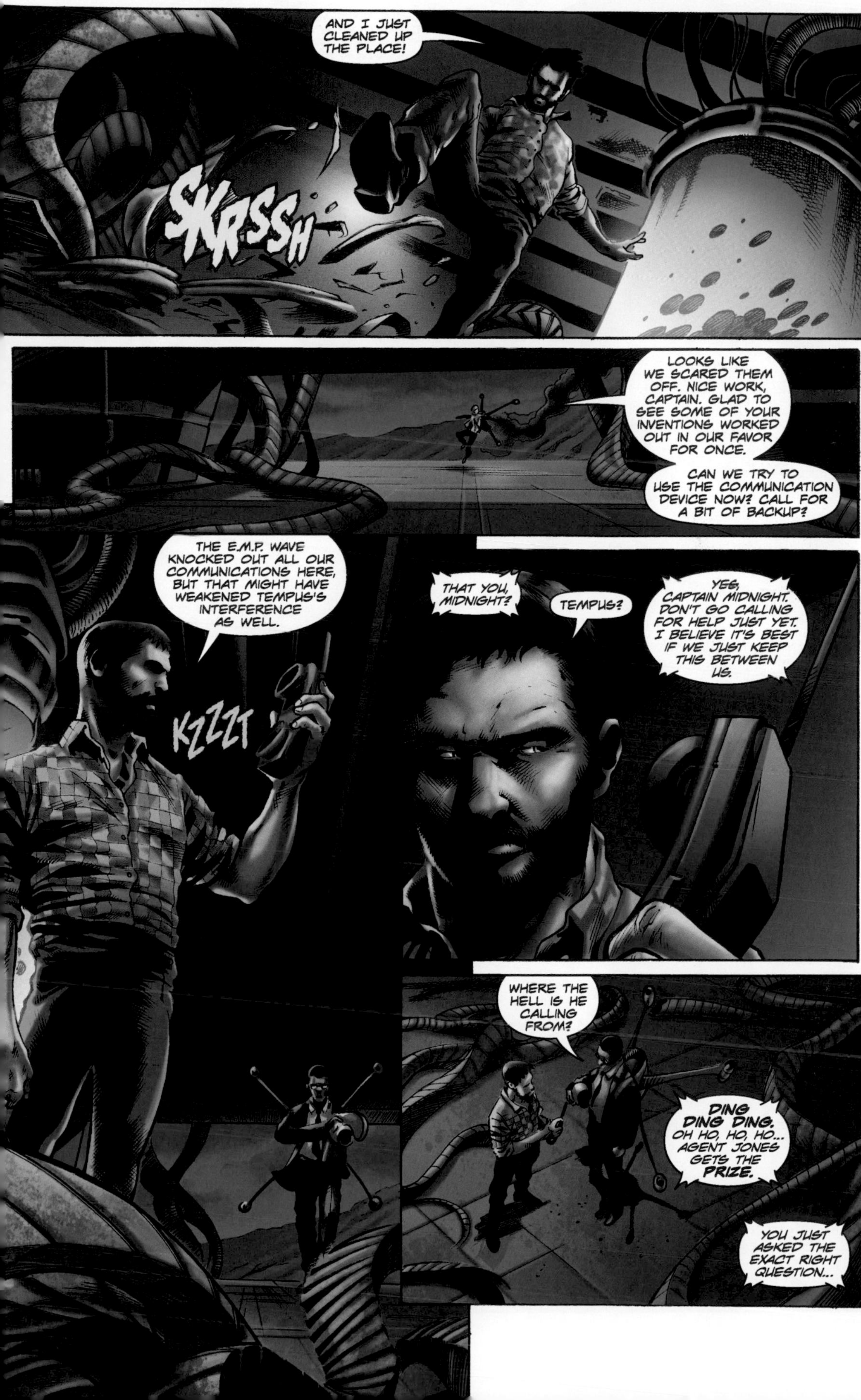
AND I JUST CLEANED UP THE PLACE!
SKRSSH
LOOKS LIKE WE SCARED THEM OFF. NICE WORK, CAPTAIN. GLAD TO SEE SOME OF YOUR INVENTIONS WORKED OUT IN OUR FAVOR FOR ONCE.
CAN WE TRY TO USE THE COMMUNICATION DEVICE NOW? CALL FOR A BIT OF BACKUP?
THE E.M.P. WAVE KNOCKED OUT ALL OUR COMMUNICATIONS HERE, BUT THAT MIGHT HAVE WEAKENED TEMPUS'S INTERFERENCE AS WELL.
KZZZT
THAT YOU, MIDNIGHT?
TEMPUS?
YES, CAPTAIN MIDNIGHT. DON'T GO CALLING FOR HELP JUST YET. I BELIEVE IT'S BEST IF WE JUST KEEP THIS BETWEEN US.
WHERE THE HELL IS HE CALLING FROM?
DING DING DING. OH HO, HO, HO... AGENT JONES GETS THE PRIZE.
YOU JUST ASKED THE EXACT RIGHT QUESTION...

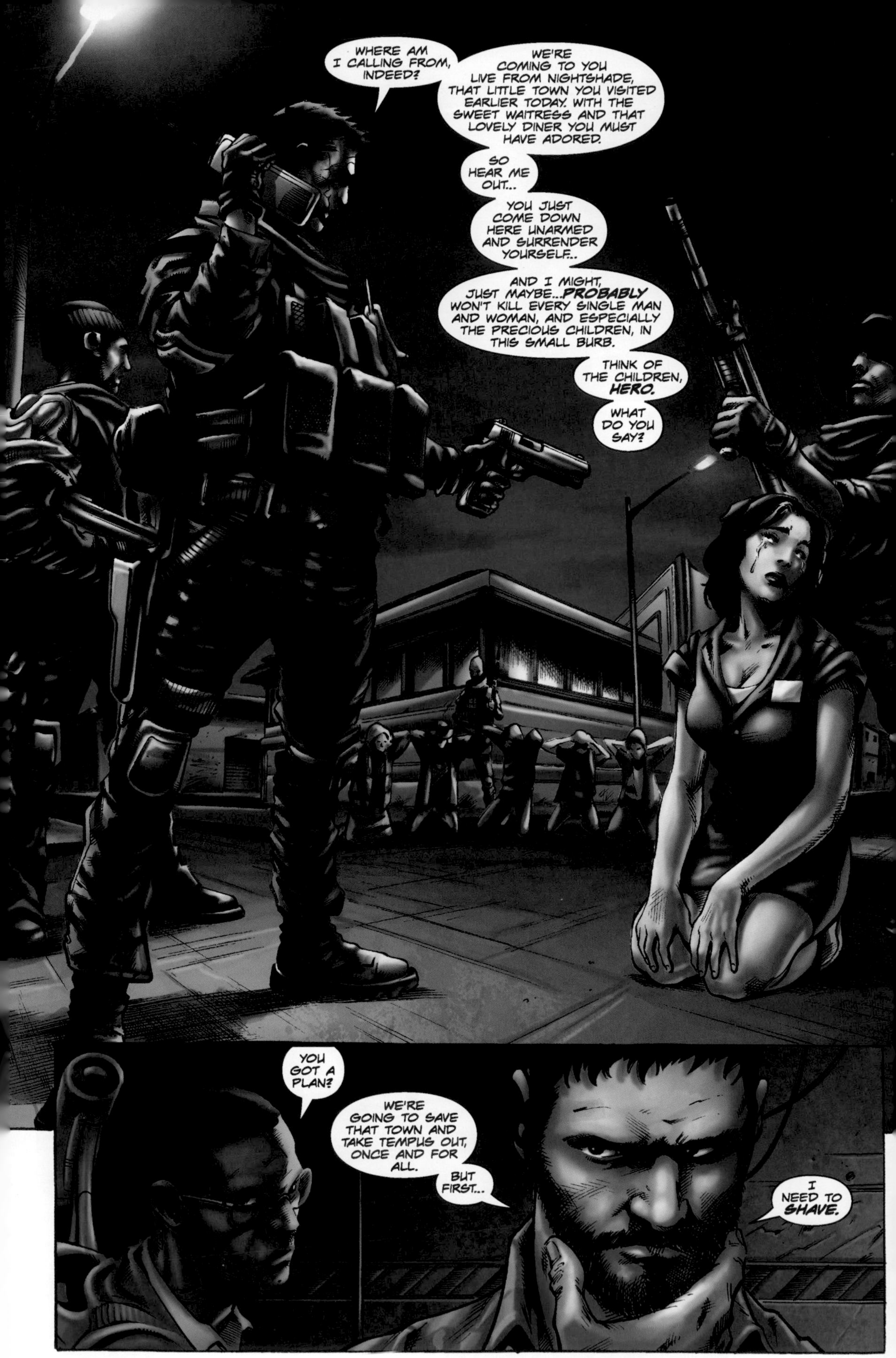
WHERE AM I CALLING FROM, INDEED?
WE'RE COMING TO YOU LIVE FROM NIGHTSHADE, THAT LITTLE TOWN YOU VISITED EARLIER TODAY. WITH THE SWEET WAITRESS AND THAT LOVELY DINER YOU MUST HAVE ADORED.
SO HEAR ME OUT...
YOU JUST COME DOWN HERE UNARMED AND SURRENDER YOURSELF...
AND I MIGHT, JUST MAYBE...PROBABLY WON'T KILL EVERY SINGLE MAN AND WOMAN, AND ESPECIALLY THE PRECIOUS CHILDREN, IN THIS SMALL BURB.
THINK OF THE CHILDREN, HERO.
WHAT DO YOU SAY?
YOU GOT A PLAN?
WE'RE GOING TO SAVE THAT TOWN AND TAKE TEMPUS OUT, ONCE AND FOR ALL.
BUT FIRST...
I NEED TO SHAVE.

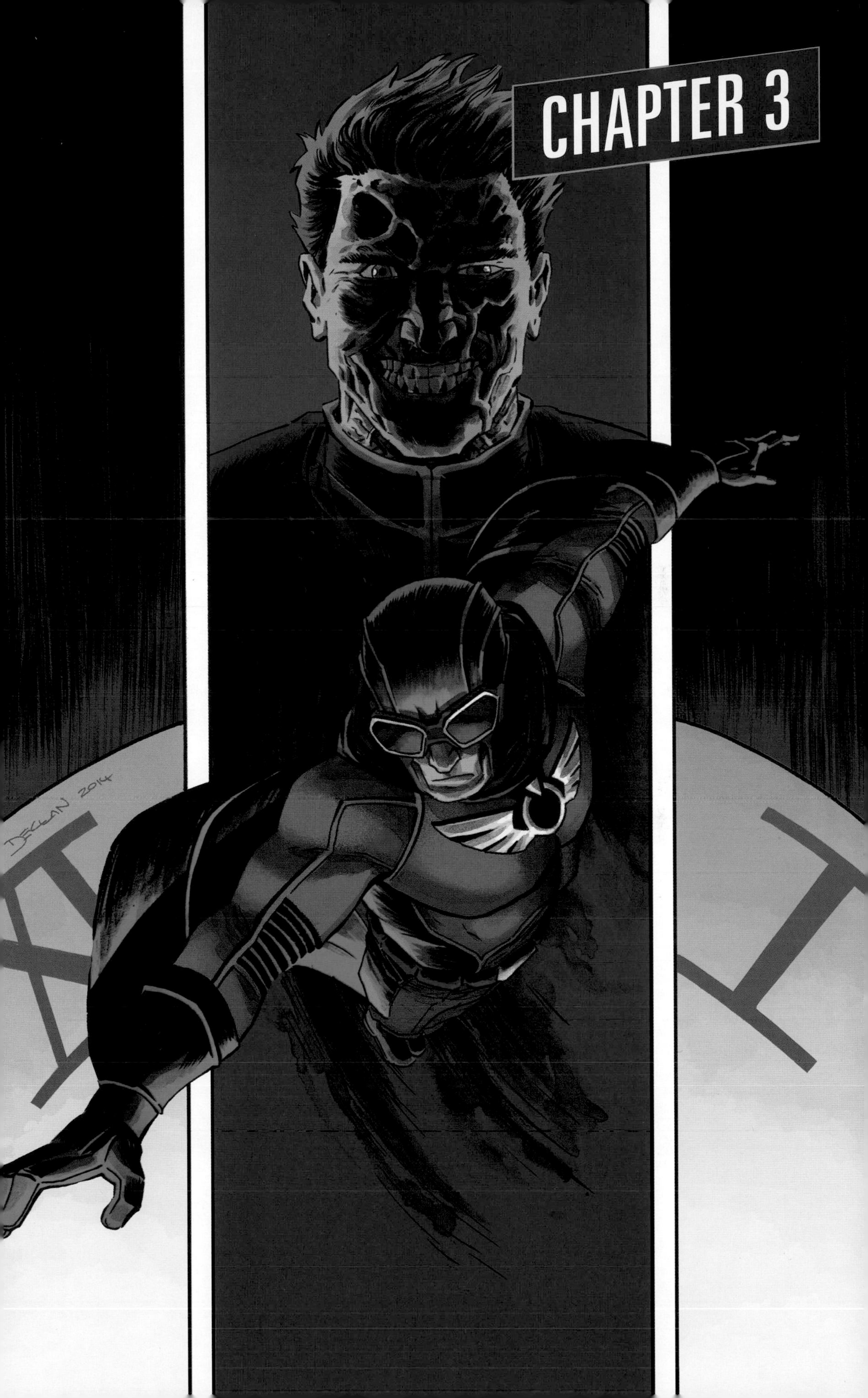
CHAPTER 3
DECLAN 2014

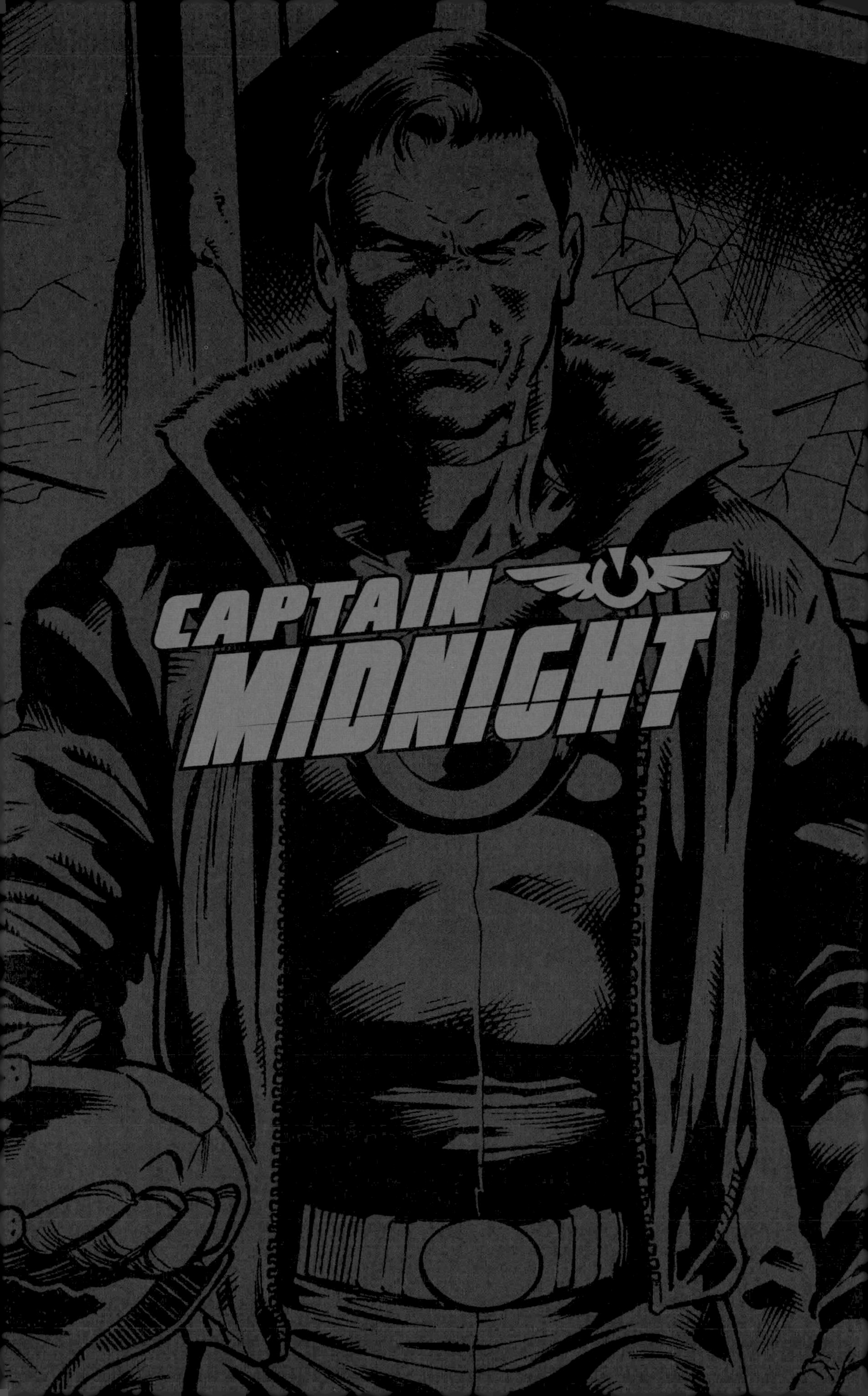
CAPTAIN
MIDNIGHT

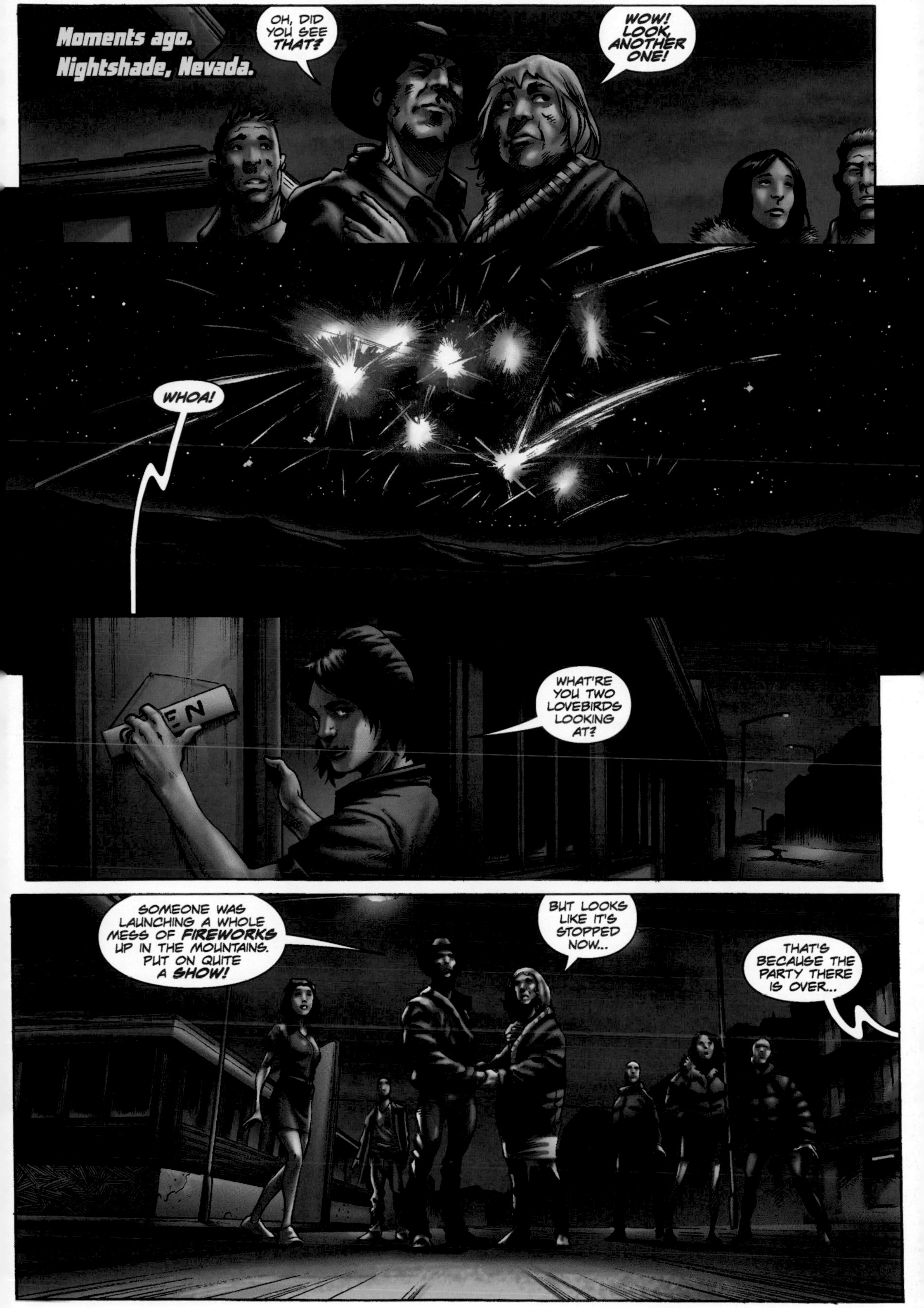
Moments ago.
Nightshade, Nevada.
OH, DID YOU SEE THAT?
WOW! LOOK, ANOTHER ONE!
WHOA!
WHAT'RE YOU TWO LOVEBIRDS LOOKING AT?
SOMEONE WAS LAUNCHING A WHOLE MESS OF FIREWORKS UP IN THE MOUNTAINS. PUT ON QUITE A SHOW!
BUT LOOKS LIKE IT'S STOPPED NOW...
THAT'S BECAUSE THE PARTY THERE IS OVER...

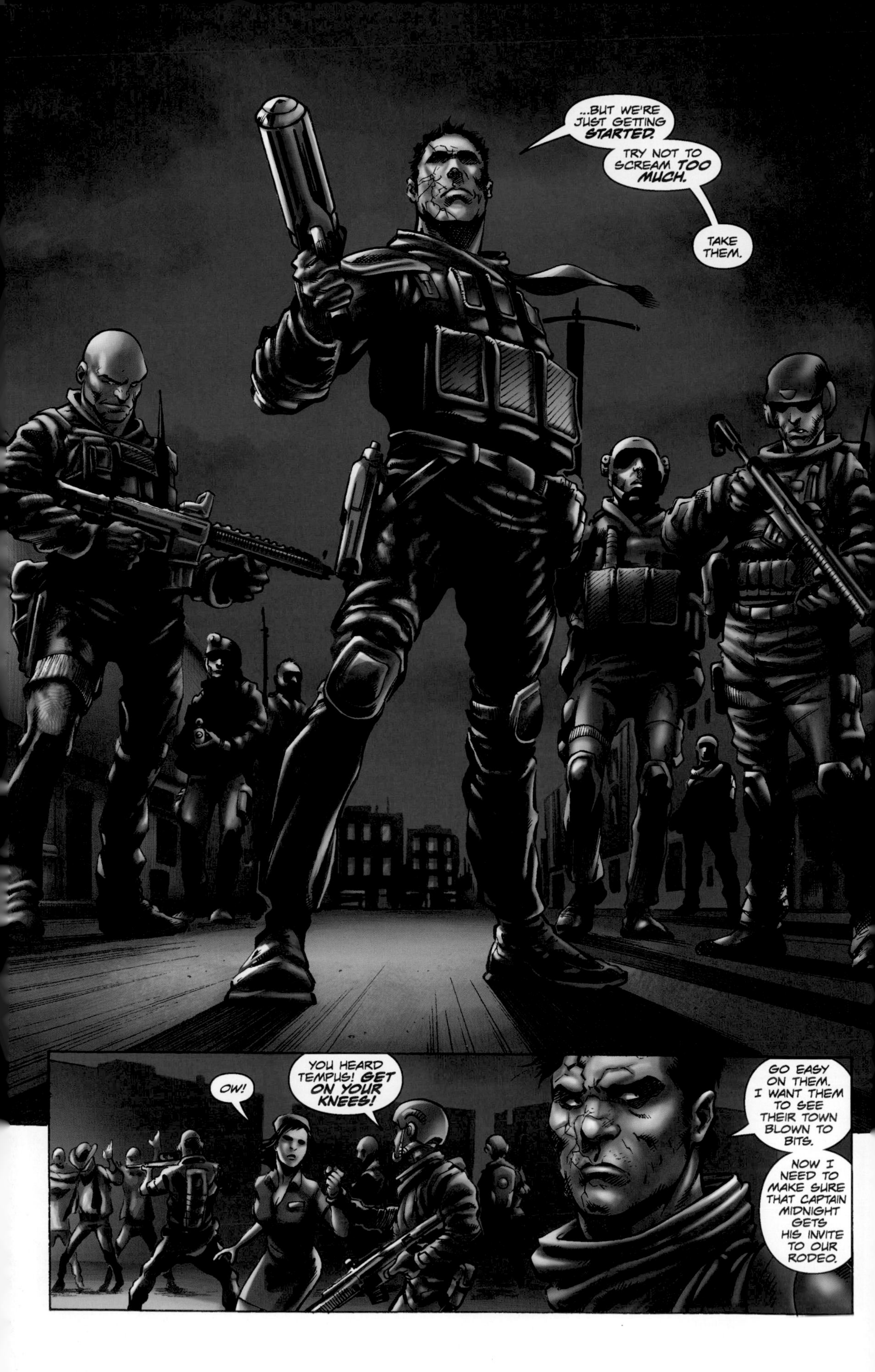
...BUT WE'RE JUST GETTING STARTED.
TRY NOT TO SCREAM TOO MUCH.
TAKE THEM.
OW!
YOU HEARD TEMPUS! GET ON YOUR KNEES!
GO EASY ON THEM. I WANT THEM TO SEE THEIR TOWN BLOWN TO BITS.
NOW I NEED TO MAKE SURE THAT CAPTAIN MIDNIGHT GETS HIS INVITE TO OUR RODEO.

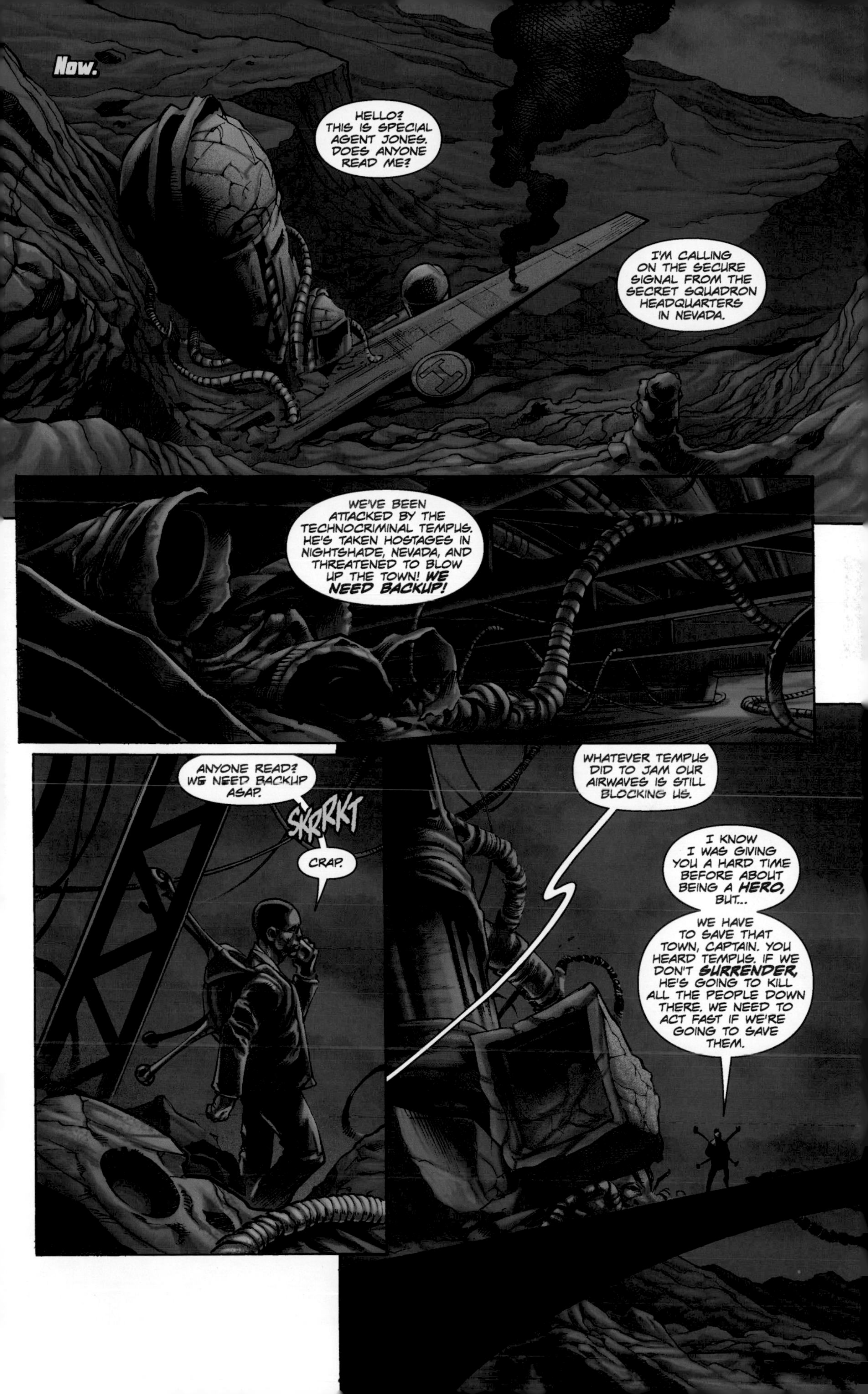
Now.
HELLO? THIS IS SPECIAL AGENT JONES. DOES ANYONE READ ME?
I'M CALLING ON THE SECURE SIGNAL FROM THE SECRET SQUADRON HEADQUARTERS IN NEVADA.
WE'VE BEEN ATTACKED BY THE TECHNOCRIMINAL TEMPUS. HE'S TAKEN HOSTAGES IN NIGHTSHADE, NEVADA, AND THREATENED TO BLOW UP THE TOWN! WE NEED BACKUP!
ANYONE READ? WE NEED BACKUP ASAP.
SKRRKT
CRAP.
WHATEVER TEMPUS DID TO JAM OUR AIRWAVES IS STILL BLOCKING US.
I KNOW I WAS GIVING YOU A HARD TIME BEFORE ABOUT BEING A HERO, BUT...
WE HAVE TO SAVE THAT TOWN, CAPTAIN. YOU HEARD TEMPUS. IF WE DON'T SURRENDER, HE'S GOING TO KILL ALL THE PEOPLE DOWN THERE. WE NEED TO ACT FAST IF WE'RE GOING TO SAVE THEM.

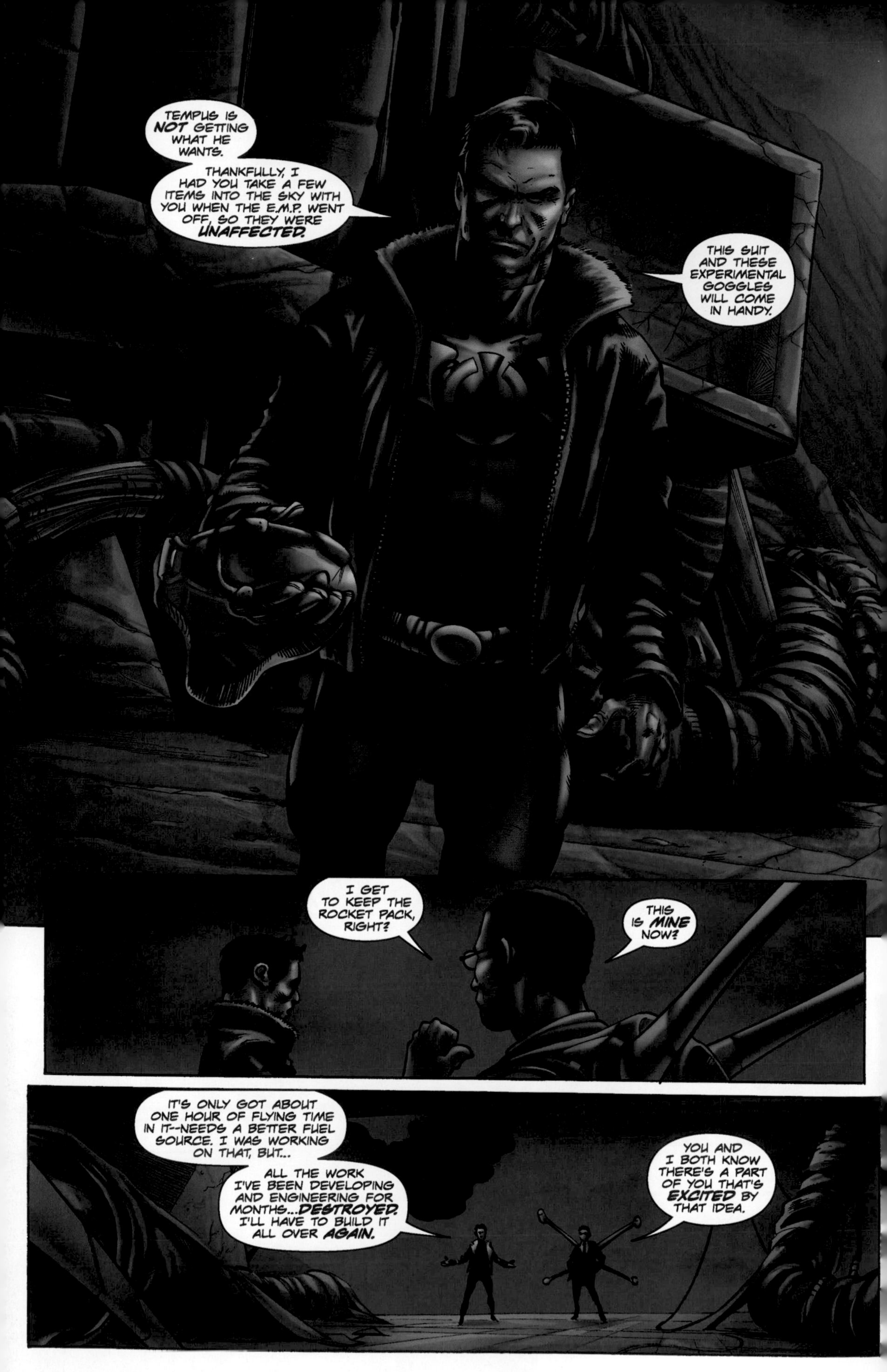
TEMPUS IS NOT GETTING WHAT HE WANTS.
THANKFULLY, I HAD YOU TAKE A FEW ITEMS INTO THE SKY WITH YOU WHEN THE E.M.P. WENT OFF, SO THEY WERE UNAFFECTED.
THIS SUIT AND THESE EXPERIMENTAL GOGGLES WILL COME IN HANDY.
I GET TO KEEP THE ROCKET PACK, RIGHT?
THIS IS MINE NOW?
IT'S ONLY GOT ABOUT ONE HOUR OF FLYING TIME IN IT--NEEDS A BETTER FUEL SOURCE. I WAS WORKING ON THAT, BUT...
ALL THE WORK I'VE BEEN DEVELOPING AND ENGINEERING FOR MONTHS...DESTROYED. I'LL HAVE TO BUILD IT ALL OVER AGAIN.
YOU AND I BOTH KNOW THERE'S A PART OF YOU THAT'S EXCITED BY THAT IDEA.

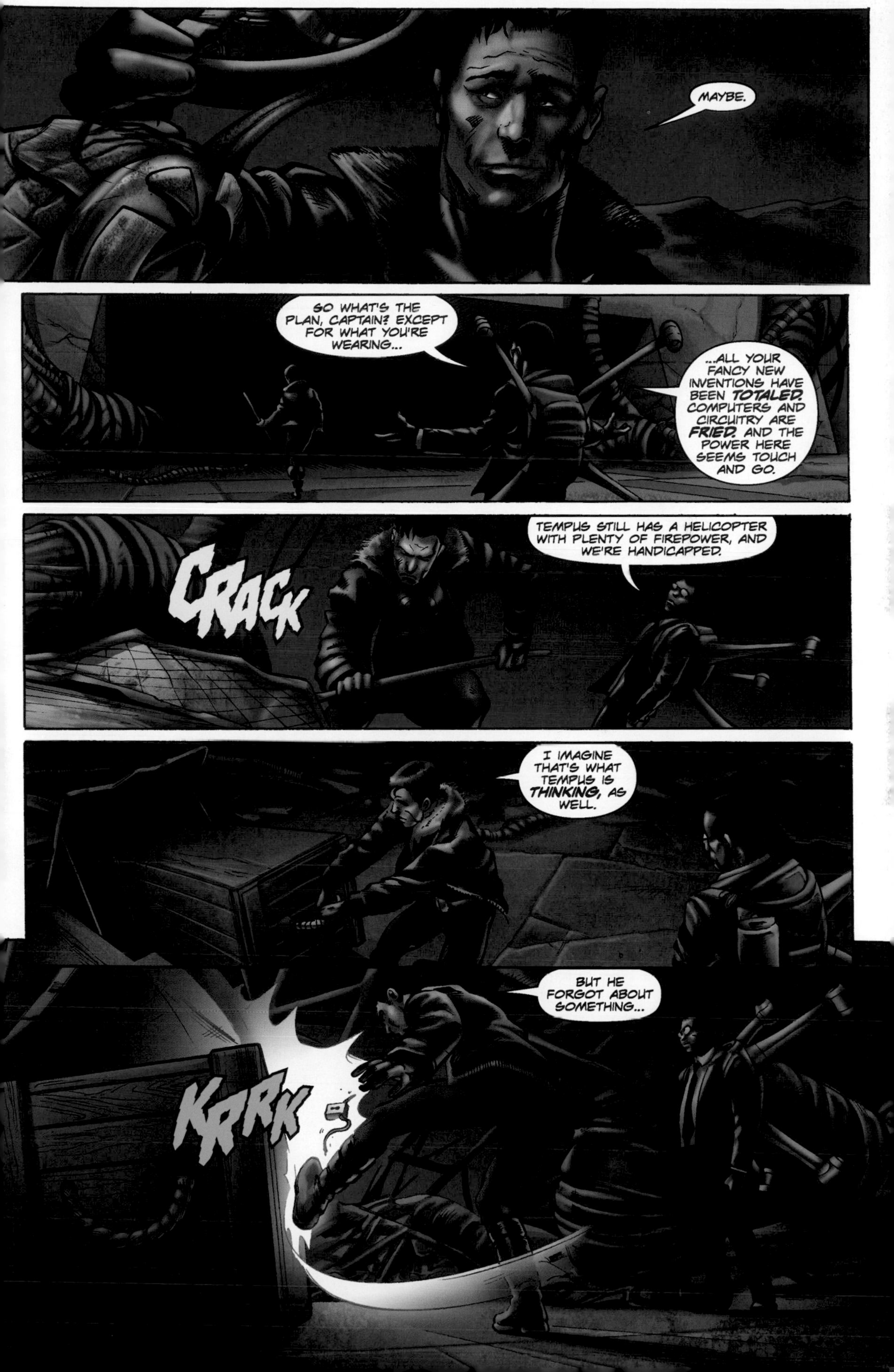
MAYBE.
SO WHAT'S THE PLAN, CAPTAIN? EXCEPT FOR WHAT YOU'RE WEARING...
...ALL YOUR FANCY NEW INVENTIONS HAVE BEEN TOTALED. COMPUTERS AND CIRCUITRY ARE FRIED. AND THE POWER HERE SEEMS TOUCH AND GO.
CRACK
TEMPUS STILL HAS A HELICOPTER WITH PLENTY OF FIREPOWER, AND WE'RE HANDICAPPED.
I IMAGINE THAT'S WHAT TEMPUS IS THINKING, AS WELL.
BUT HE FORGOT ABOUT SOMETHING...
KRRK

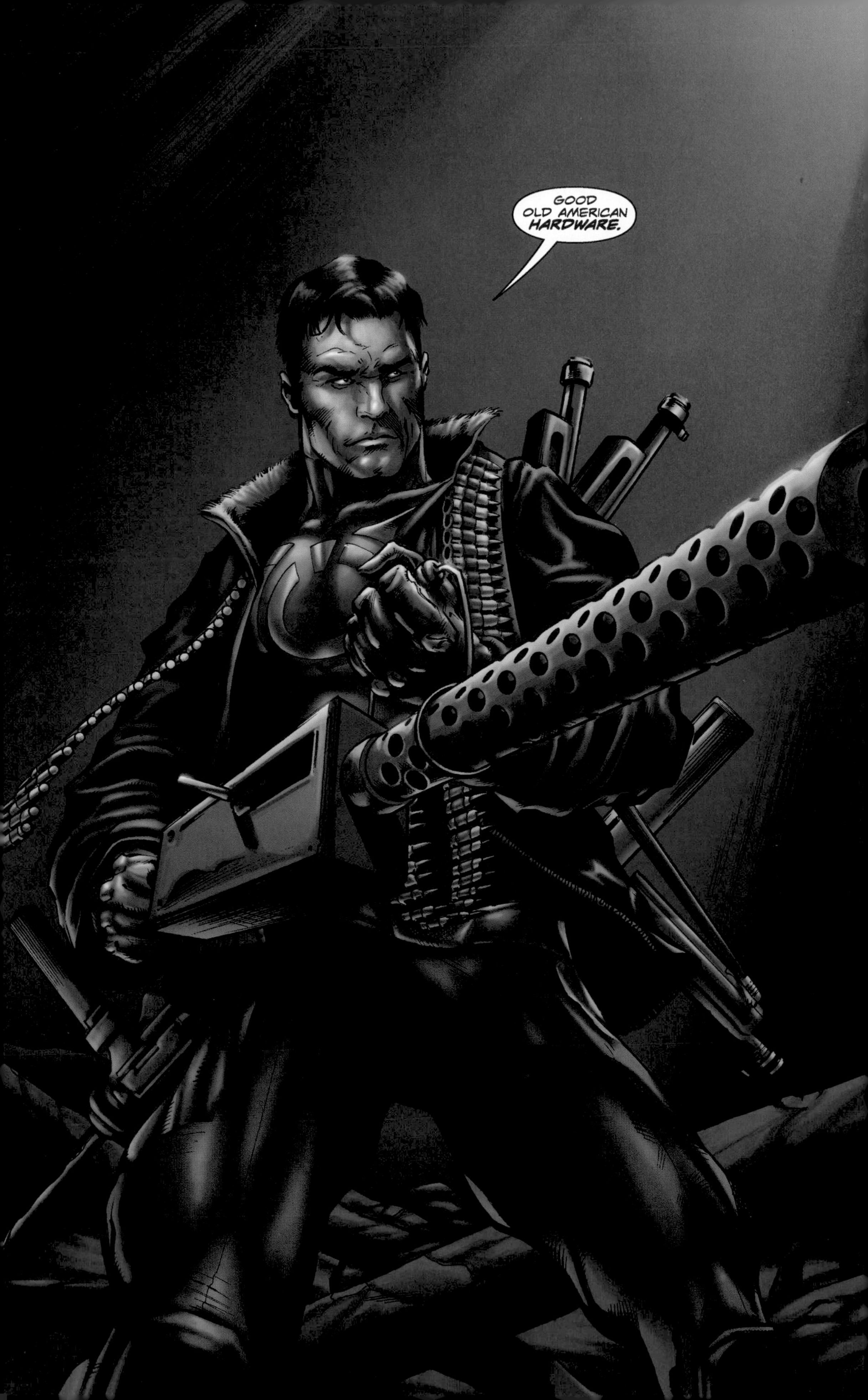
GOOD OLD AMERICAN HARDWARE.

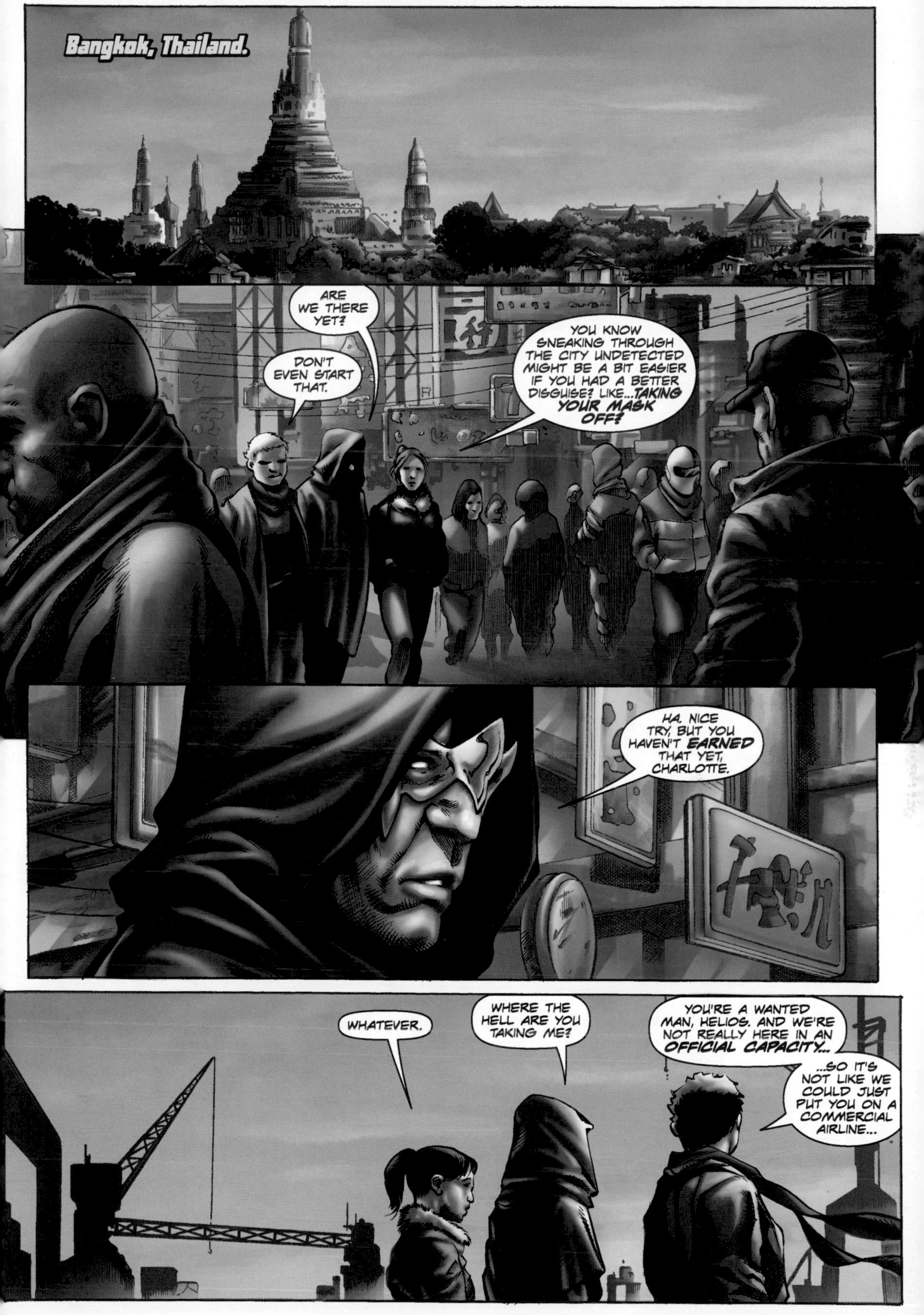
Bangkok, Thailand.
ARE WE THERE YET?
DON'T EVEN START THAT.
YOU KNOW SNEAKING THROUGH THE CITY UNDETECTED MIGHT BE A BIT EASIER IF YOU HAD A BETTER DISGUISE? LIKE...TAKING YOUR MASK OFF?
HA. NICE TRY, BUT YOU HAVEN'T EARNED THAT YET, CHARLOTTE.
WHATEVER.
WHERE THE HELL ARE YOU TAKING ME?
YOU'RE A WANTED MAN, HELIOS. AND WE'RE NOT REALLY HERE IN AN OFFICIAL CAPACITY...
...SO IT'S NOT LIKE WE COULD JUST PUT YOU ON A COMMERCIAL AIRLINE...

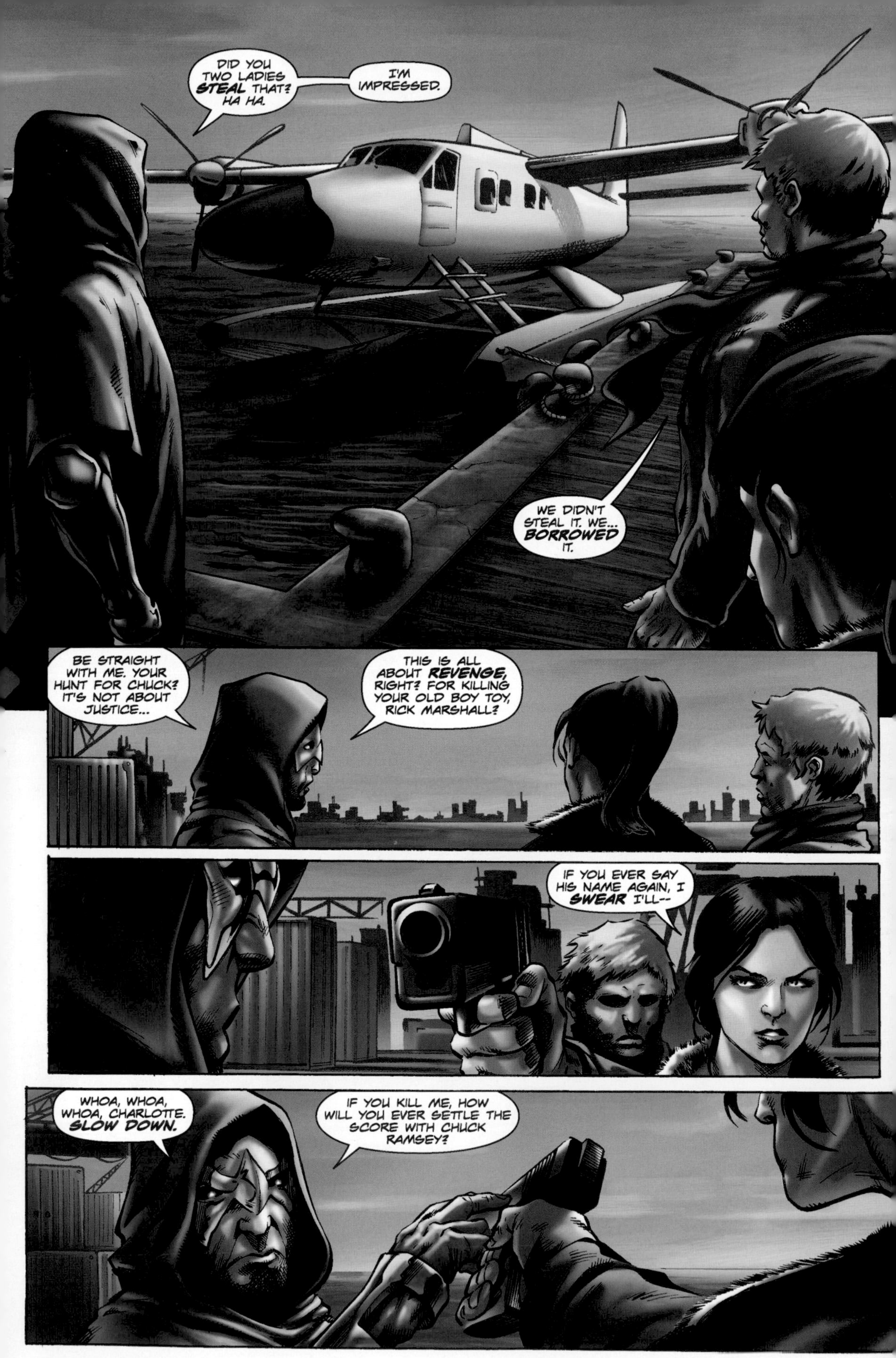
DID YOU TWO LADIES **STEAL** THAT? HA HA.
I'M IMPRESSED.
WE DIDN'T STEAL IT. WE... **BORROWED** IT.
BE STRAIGHT WITH ME. YOUR HUNT FOR CHUCK? IT'S NOT ABOUT JUSTICE...
THIS IS ALL ABOUT **REVENGE,** RIGHT? FOR KILLING YOUR OLD BOY TOY, RICK MARSHALL?
IF YOU EVER SAY HIS NAME AGAIN, I **SWEAR** I'LL--
WHOA, WHOA, WHOA, CHARLOTTE. **SLOW DOWN.**
IF YOU KILL ME, HOW WILL YOU EVER SETTLE THE SCORE WITH CHUCK RAMSEY?

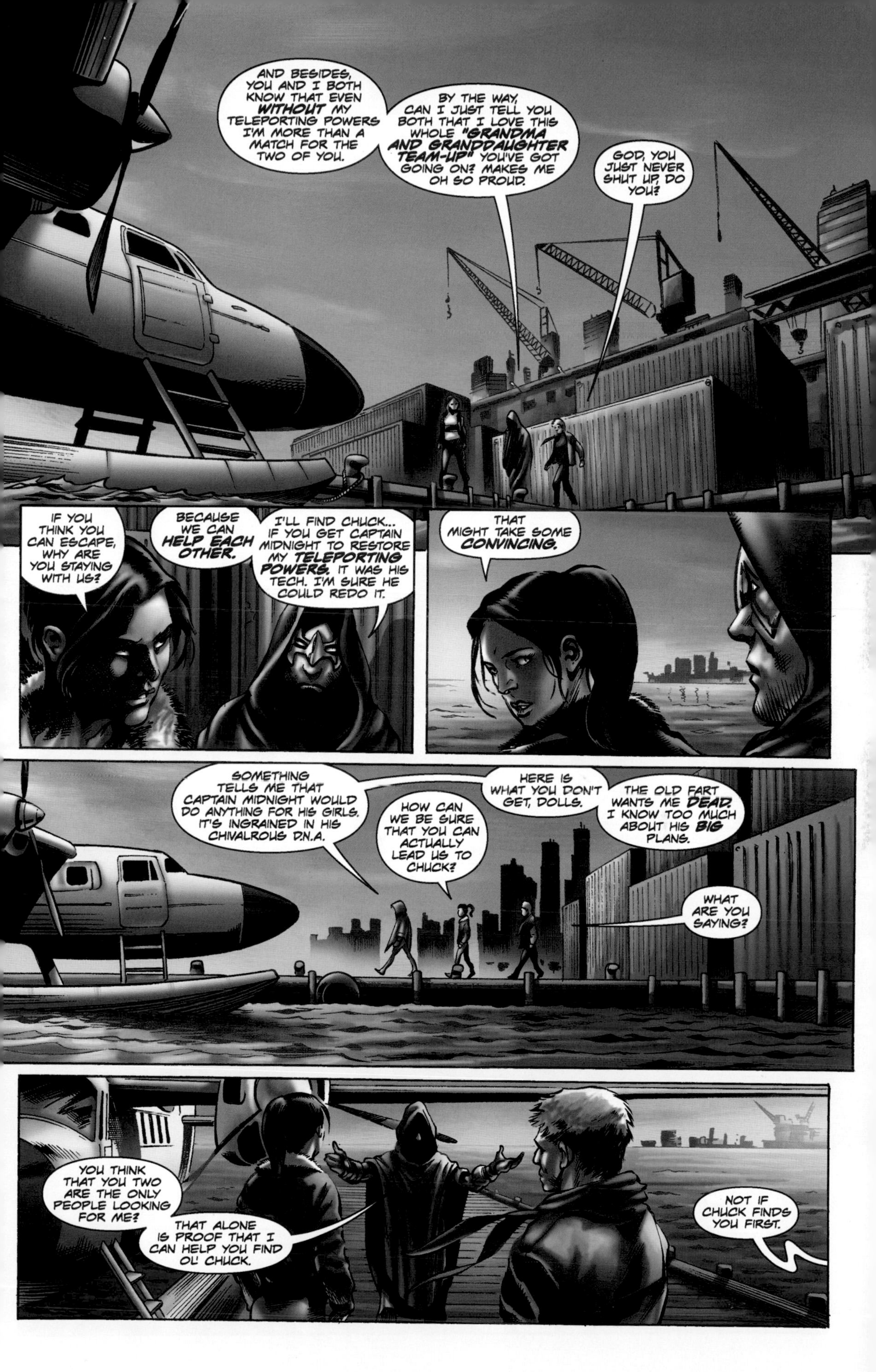
AND BESIDES, YOU AND I BOTH KNOW THAT EVEN WITHOUT MY TELEPORTING POWERS I'M MORE THAN A MATCH FOR THE TWO OF YOU.
BY THE WAY, CAN I JUST TELL YOU BOTH THAT I LOVE THIS WHOLE "GRANDMA AND GRANDDAUGHTER TEAM-UP" YOU'VE GOT GOING ON? MAKES ME OH SO PROUD.
GOD, YOU JUST NEVER SHUT UP, DO YOU?
IF YOU THINK YOU CAN ESCAPE, WHY ARE YOU STAYING WITH US?
BECAUSE WE CAN HELP EACH OTHER.
I'LL FIND CHUCK... IF YOU GET CAPTAIN MIDNIGHT TO RESTORE MY TELEPORTING POWERS. IT WAS HIS TECH. I'M SURE HE COULD REDO IT.
THAT MIGHT TAKE SOME CONVINCING.
SOMETHING TELLS ME THAT CAPTAIN MIDNIGHT WOULD DO ANYTHING FOR HIS GIRLS. IT'S INGRAINED IN HIS CHIVALROUS D.N.A.
HOW CAN WE BE SURE THAT YOU CAN ACTUALLY LEAD US TO CHUCK?
HERE IS WHAT YOU DON'T GET, DOLLS.
THE OLD FART WANTS ME DEAD. I KNOW TOO MUCH ABOUT HIS BIG PLANS.
WHAT ARE YOU SAYING?
YOU THINK THAT YOU TWO ARE THE ONLY PEOPLE LOOKING FOR ME?
THAT ALONE IS PROOF THAT I CAN HELP YOU FIND OL' CHUCK.
NOT IF CHUCK FINDS YOU FIRST.

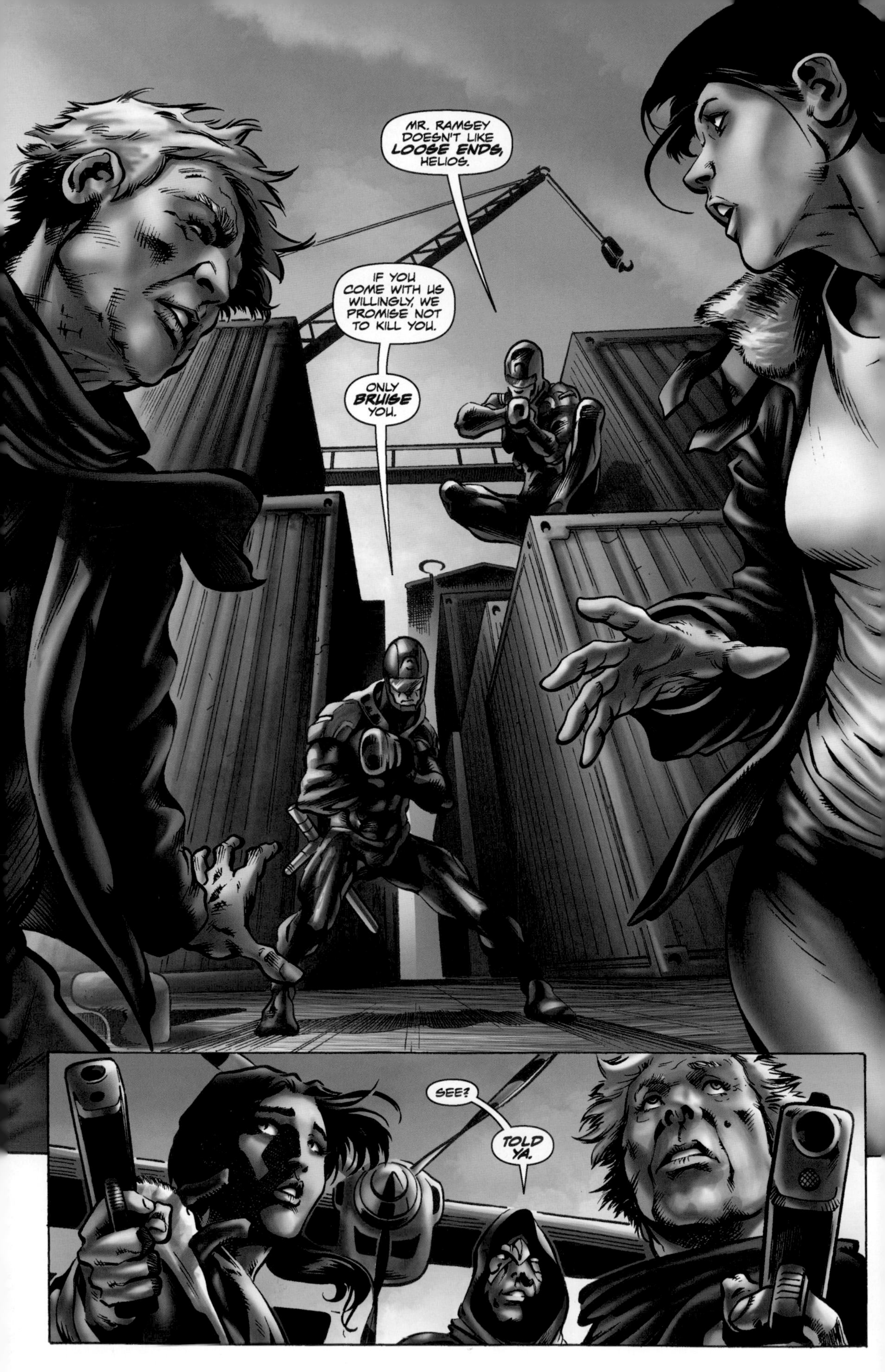
MR. RAMSEY DOESN'T LIKE **LOOSE ENDS,** HELIOS.
IF YOU COME WITH US WILLINGLY, WE PROMISE NOT TO KILL YOU.
ONLY **BRUISE** YOU.
SEE?
TOLD YA.

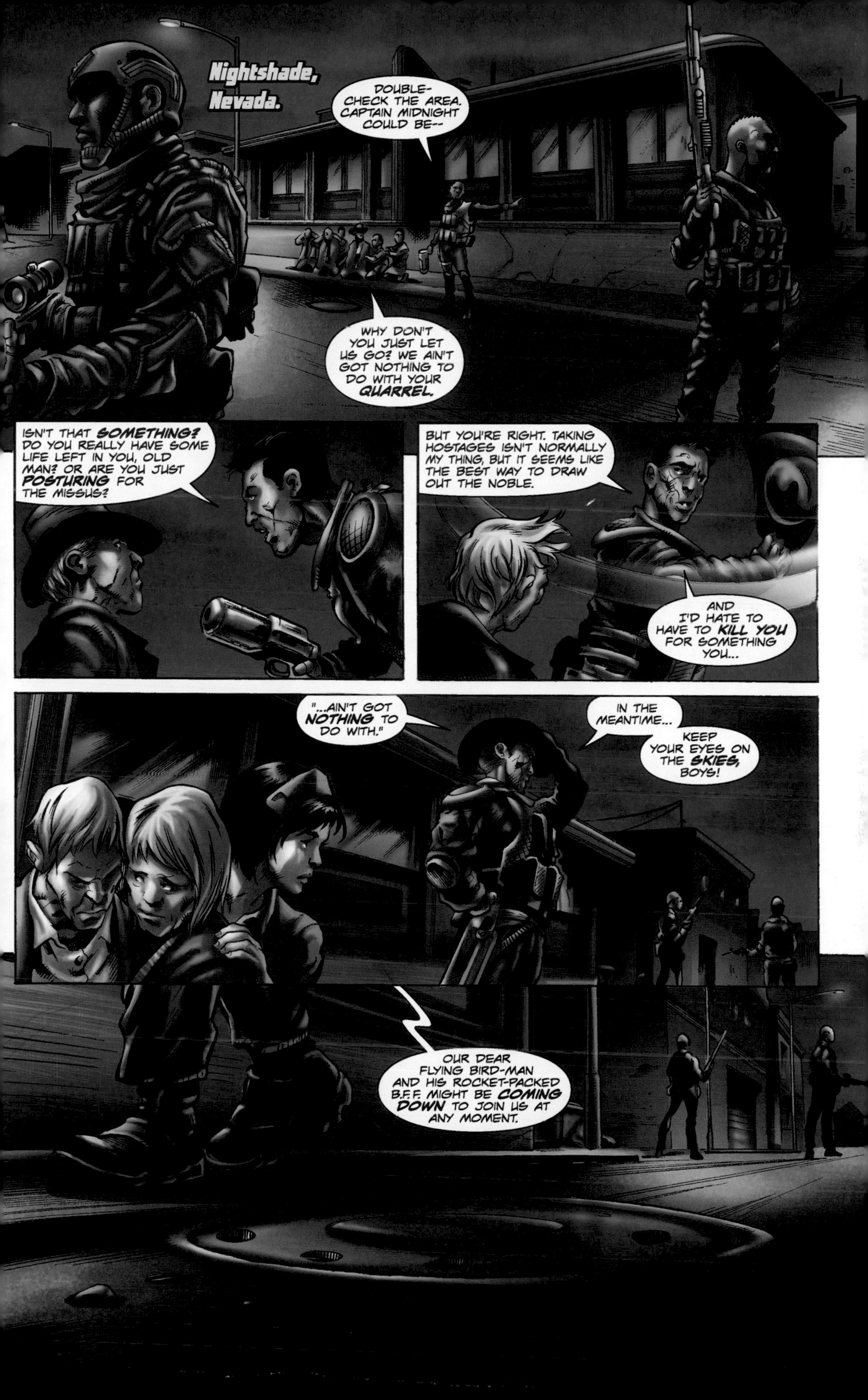
Nightshade, Nevada.
DOUBLE-CHECK THE AREA. CAPTAIN MIDNIGHT COULD BE--
WHY DON'T YOU JUST LET US GO? WE AIN'T GOT NOTHING TO DO WITH YOUR QUARREL.
ISN'T THAT SOMETHING? DO YOU REALLY HAVE SOME LIFE LEFT IN YOU, OLD MAN? OR ARE YOU JUST POSTURING FOR THE MISSUS?
BUT YOU'RE RIGHT. TAKING HOSTAGES ISN'T NORMALLY MY THING, BUT IT SEEMS LIKE THE BEST WAY TO DRAW OUT THE NOBLE.
AND I'D HATE TO HAVE TO KILL YOU FOR SOMETHING YOU...
"...AIN'T GOT NOTHING TO DO WITH."
IN THE MEANTIME...
KEEP YOUR EYES ON THE SKIES, BOYS!
OUR DEAR FLYING BIRD-MAN AND HIS ROCKET-PACKED B.F.F. MIGHT BE COMING DOWN TO JOIN US AT ANY MOMENT.

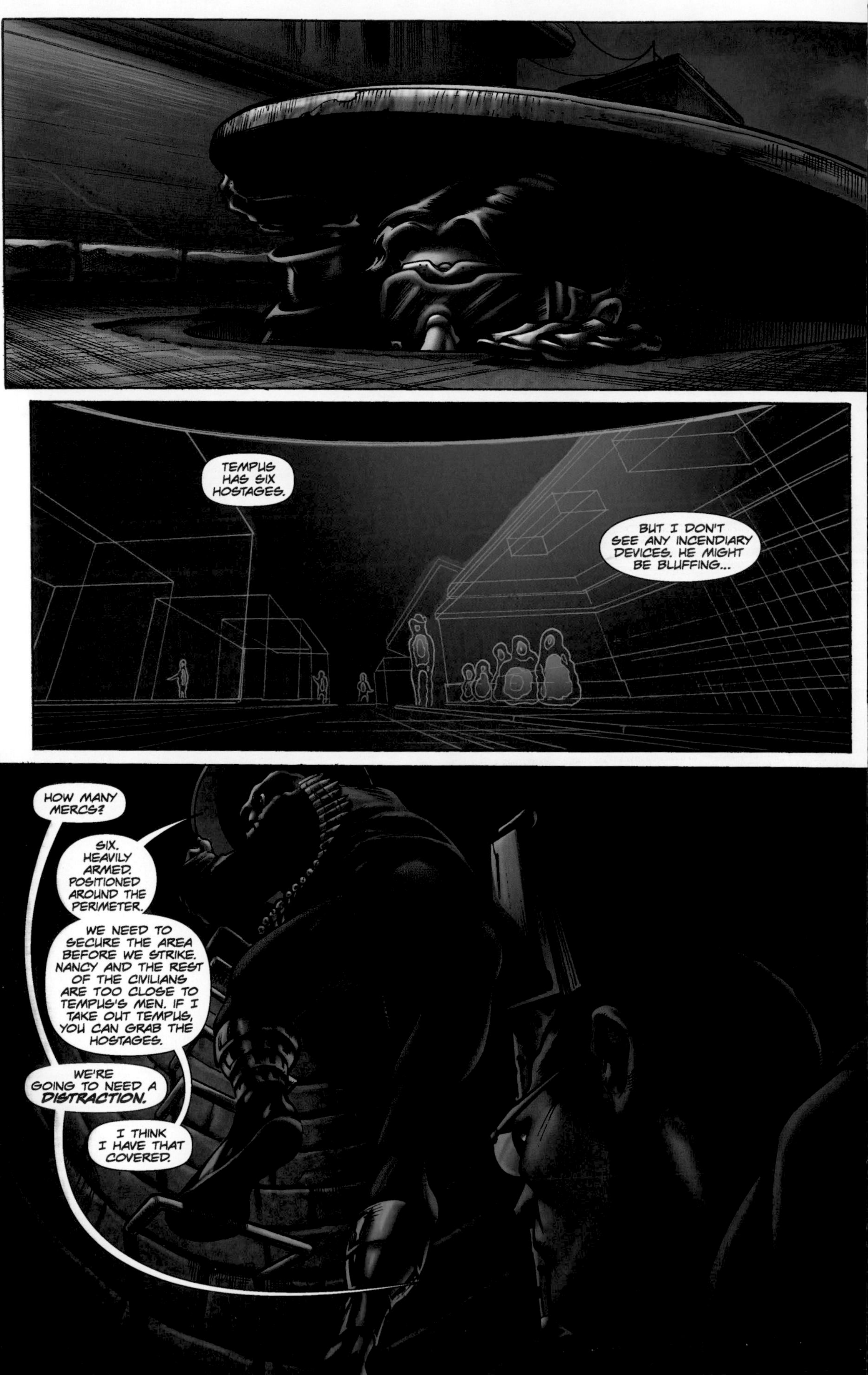
TEMPUS HAS SIX HOSTAGES.
BUT I DON'T SEE ANY INCENDIARY DEVICES. HE MIGHT BE BLUFFING...
HOW MANY MERCS?
SIX. HEAVILY ARMED. POSITIONED AROUND THE PERIMETER.
WE NEED TO SECURE THE AREA BEFORE WE STRIKE. NANCY AND THE REST OF THE CIVILIANS ARE TOO CLOSE TO TEMPUS'S MEN. IF I TAKE OUT TEMPUS, YOU CAN GRAB THE HOSTAGES.
WE'RE GOING TO NEED A DISTRACTION.
I THINK I HAVE THAT COVERED.

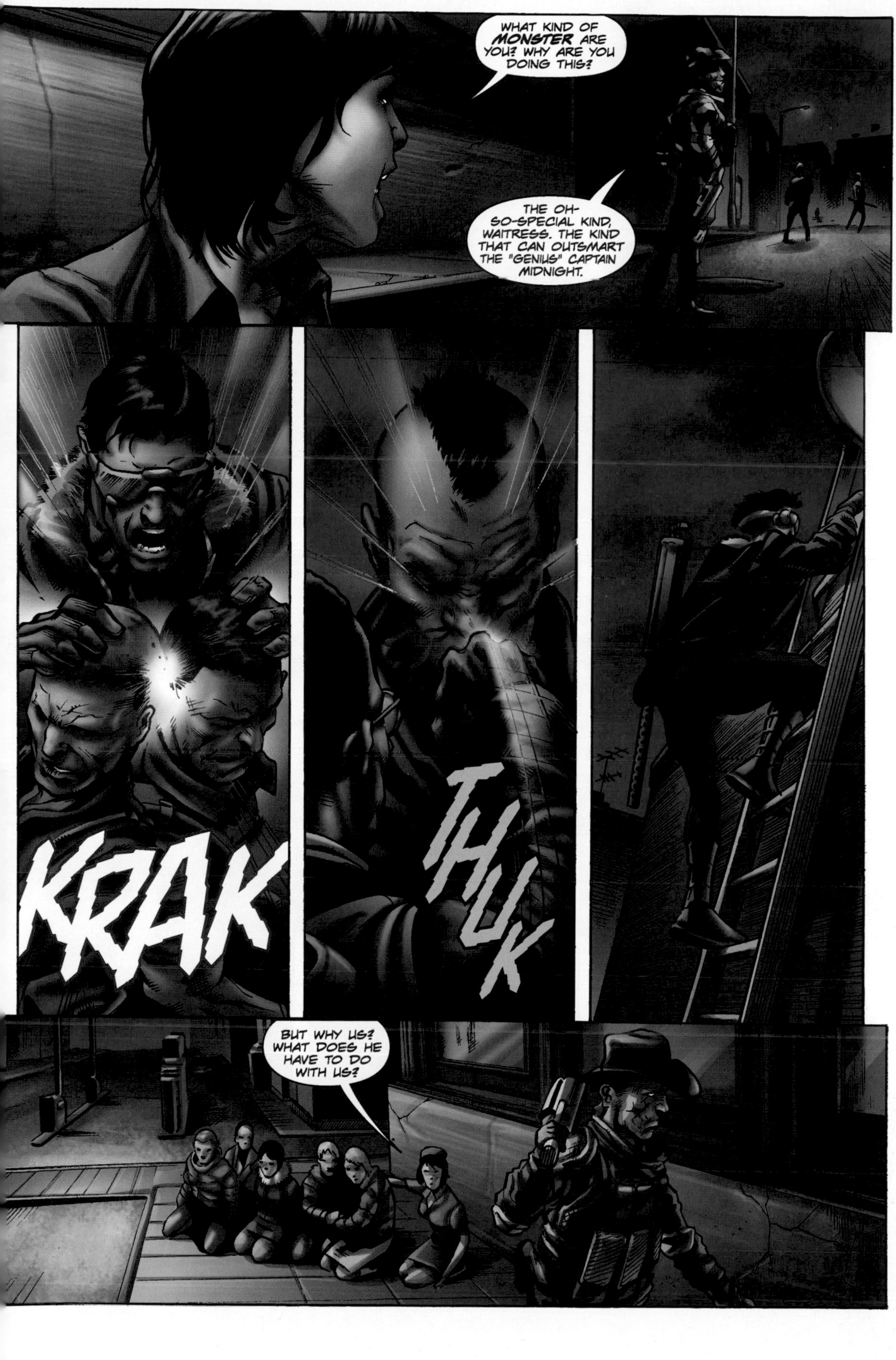
WHAT KIND OF MONSTER ARE YOU? WHY ARE YOU DOING THIS?
THE OH-SO-SPECIAL KIND, WAITRESS. THE KIND THAT CAN OUTSMART THE "GENIUS" CAPTAIN MIDNIGHT.
KRAK
THUK
BUT WHY US? WHAT DOES HE HAVE TO DO WITH US?

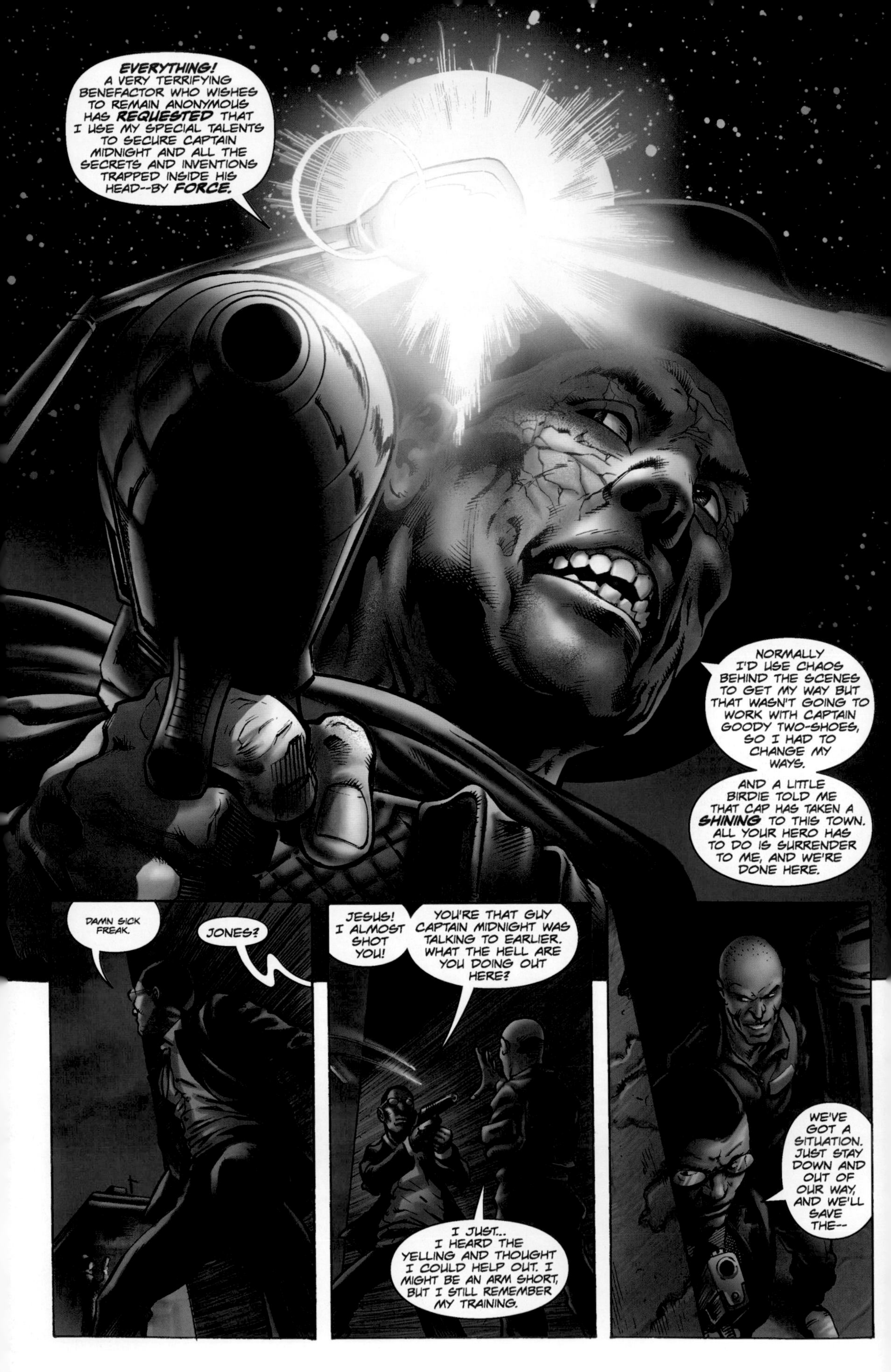
EVERYTHING! A VERY TERRIFYING BENEFACTOR WHO WISHES TO REMAIN ANONYMOUS HAS REQUESTED THAT I USE MY SPECIAL TALENTS TO SECURE CAPTAIN MIDNIGHT AND ALL THE SECRETS AND INVENTIONS TRAPPED INSIDE HIS HEAD--BY FORCE.
NORMALLY I'D USE CHAOS BEHIND THE SCENES TO GET MY WAY BUT THAT WASN'T GOING TO WORK WITH CAPTAIN GOODY TWO-SHOES, SO I HAD TO CHANGE MY WAYS.
AND A LITTLE BIRDIE TOLD ME THAT CAP HAS TAKEN A SHINING TO THIS TOWN. ALL YOUR HERO HAS TO DO IS SURRENDER TO ME, AND WE'RE DONE HERE.
DAMN SICK FREAK.
JONES?
JESUS! I ALMOST SHOT YOU!
YOU'RE THAT GUY CAPTAIN MIDNIGHT WAS TALKING TO EARLIER. WHAT THE HELL ARE YOU DOING OUT HERE?
I JUST... I HEARD THE YELLING AND THOUGHT I COULD HELP OUT. I MIGHT BE AN ARM SHORT, BUT I STILL REMEMBER MY TRAINING.
WE'VE GOT A SITUATION. JUST STAY DOWN AND OUT OF OUR WAY, AND WE'LL SAVE THE--

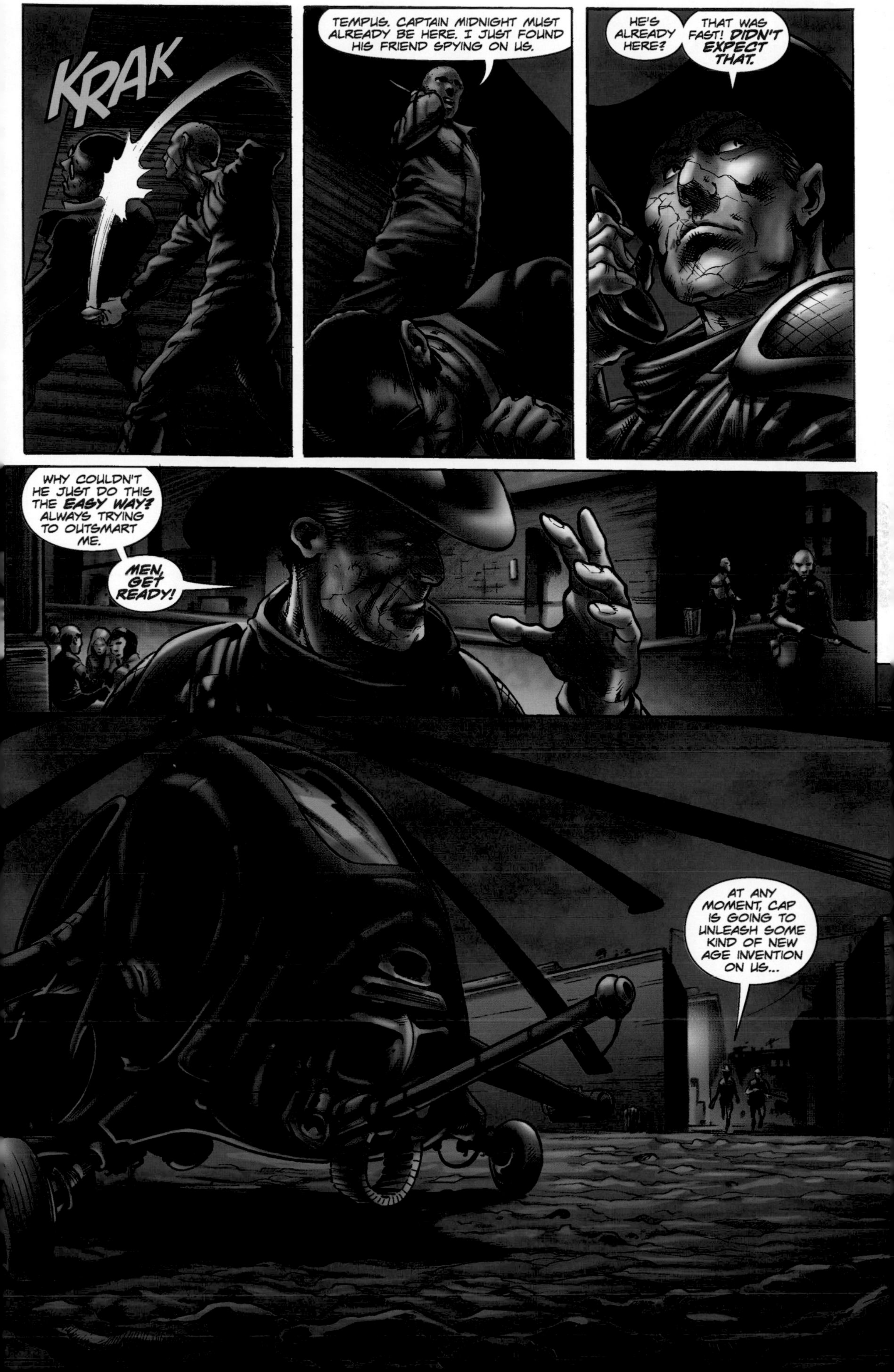
KRAK
TEMPUS. CAPTAIN MIDNIGHT MUST ALREADY BE HERE. I JUST FOUND HIS FRIEND SPYING ON US.
HE'S ALREADY HERE?
THAT WAS FAST! DIDN'T EXPECT THAT.
WHY COULDN'T HE JUST DO THIS THE EASY WAY? ALWAYS TRYING TO OUTSMART ME.
MEN, GET READY!
AT ANY MOMENT, CAP IS GOING TO UNLEASH SOME KIND OF NEW AGE INVENTION ON US...

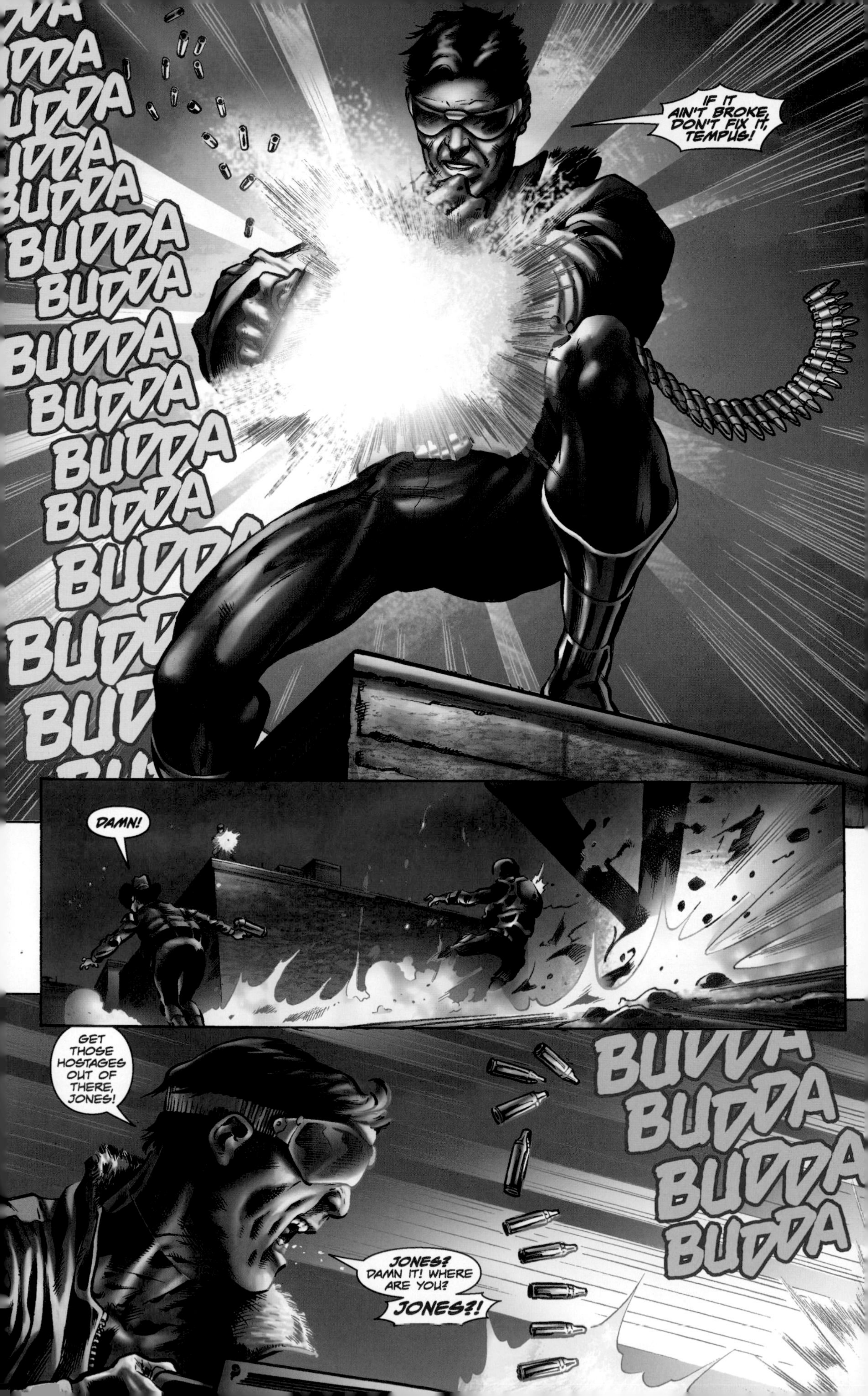
BUDDA
BUDDA
BUDDA
BUDDA
BUDDA
BUDDA
BUDDA
BUDDA
IF IT AIN'T BROKE, DON'T FIX IT, TEMPUS!
DAMN!
GET THOSE HOSTAGES OUT OF THERE, JONES!
BUDDA
BUDDA
BUDDA
JONES? DAMN IT! WHERE ARE YOU?
JONES?!

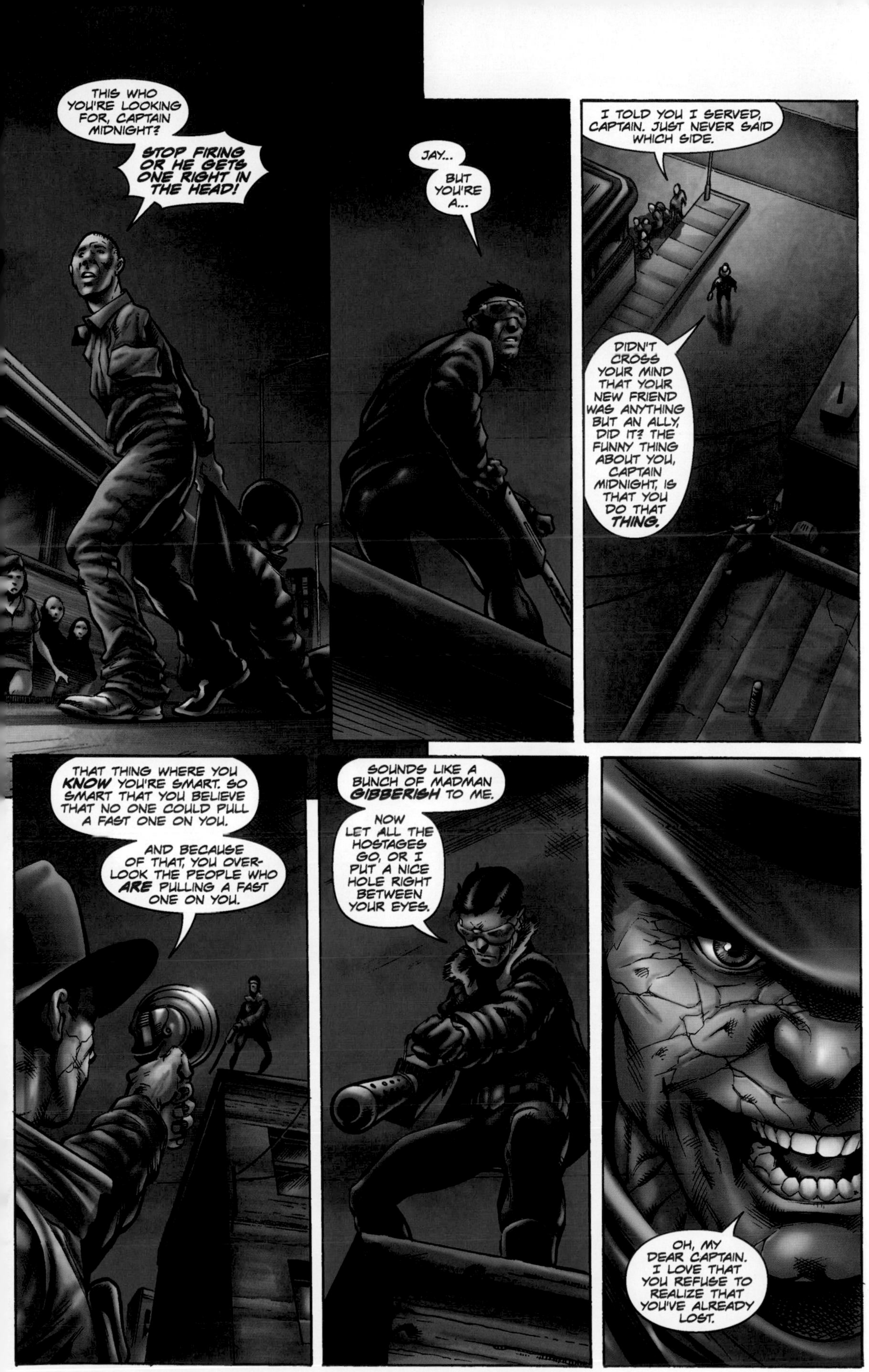
THIS WHO YOU'RE LOOKING FOR, CAPTAIN MIDNIGHT?
STOP FIRING OR HE GETS ONE RIGHT IN THE HEAD!
JAY...
BUT YOU'RE A...
I TOLD YOU I SERVED, CAPTAIN. JUST NEVER SAID WHICH SIDE.
DIDN'T CROSS YOUR MIND THAT YOUR NEW FRIEND WAS ANYTHING BUT AN ALLY, DID IT? THE FUNNY THING ABOUT YOU, CAPTAIN MIDNIGHT, IS THAT YOU DO THAT THING.
THAT THING WHERE YOU KNOW YOU'RE SMART. SO SMART THAT YOU BELIEVE THAT NO ONE COULD PULL A FAST ONE ON YOU.
AND BECAUSE OF THAT, YOU OVER-LOOK THE PEOPLE WHO ARE PULLING A FAST ONE ON YOU.
SOUNDS LIKE A BUNCH OF MADMAN GIBBERISH TO ME.
NOW LET ALL THE HOSTAGES GO, OR I PUT A NICE HOLE RIGHT BETWEEN YOUR EYES.
OH, MY DEAR CAPTAIN. I LOVE THAT YOU REFUSE TO REALIZE THAT YOU'VE ALREADY LOST.

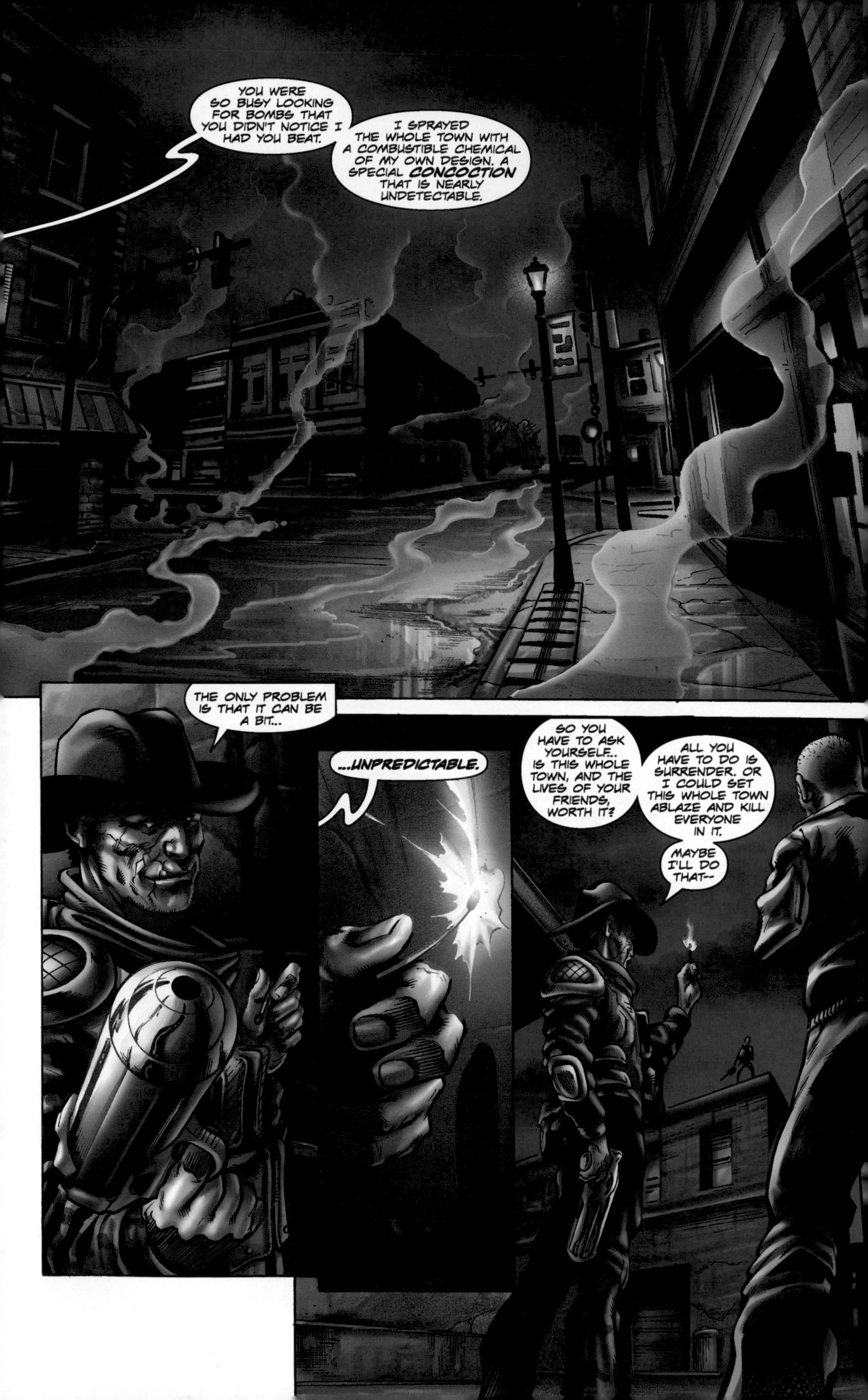
YOU WERE SO BUSY LOOKING FOR BOMBS THAT YOU DIDN'T NOTICE I HAD YOU BEAT.
I SPRAYED THE WHOLE TOWN WITH A COMBUSTIBLE CHEMICAL OF MY OWN DESIGN. A SPECIAL CONCOCTION THAT IS NEARLY UNDETECTABLE.
THE ONLY PROBLEM IS THAT IT CAN BE A BIT...
...UNPREDICTABLE.
SO YOU HAVE TO ASK YOURSELF.. IS THIS WHOLE TOWN, AND THE LIVES OF YOUR FRIENDS, WORTH IT?
ALL YOU HAVE TO DO IS SURRENDER. OR I COULD SET THIS WHOLE TOWN ABLAZE AND KILL EVERYONE IN IT.
MAYBE I'LL DO THAT--

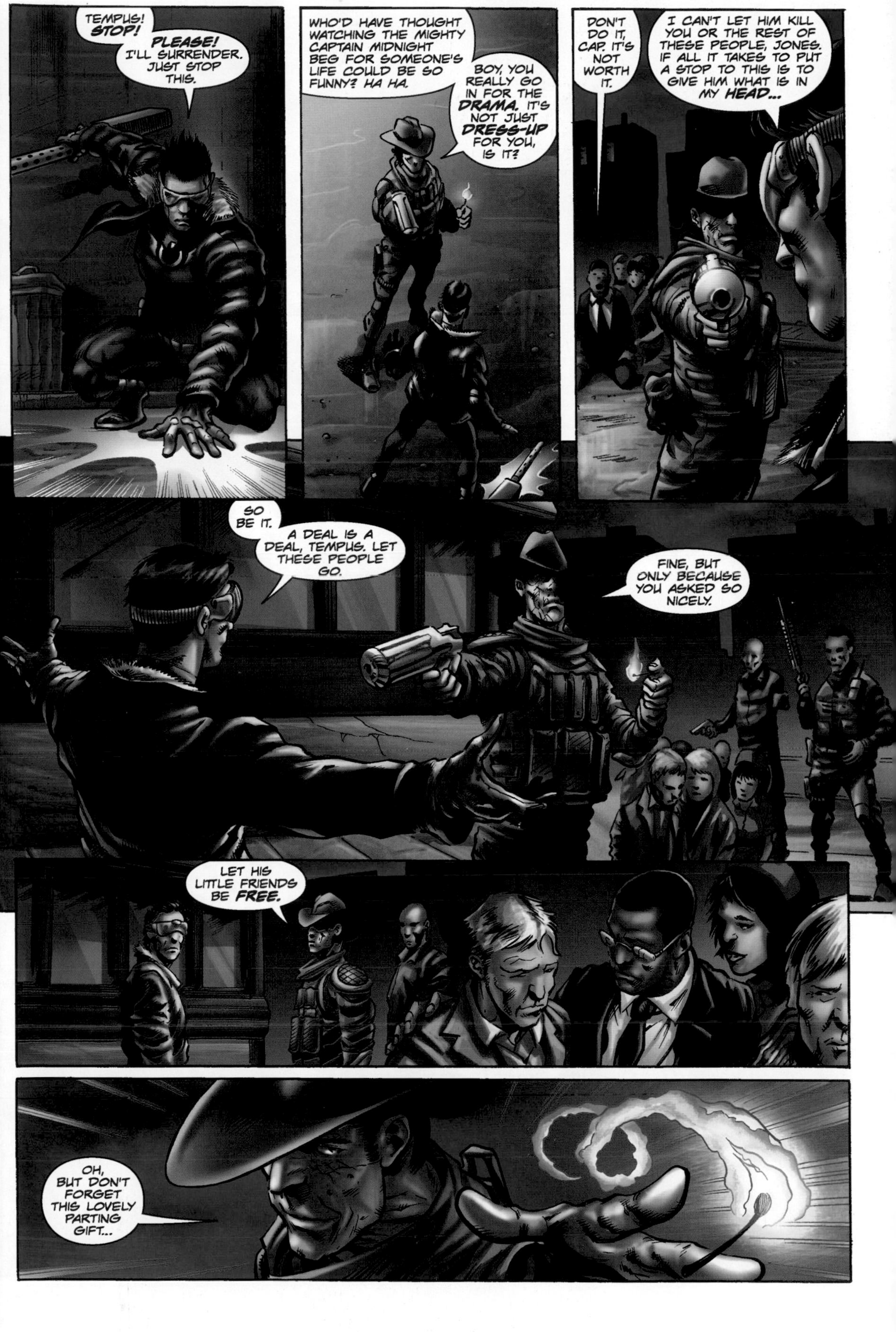
TEMPUS! STOP!
PLEASE! I'LL SURRENDER. JUST STOP THIS.
WHO'D HAVE THOUGHT WATCHING THE MIGHTY CAPTAIN MIDNIGHT BEG FOR SOMEONE'S LIFE COULD BE SO FUNNY? HA HA.
BOY, YOU REALLY GO IN FOR THE DRAMA. IT'S NOT JUST DRESS-UP FOR YOU, IS IT?
DON'T DO IT, CAP. IT'S NOT WORTH IT.
I CAN'T LET HIM KILL YOU OR THE REST OF THESE PEOPLE, JONES. IF ALL IT TAKES TO PUT A STOP TO THIS IS TO GIVE HIM WHAT IS IN MY HEAD...
SO BE IT.
A DEAL IS A DEAL, TEMPUS. LET THESE PEOPLE GO.
FINE, BUT ONLY BECAUSE YOU ASKED SO NICELY.
LET HIS LITTLE FRIENDS BE FREE.
OH, BUT DON'T FORGET THIS LOVELY PARTING GIFT...

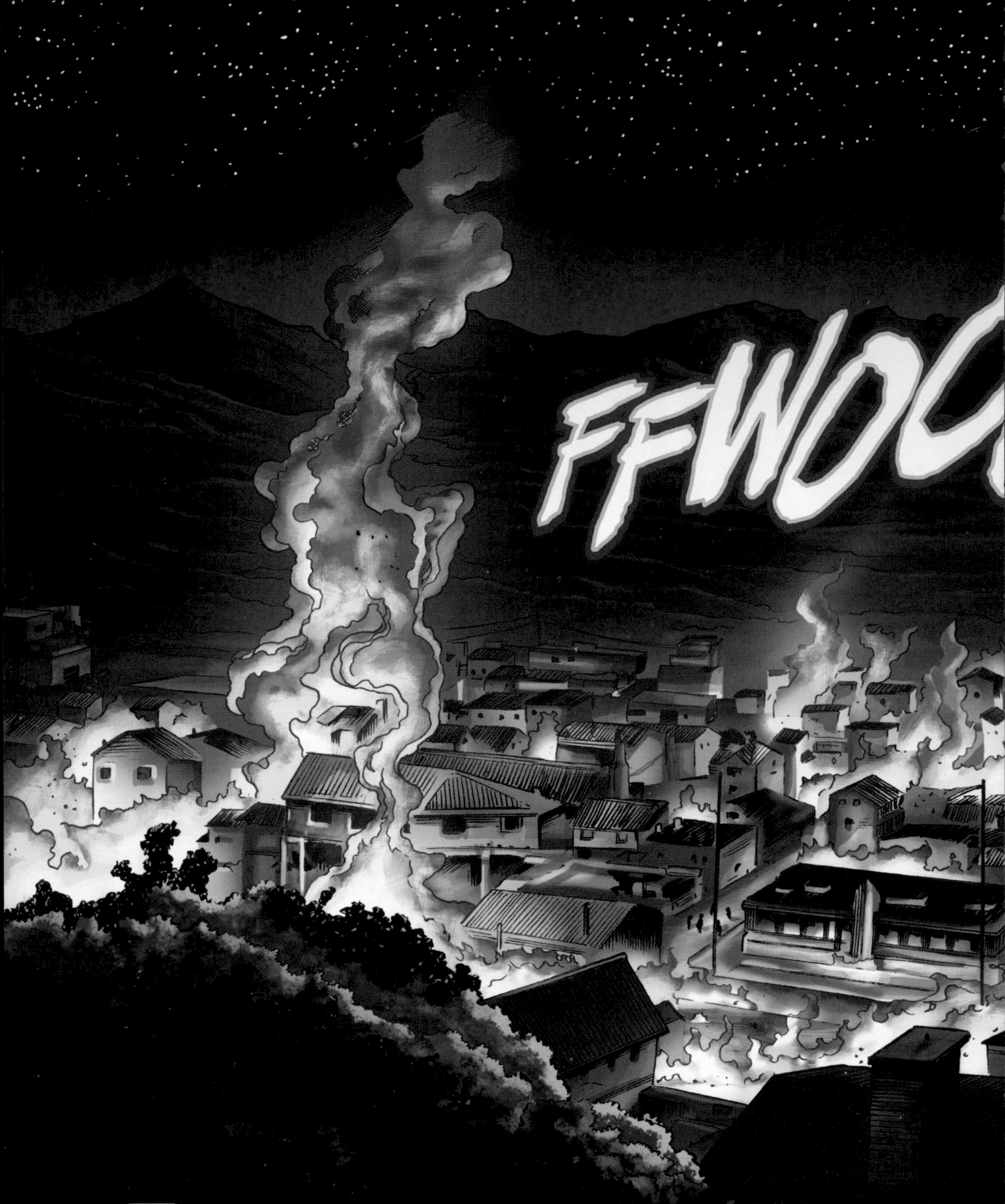
FFWOO

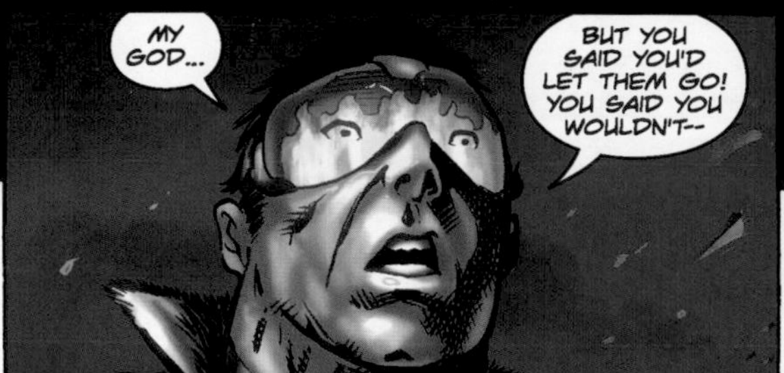
MY GOD...
BUT YOU SAID YOU'D LET THEM GO! YOU SAID YOU WOULDN'T--

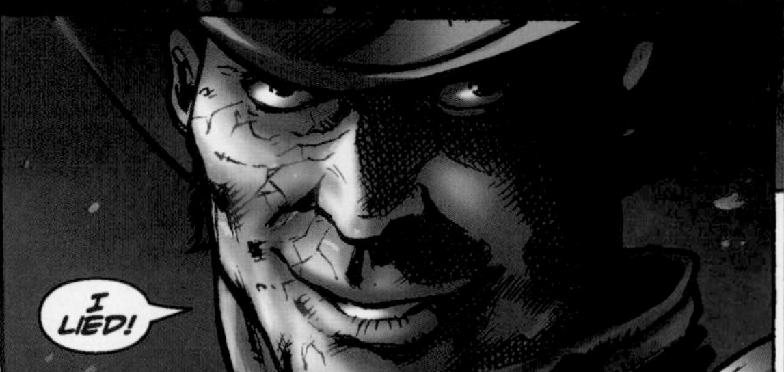
I LIED!

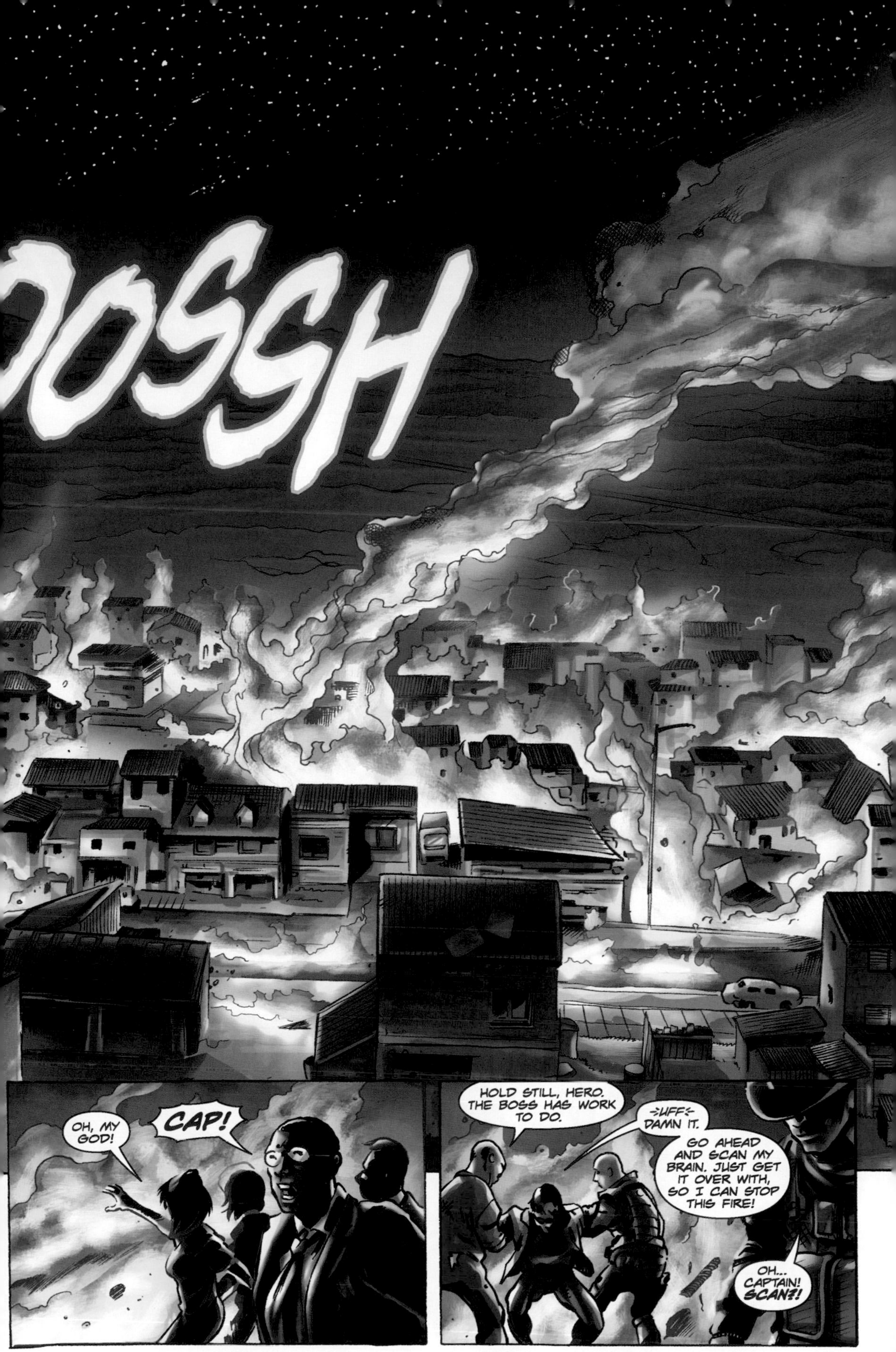

OOSSH
OH, MY GOD!
CAP!
HOLD STILL, HERO. THE BOSS HAS WORK TO DO.
-UFF- DAMN IT.
GO AHEAD AND SCAN MY BRAIN. JUST GET IT OVER WITH, SO I CAN STOP THIS FIRE!
OH... CAPTAIN! SCAN?!

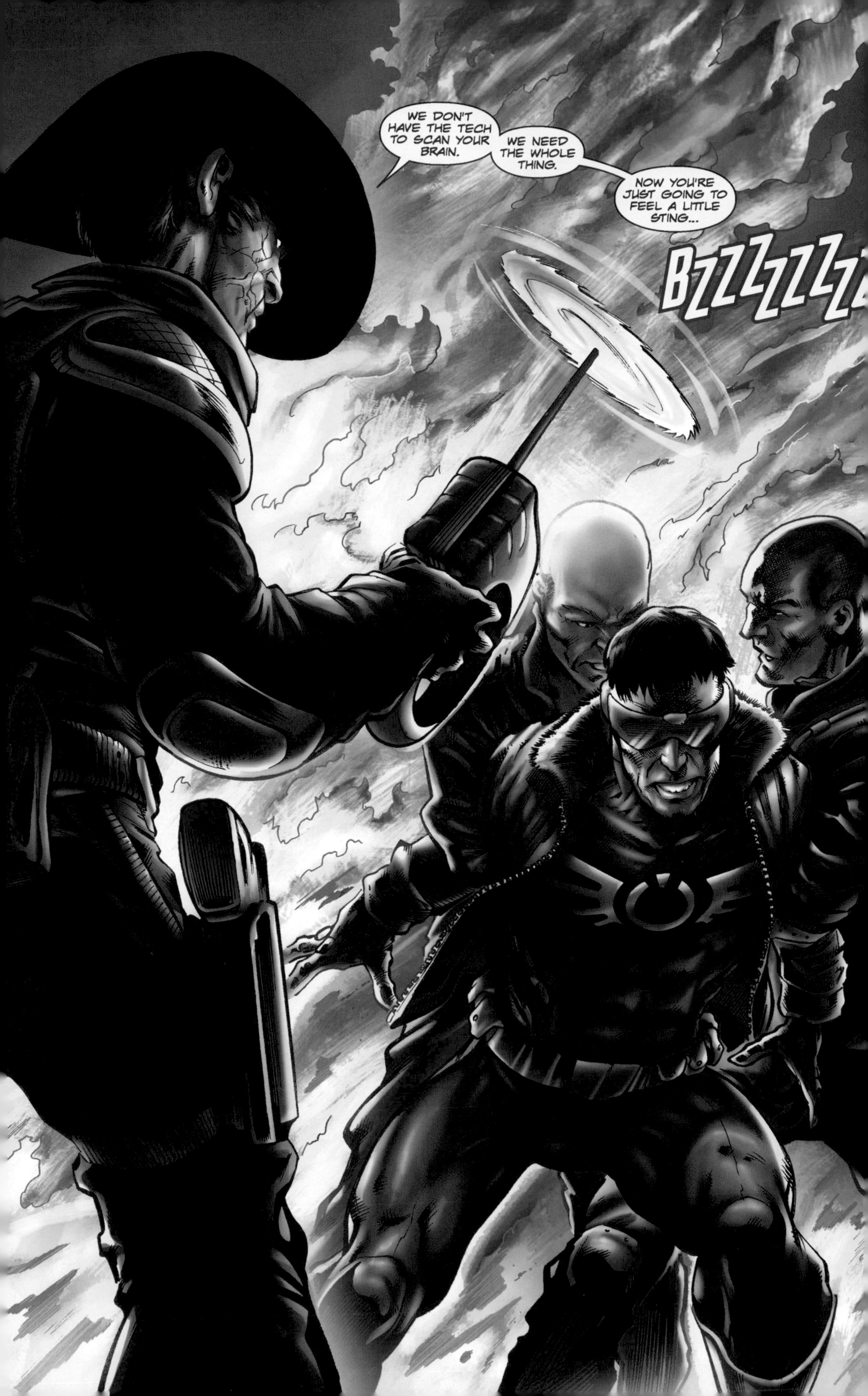
WE DON'T HAVE THE TECH TO SCAN YOUR BRAIN.
WE NEED THE WHOLE THING.
NOW YOU'RE JUST GOING TO FEEL A LITTLE STING...
BZZZZZZZ

CHAPTER 4

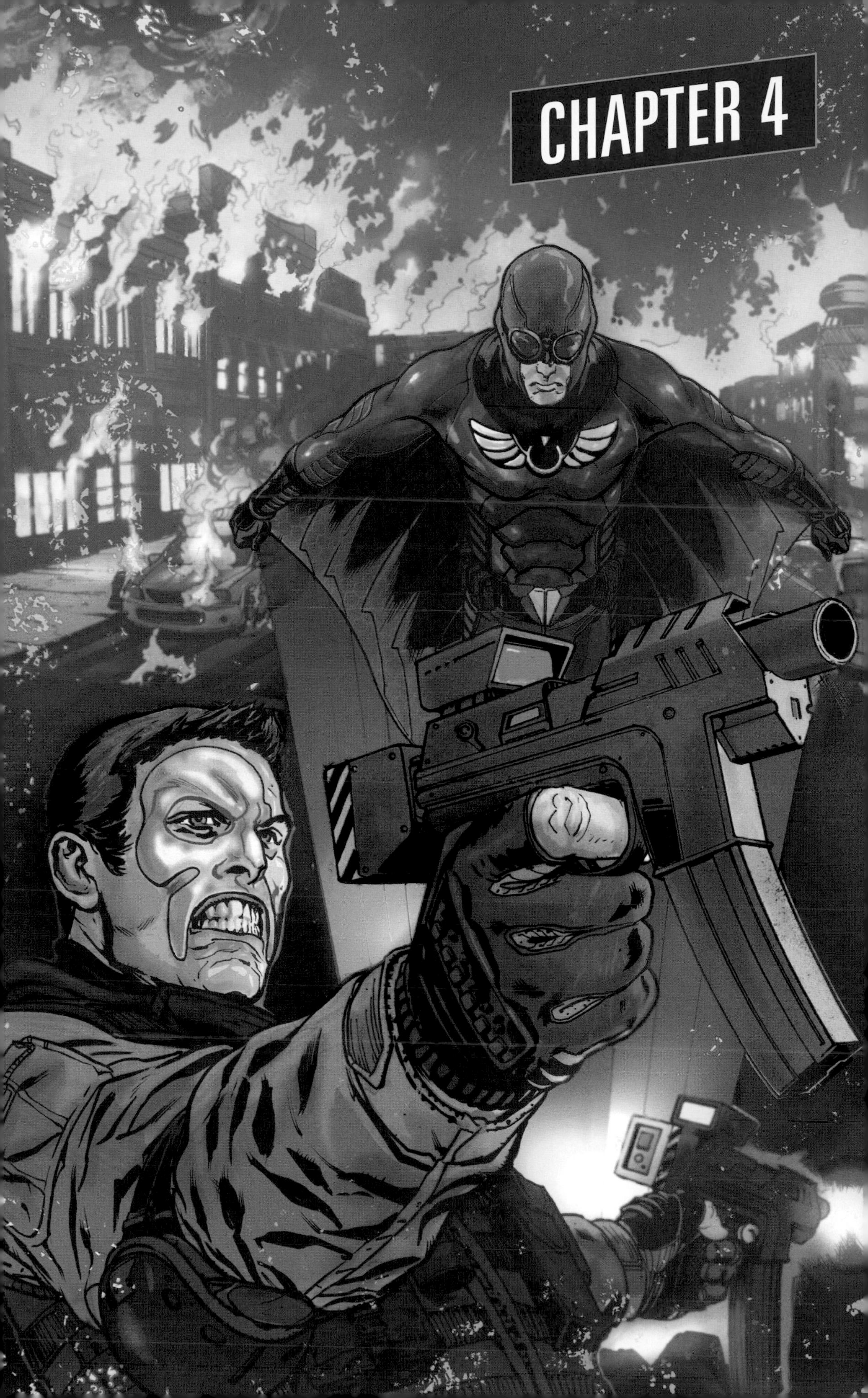

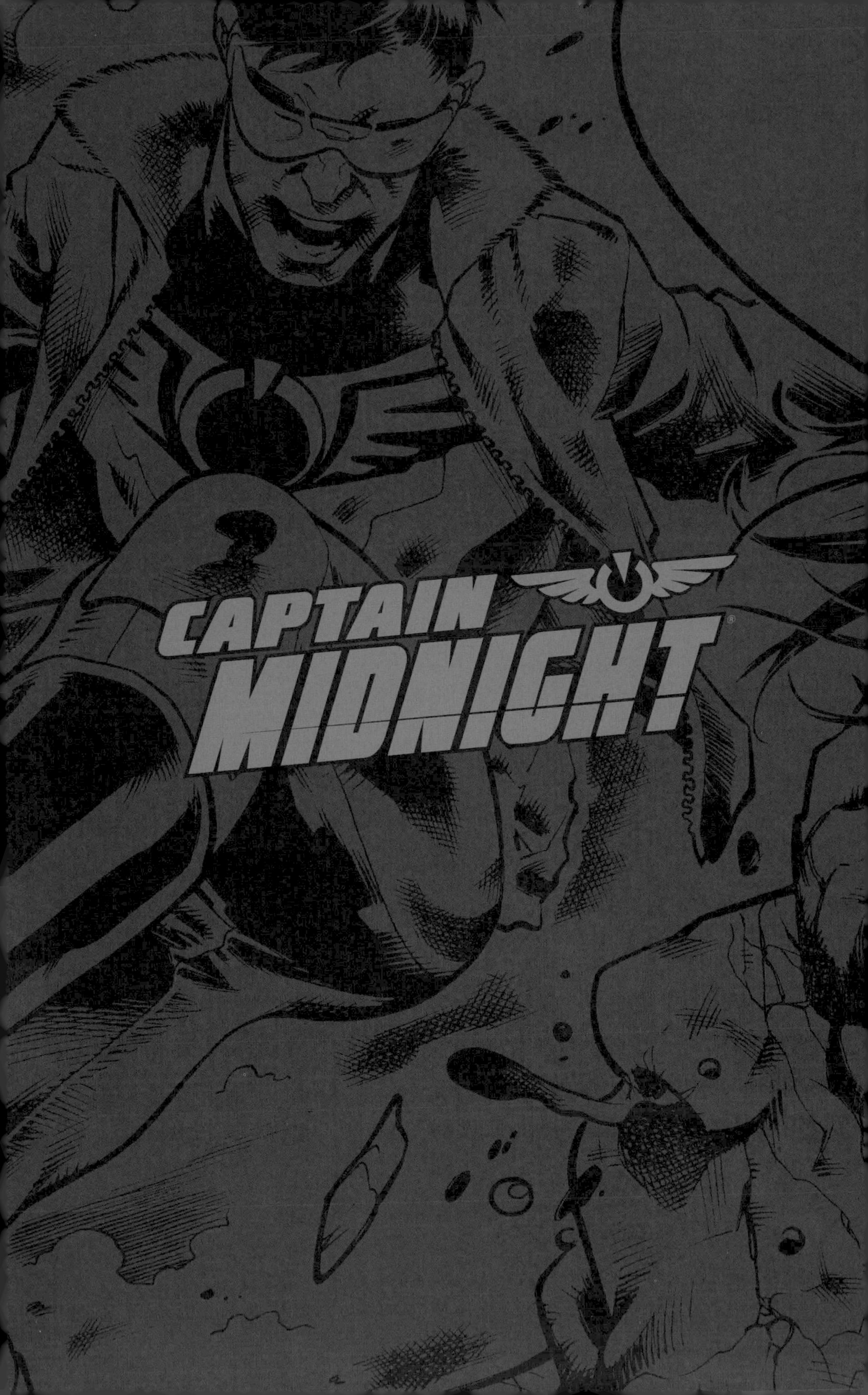
CAPTAIN MIDNIGHT

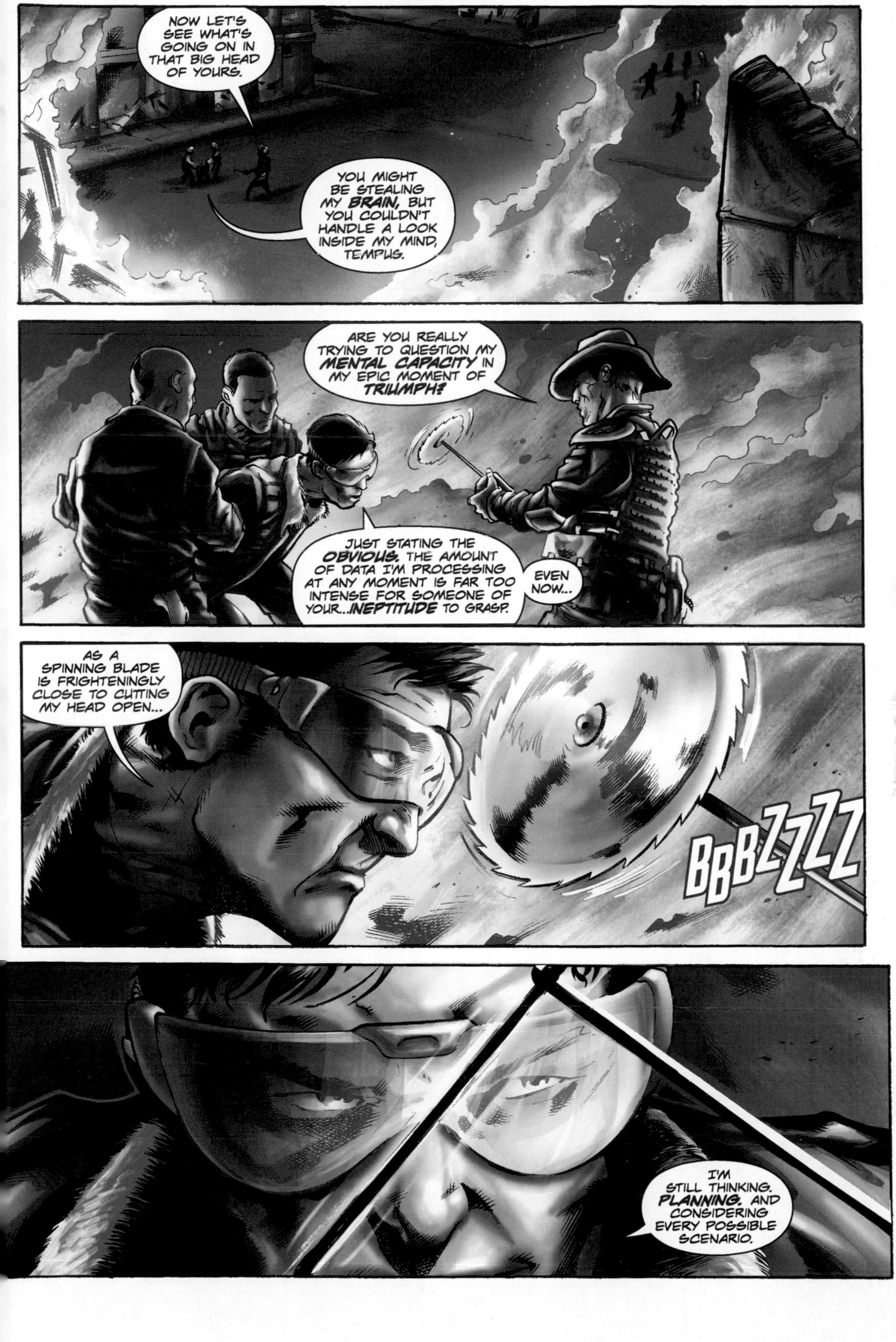
NOW LET'S SEE WHAT'S GOING ON IN THAT BIG HEAD OF YOURS.
YOU MIGHT BE STEALING MY BRAIN, BUT YOU COULDN'T HANDLE A LOOK INSIDE MY MIND, TEMPUS.
ARE YOU REALLY TRYING TO QUESTION MY MENTAL CAPACITY IN MY EPIC MOMENT OF TRIUMPH?
JUST STATING THE OBVIOUS. THE AMOUNT OF DATA I'M PROCESSING AT ANY MOMENT IS FAR TOO INTENSE FOR SOMEONE OF YOUR...INEPTITUDE TO GRASP.
EVEN NOW...
AS A SPINNING BLADE IS FRIGHTENINGLY CLOSE TO CUTTING MY HEAD OPEN...
BBBZZZZ
I'M STILL THINKING. PLANNING. AND CONSIDERING EVERY POSSIBLE SCENARIO.

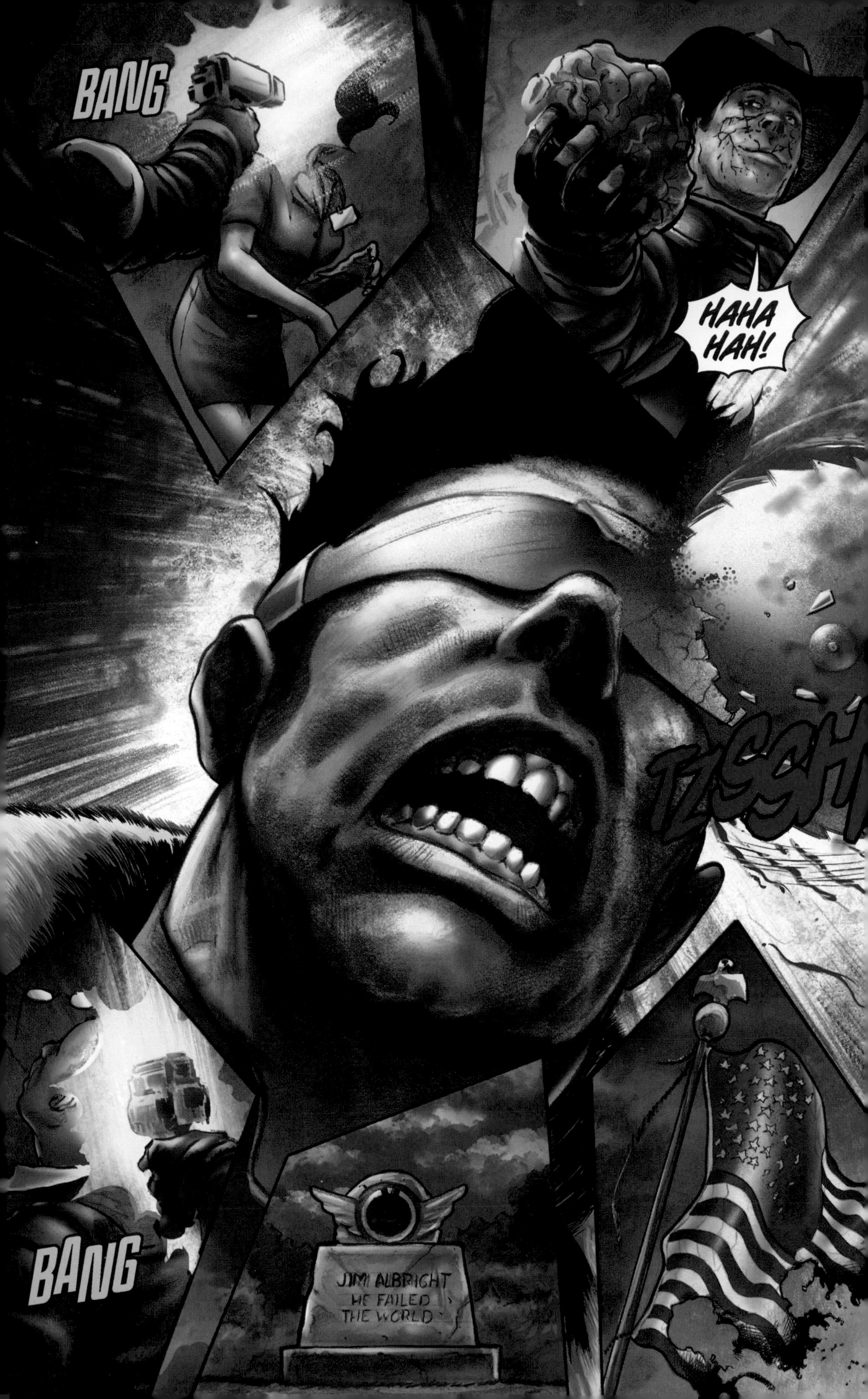
BANG
HAHA
HAH!
TZSSH
BANG
JIM ALBRIGHT
HE FAILED
THE WORLD

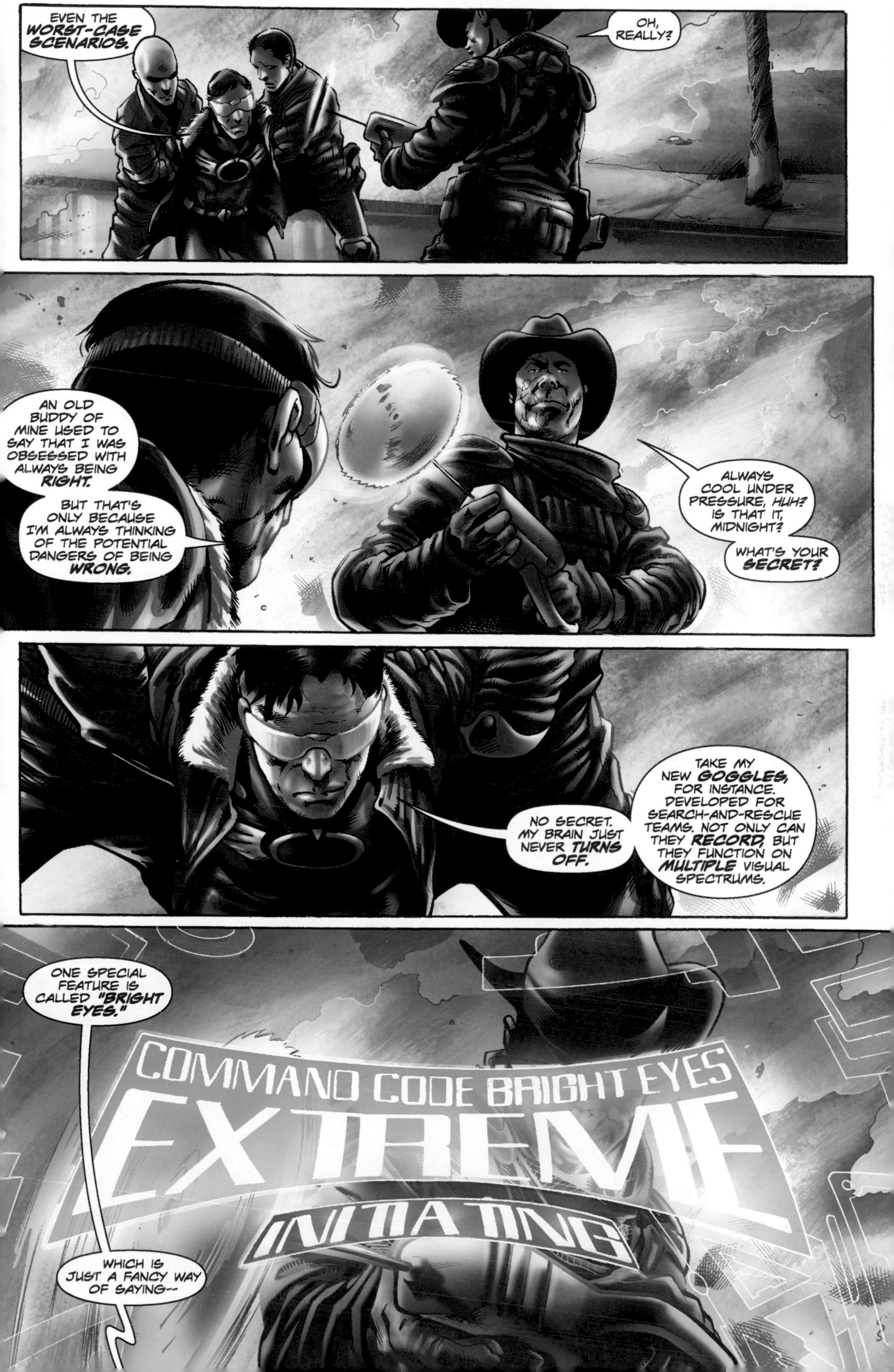
EVEN THE WORST-CASE SCENARIOS.
OH, REALLY?
AN OLD BUDDY OF MINE USED TO SAY THAT I WAS OBSESSED WITH ALWAYS BEING RIGHT.
BUT THAT'S ONLY BECAUSE I'M ALWAYS THINKING OF THE POTENTIAL DANGERS OF BEING WRONG.
ALWAYS COOL UNDER PRESSURE, HUH? IS THAT IT, MIDNIGHT?
WHAT'S YOUR SECRET?
NO SECRET. MY BRAIN JUST NEVER TURNS OFF.
TAKE MY NEW GOGGLES, FOR INSTANCE. DEVELOPED FOR SEARCH-AND-RESCUE TEAMS. NOT ONLY CAN THEY RECORD, BUT THEY FUNCTION ON MULTIPLE VISUAL SPECTRUMS.
ONE SPECIAL FEATURE IS CALLED "BRIGHT EYES."
COMMAND CODE BRIGHT EYES
EXTREME
INITIATING
WHICH IS JUST A FANCY WAY OF SAYING--

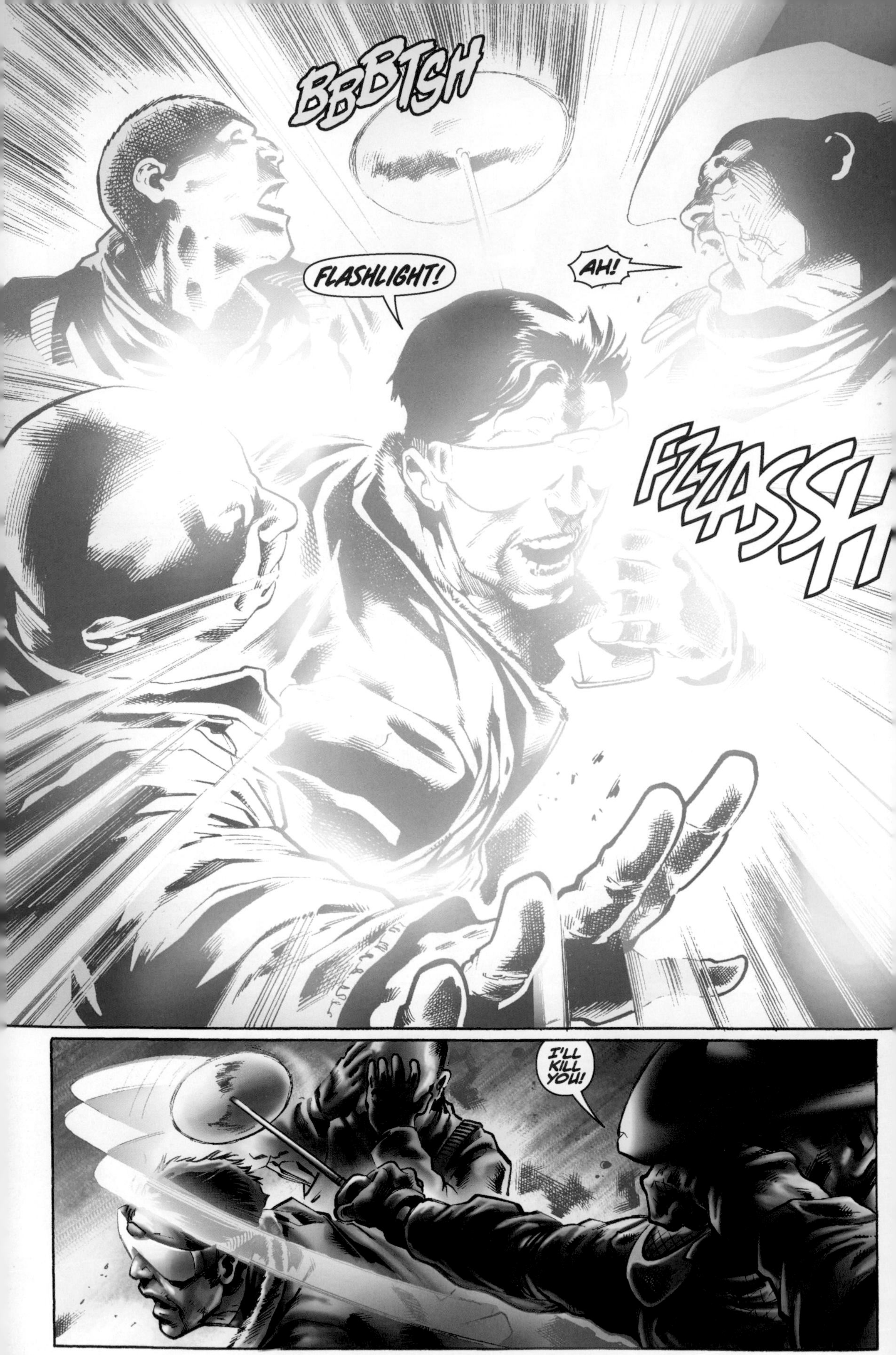
BBBTSH
FLASHLIGHT!
AH!
FZZASSH
I'LL KILL YOU!

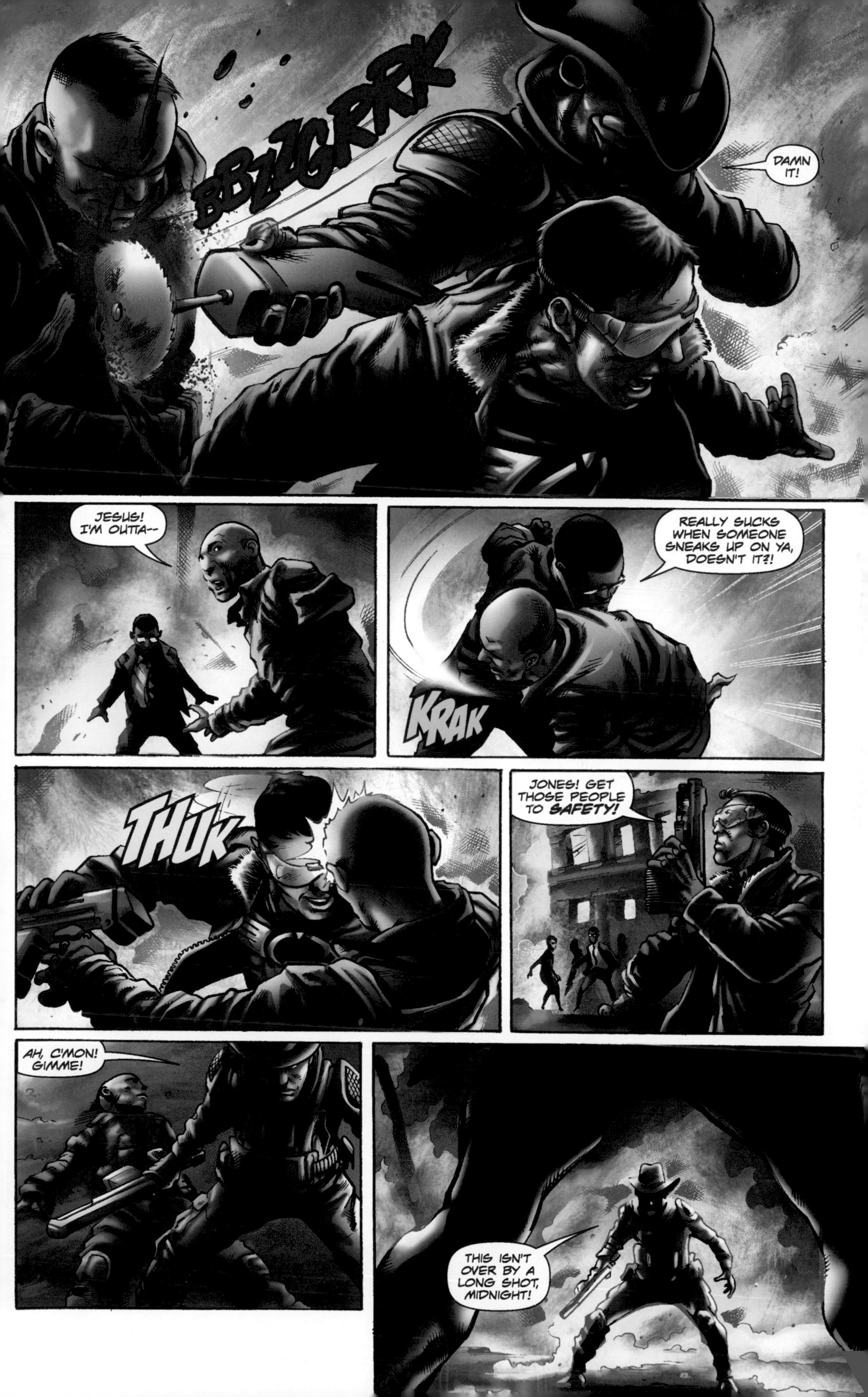
BBZZGRRK
DAMN IT!
JESUS! I'M OUTTA--
REALLY SUCKS WHEN SOMEONE SNEAKS UP ON YA, DOESN'T IT?!
KRAK
THUK
JONES! GET THOSE PEOPLE TO SAFETY!
AH, C'MON! GIMME!
THIS ISN'T OVER BY A LONG SHOT, MIDNIGHT!

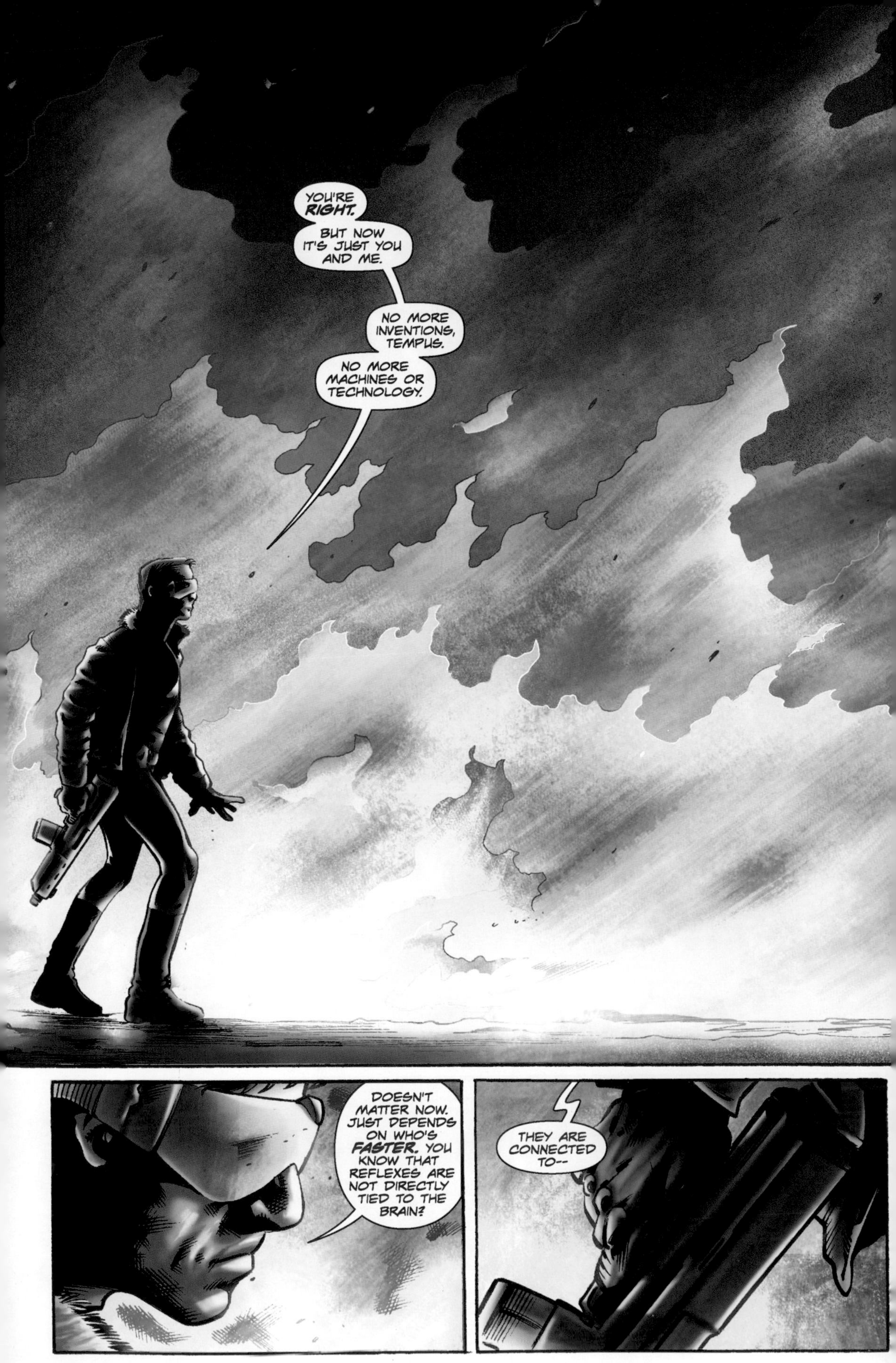
YOU'RE RIGHT.
BUT NOW IT'S JUST YOU AND ME.
NO MORE INVENTIONS, TEMPUS.
NO MORE MACHINES OR TECHNOLOGY.
DOESN'T MATTER NOW. JUST DEPENDS ON WHO'S FASTER. YOU KNOW THAT REFLEXES ARE NOT DIRECTLY TIED TO THE BRAIN?
THEY ARE CONNECTED TO--

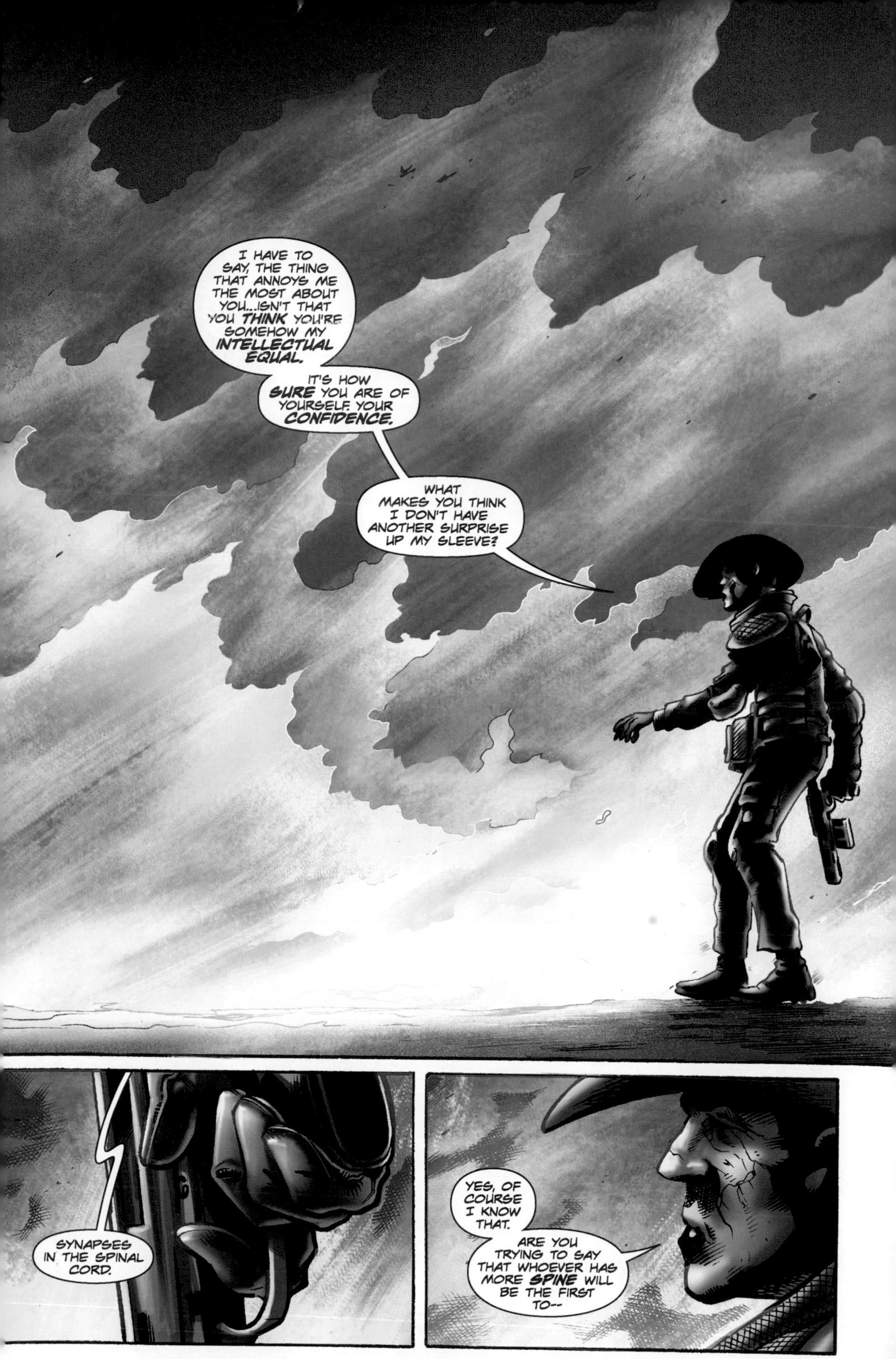
I HAVE TO SAY, THE THING THAT ANNOYS ME THE MOST ABOUT YOU...ISN'T THAT YOU THINK YOU'RE SOMEHOW MY INTELLECTUAL EQUAL.
IT'S HOW SURE YOU ARE OF YOURSELF. YOUR CONFIDENCE.
WHAT MAKES YOU THINK I DON'T HAVE ANOTHER SURPRISE UP MY SLEEVE?
SYNAPSES IN THE SPINAL CORD.
YES, OF COURSE I KNOW THAT.
ARE YOU TRYING TO SAY THAT WHOEVER HAS MORE SPINE WILL BE THE FIRST TO--

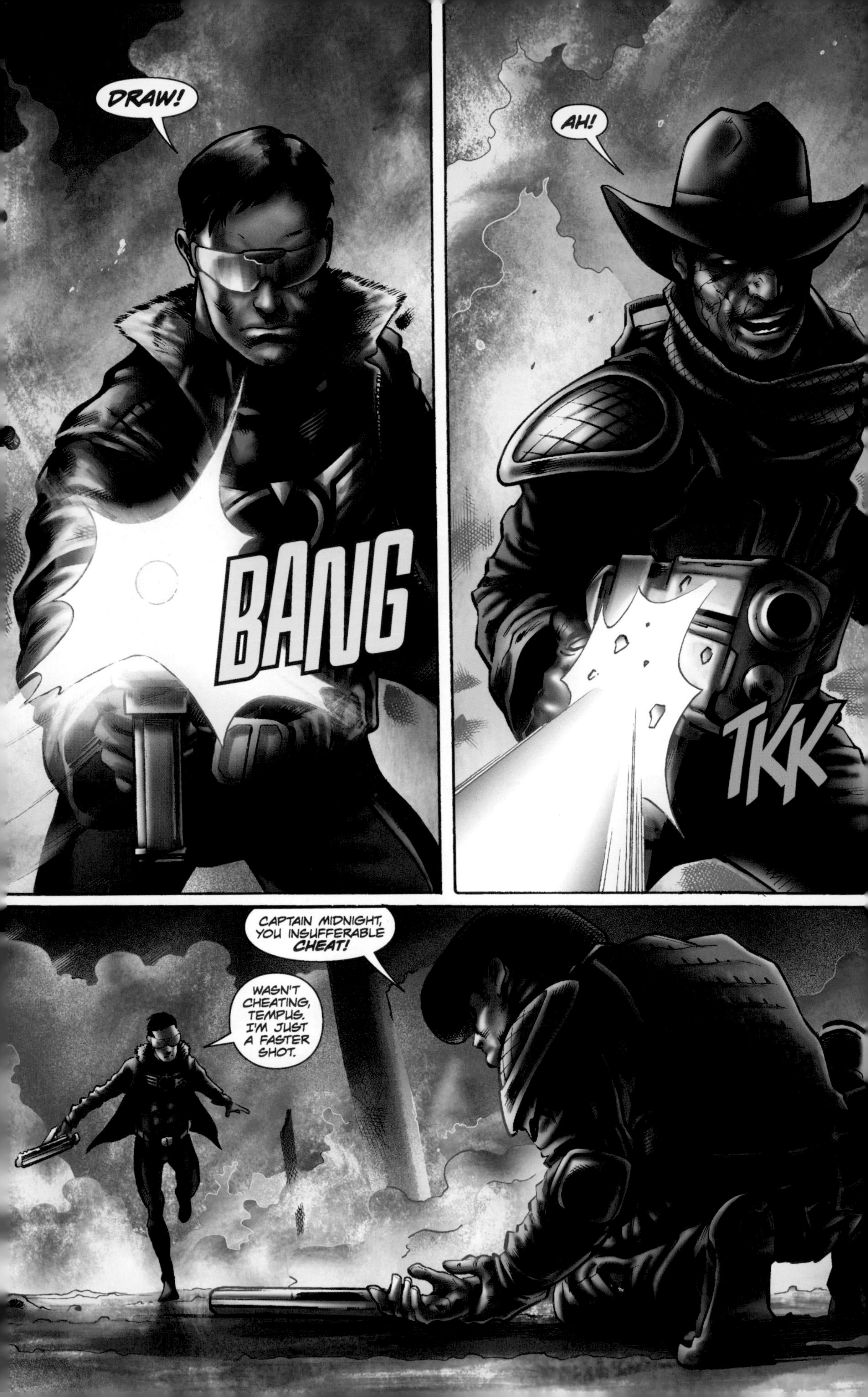
DRAW!
BANG
AH!
TKK
CAPTAIN MIDNIGHT, YOU INSUFFERABLE CHEAT!
WASN'T CHEATING, TEMPUS. I'M JUST A FASTER SHOT.

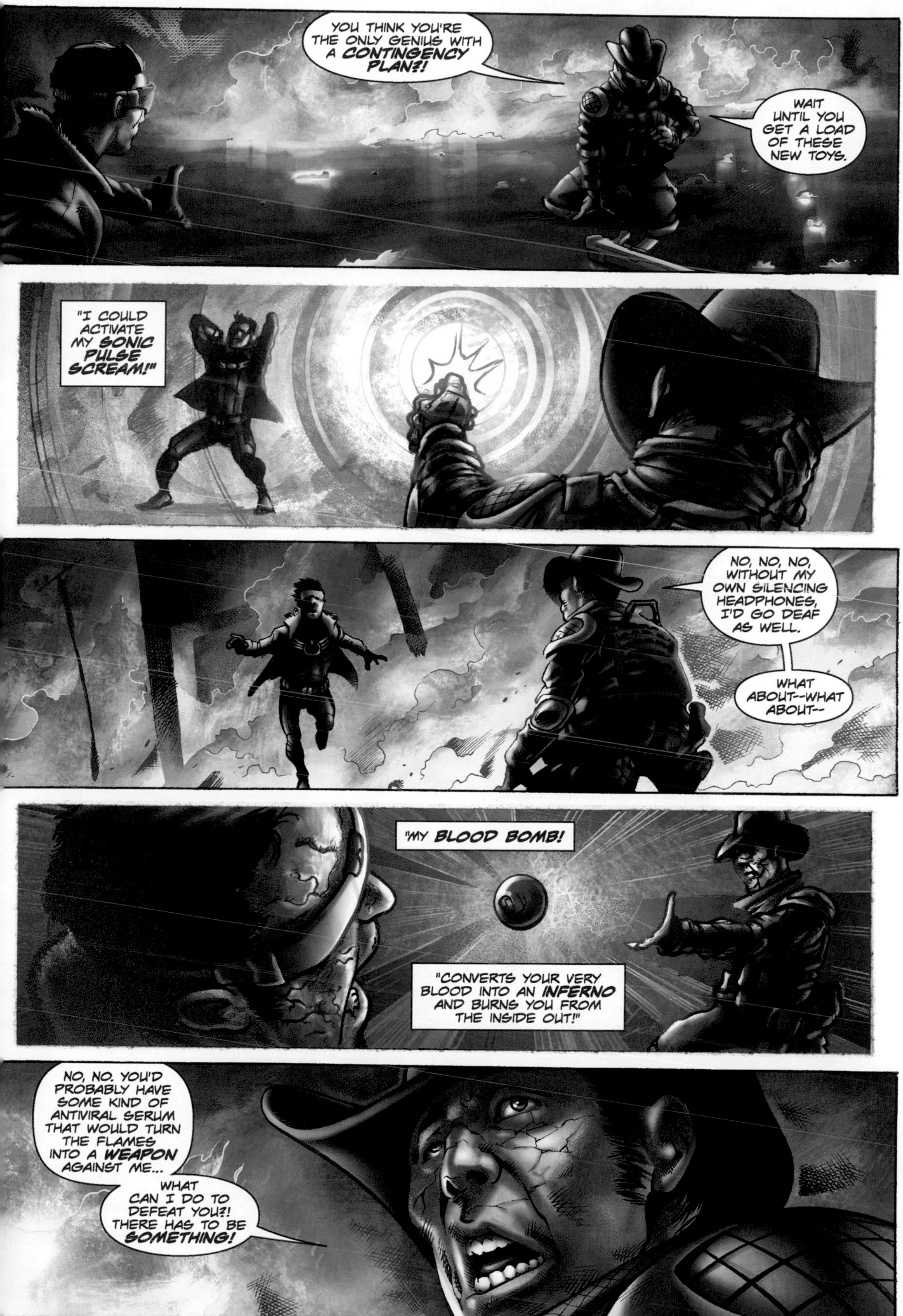
YOU THINK YOU'RE THE ONLY GENIUS WITH A CONTINGENCY PLAN?!
WAIT UNTIL YOU GET A LOAD OF THESE NEW TOYS.
"I COULD ACTIVATE MY SONIC PULSE SCREAM!"
NO, NO, NO, WITHOUT MY OWN SILENCING HEADPHONES, I'D GO DEAF AS WELL.
WHAT ABOUT--WHAT ABOUT--
"MY BLOOD BOMB!
"CONVERTS YOUR VERY BLOOD INTO AN INFERNO AND BURNS YOU FROM THE INSIDE OUT!"
NO, NO. YOU'D PROBABLY HAVE SOME KIND OF ANTIVIRAL SERUM THAT WOULD TURN THE FLAMES INTO A WEAPON AGAINST ME...
WHAT CAN I DO TO DEFEAT YOU?! THERE HAS TO BE SOMETHING!

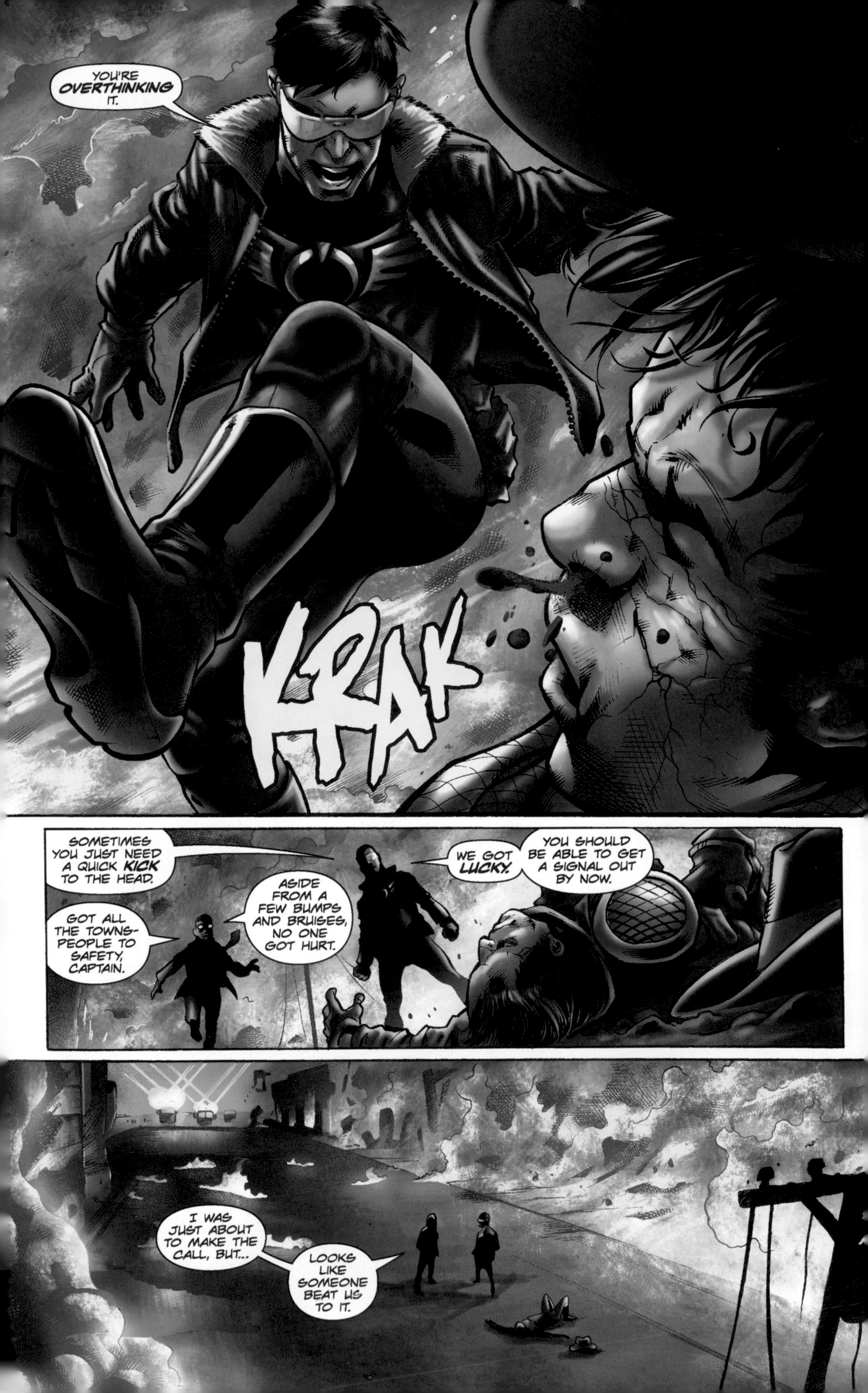
YOU'RE OVERTHINKING IT.
KRAK
SOMETIMES YOU JUST NEED A QUICK KICK TO THE HEAD.
WE GOT LUCKY.
YOU SHOULD BE ABLE TO GET A SIGNAL OUT BY NOW.
GOT ALL THE TOWNS-PEOPLE TO SAFETY, CAPTAIN.
ASIDE FROM A FEW BUMPS AND BRUISES, NO ONE GOT HURT.
I WAS JUST ABOUT TO MAKE THE CALL, BUT...
LOOKS LIKE SOMEONE BEAT US TO IT.

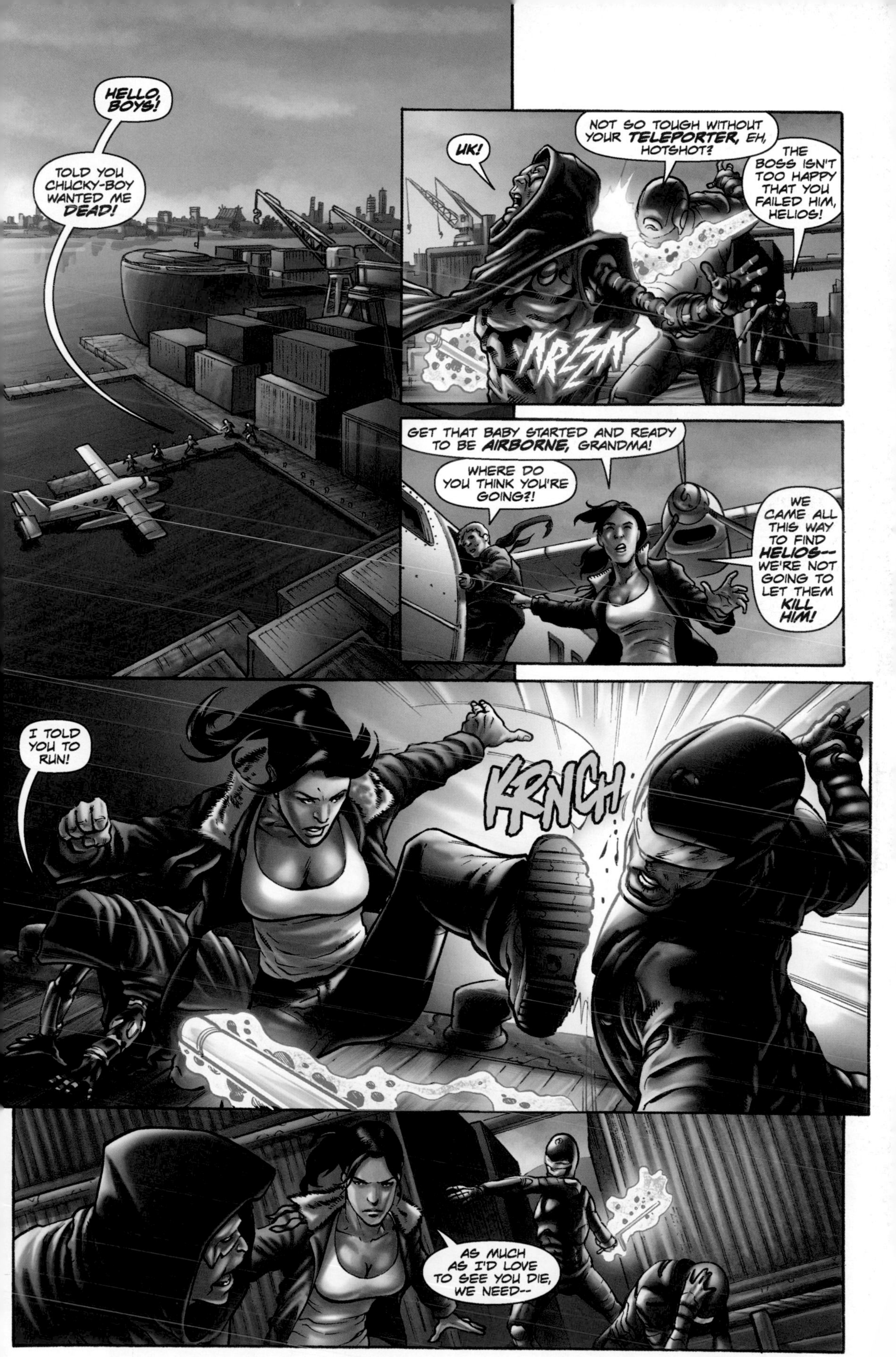
HELLO, BOYS!
TOLD YOU CHUCKY-BOY WANTED ME DEAD!
UK!
NOT SO TOUGH WITHOUT YOUR TELEPORTER, EH, HOTSHOT?
THE BOSS ISN'T TOO HAPPY THAT YOU FAILED HIM, HELIOS!
KRZZK
GET THAT BABY STARTED AND READY TO BE AIRBORNE, GRANDMA!
WHERE DO YOU THINK YOU'RE GOING?!
WE CAME ALL THIS WAY TO FIND HELIOS-- WE'RE NOT GOING TO LET THEM KILL HIM!
I TOLD YOU TO RUN!
KRNCH
AS MUCH AS I'D LOVE TO SEE YOU DIE, WE NEED--

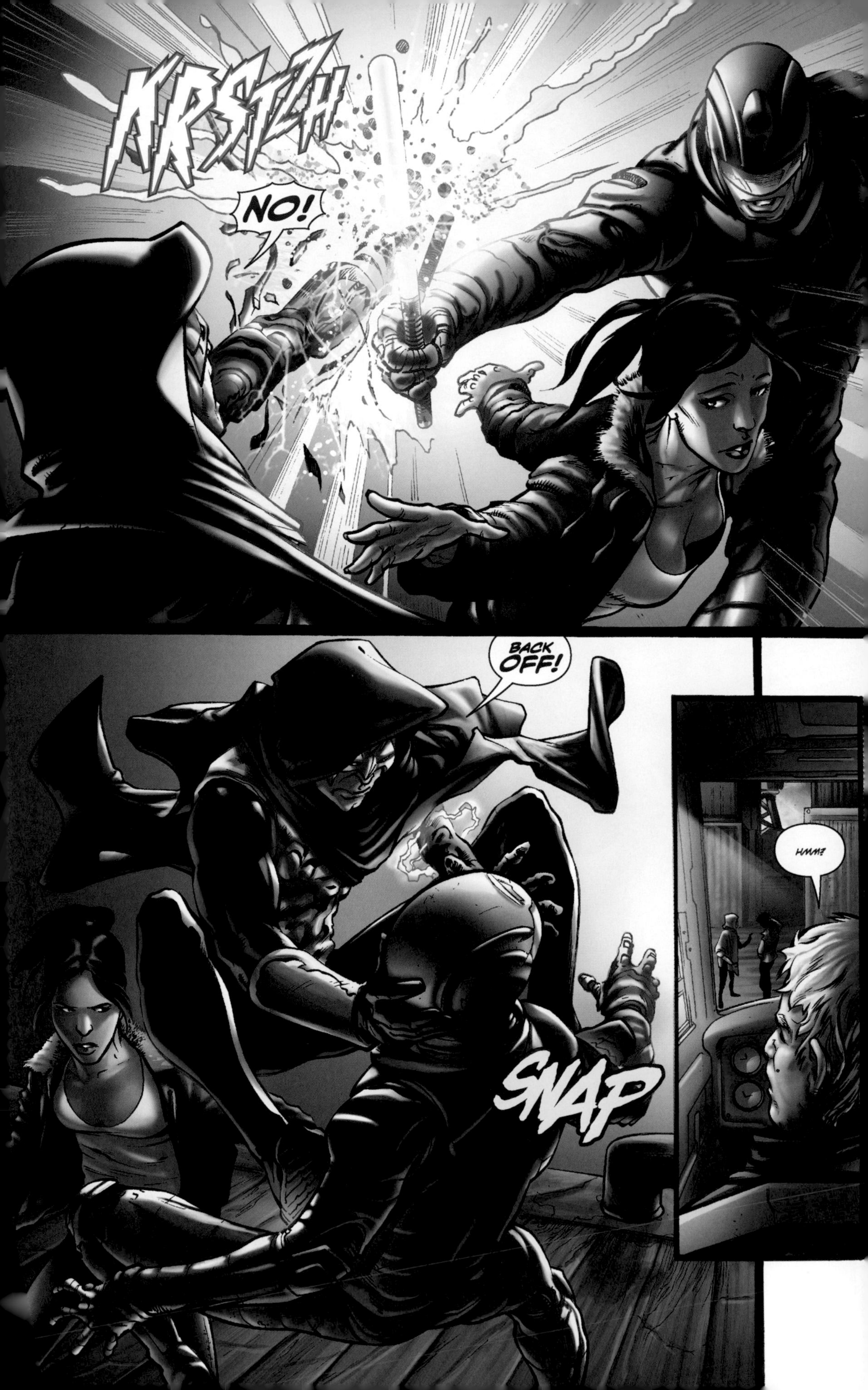
KRSTZH
NO!
BACK OFF!
HMM?
SNAP

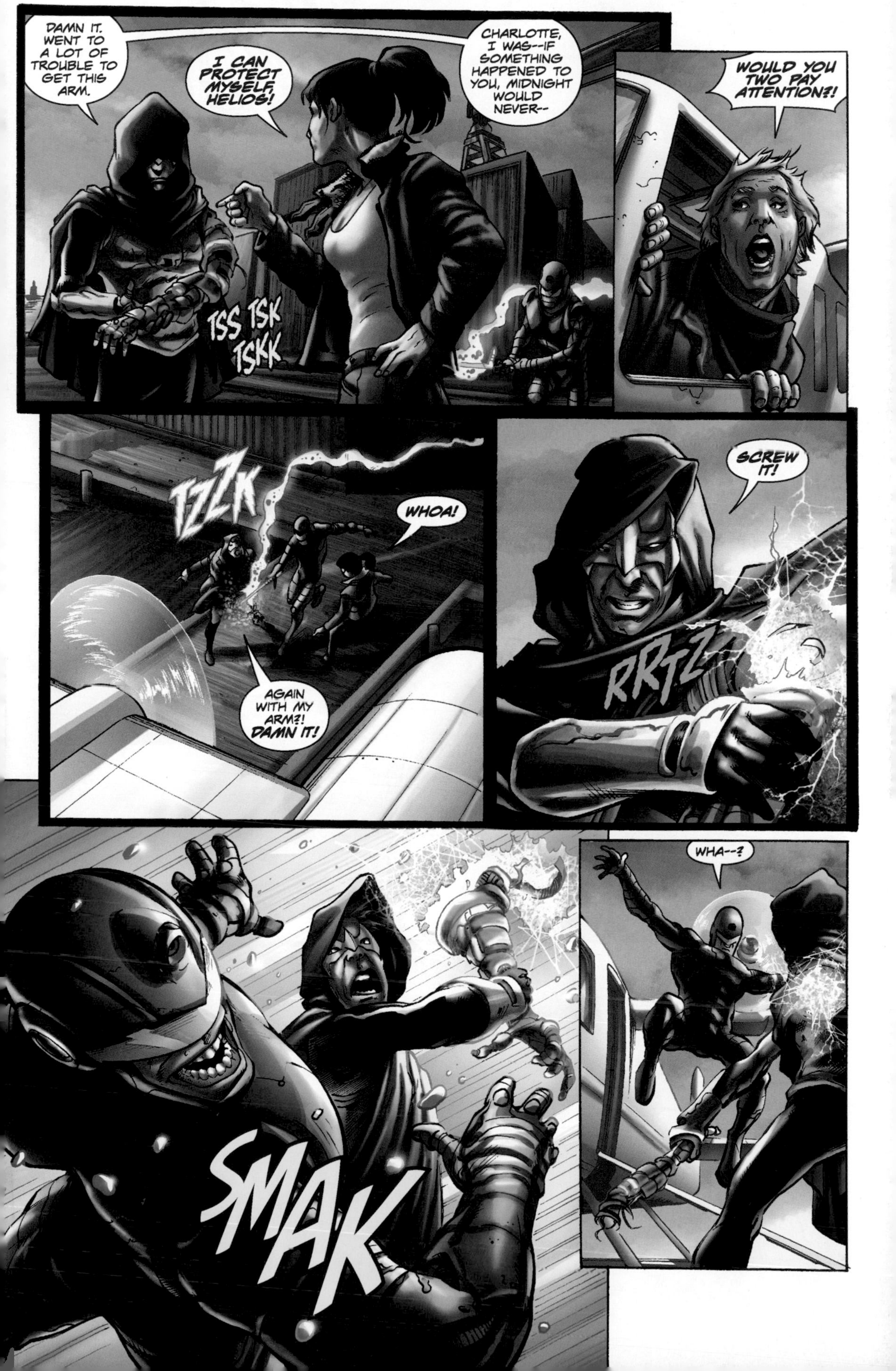
DAMN IT. WENT TO A LOT OF TROUBLE TO GET THIS ARM.
I CAN PROTECT MYSELF, HELIOS!
CHARLOTTE, I WAS--IF SOMETHING HAPPENED TO YOU, MIDNIGHT WOULD NEVER--
TSS TSK TSKK
WOULD YOU TWO PAY ATTENTION?!
TZZK
WHOA!
AGAIN WITH MY ARM?! DAMN IT!
SCREW IT!
RRTZ
SMAK
WHA--?

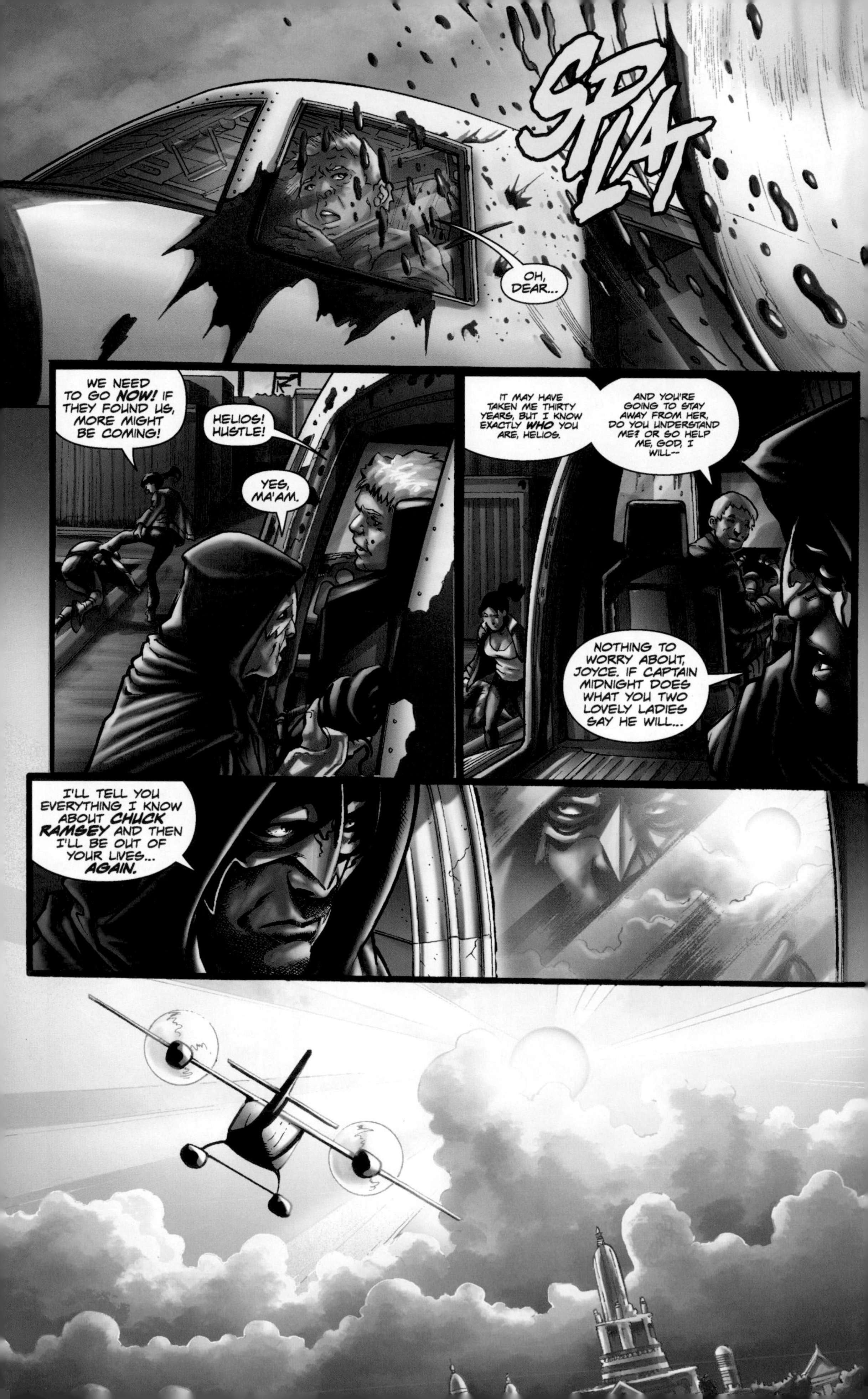
SPLAT
OH, DEAR...
WE NEED TO GO NOW! IF THEY FOUND US, MORE MIGHT BE COMING!
HELIOS! HUSTLE!
YES, MA'AM.
IT MAY HAVE TAKEN ME THIRTY YEARS, BUT I KNOW EXACTLY WHO YOU ARE, HELIOS.
AND YOU'RE GOING TO STAY AWAY FROM HER, DO YOU UNDERSTAND ME? OR SO HELP ME, GOD, I WILL--
NOTHING TO WORRY ABOUT, JOYCE. IF CAPTAIN MIDNIGHT DOES WHAT YOU TWO LOVELY LADIES SAY HE WILL...
I'LL TELL YOU EVERYTHING I KNOW ABOUT CHUCK RAMSEY AND THEN I'LL BE OUT OF YOUR LIVES... AGAIN.

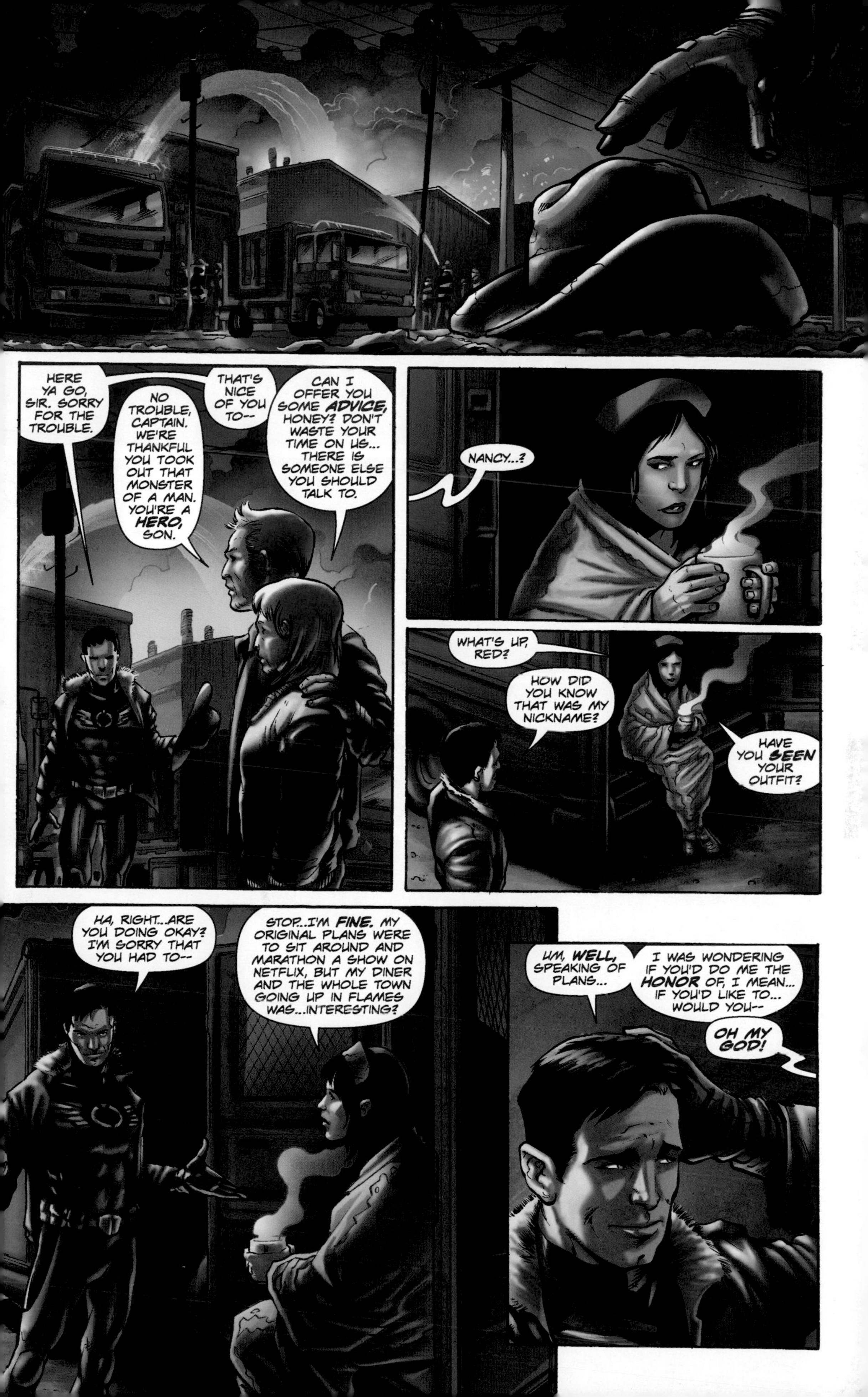
HERE YA GO, SIR. SORRY FOR THE TROUBLE.
NO TROUBLE, CAPTAIN. WE'RE THANKFUL YOU TOOK OUT THAT MONSTER OF A MAN. YOU'RE A HERO, SON.
THAT'S NICE OF YOU TO--
CAN I OFFER YOU SOME ADVICE, HONEY? DON'T WASTE YOUR TIME ON US... THERE IS SOMEONE ELSE YOU SHOULD TALK TO.
NANCY...?
WHAT'S UP, RED?
HOW DID YOU KNOW THAT WAS MY NICKNAME?
HAVE YOU SEEN YOUR OUTFIT?
HA, RIGHT...ARE YOU DOING OKAY? I'M SORRY THAT YOU HAD TO--
STOP...I'M FINE. MY ORIGINAL PLANS WERE TO SIT AROUND AND MARATHON A SHOW ON NETFLIX, BUT MY DINER AND THE WHOLE TOWN GOING UP IN FLAMES WAS...INTERESTING?
UM, WELL, SPEAKING OF PLANS...
I WAS WONDERING IF YOU'D DO ME THE HONOR OF, I MEAN... IF YOU'D LIKE TO... WOULD YOU--
OH MY GOD!

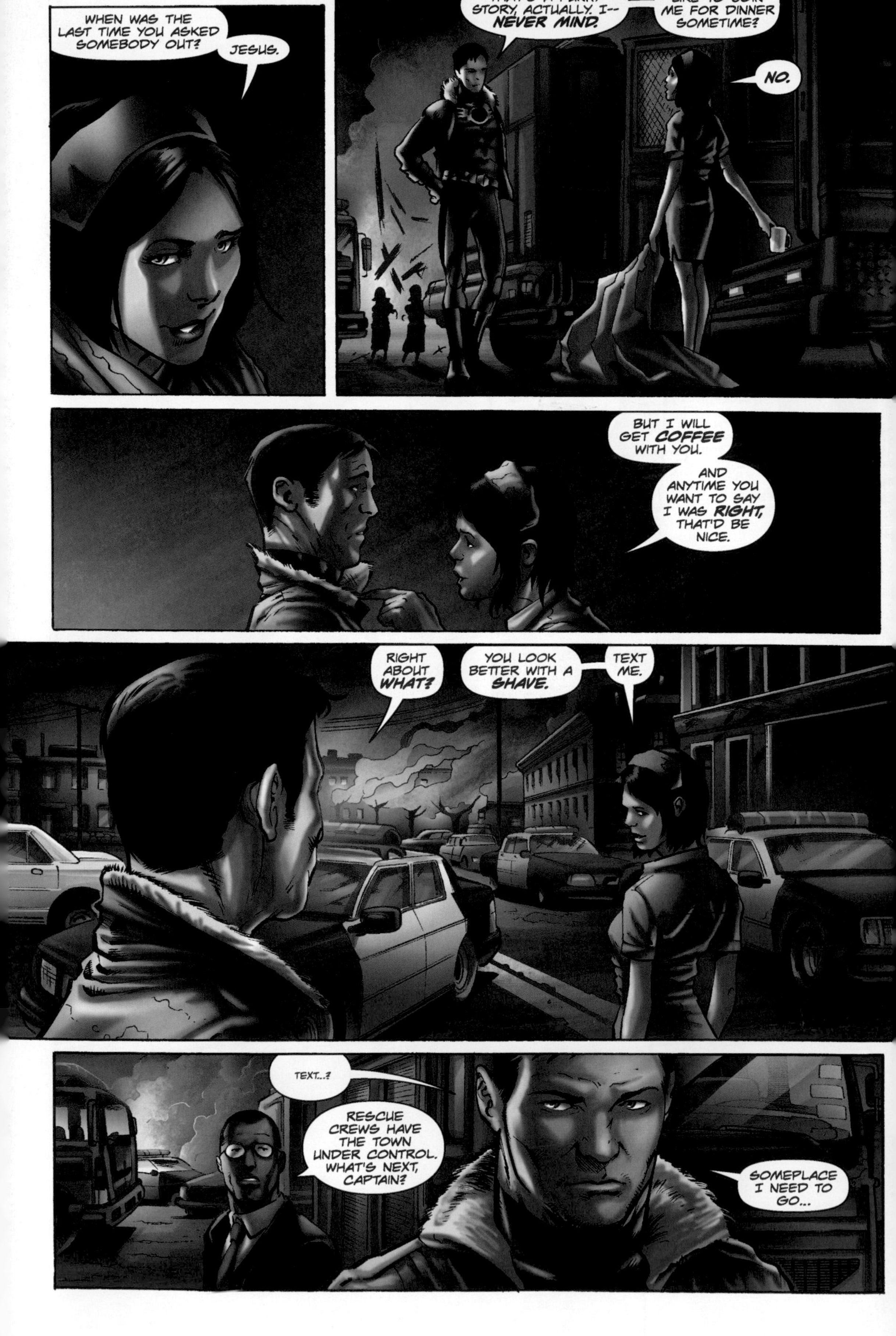
WHEN WAS THE LAST TIME YOU ASKED SOMEBODY OUT?
JESUS.
WELL, THAT'S A FUNNY STORY, ACTUALLY. I-- NEVER MIND.
WOULD YOU LIKE TO JOIN ME FOR DINNER SOMETIME?
NO.
BUT I WILL GET COFFEE WITH YOU.
AND ANYTIME YOU WANT TO SAY I WAS RIGHT, THAT'D BE NICE.
RIGHT ABOUT WHAT?
YOU LOOK BETTER WITH A SHAVE.
TEXT ME.
TEXT...?
RESCUE CREWS HAVE THE TOWN UNDER CONTROL. WHAT'S NEXT, CAPTAIN?
SOMEPLACE I NEED TO GO...

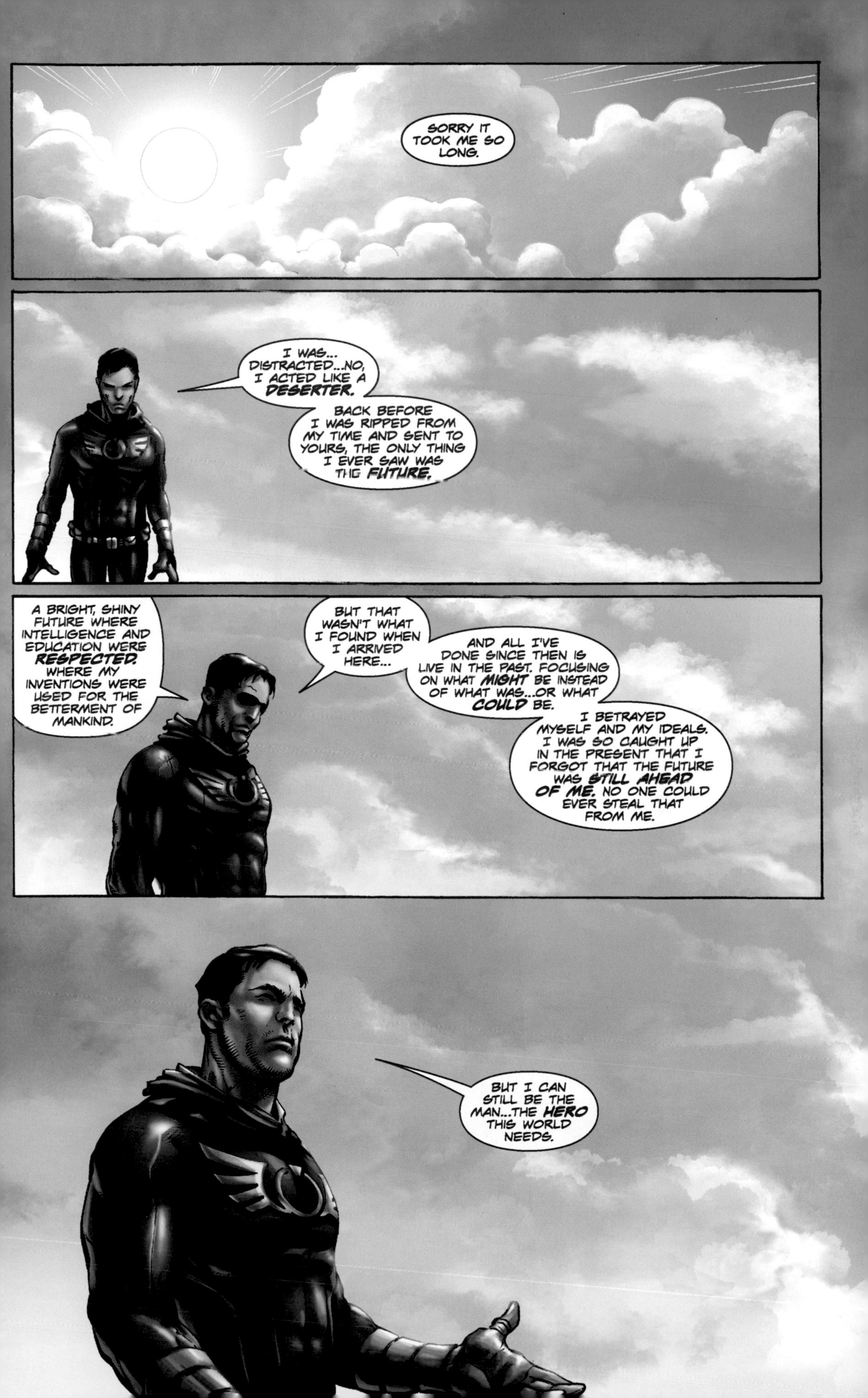
SORRY IT TOOK ME SO LONG.
I WAS... DISTRACTED...NO, I ACTED LIKE A DESERTER.
BACK BEFORE I WAS RIPPED FROM MY TIME AND SENT TO YOURS, THE ONLY THING I EVER SAW WAS THE FUTURE.
A BRIGHT, SHINY FUTURE WHERE INTELLIGENCE AND EDUCATION WERE RESPECTED. WHERE MY INVENTIONS WERE USED FOR THE BETTERMENT OF MANKIND.
BUT THAT WASN'T WHAT I FOUND WHEN I ARRIVED HERE...
AND ALL I'VE DONE SINCE THEN IS LIVE IN THE PAST. FOCUSING ON WHAT MIGHT BE INSTEAD OF WHAT WAS...OR WHAT COULD BE.
I BETRAYED MYSELF AND MY IDEALS. I WAS SO CAUGHT UP IN THE PRESENT THAT I FORGOT THAT THE FUTURE WAS STILL AHEAD OF ME. NO ONE COULD EVER STEAL THAT FROM ME.
BUT I CAN STILL BE THE MAN...THE HERO THIS WORLD NEEDS.

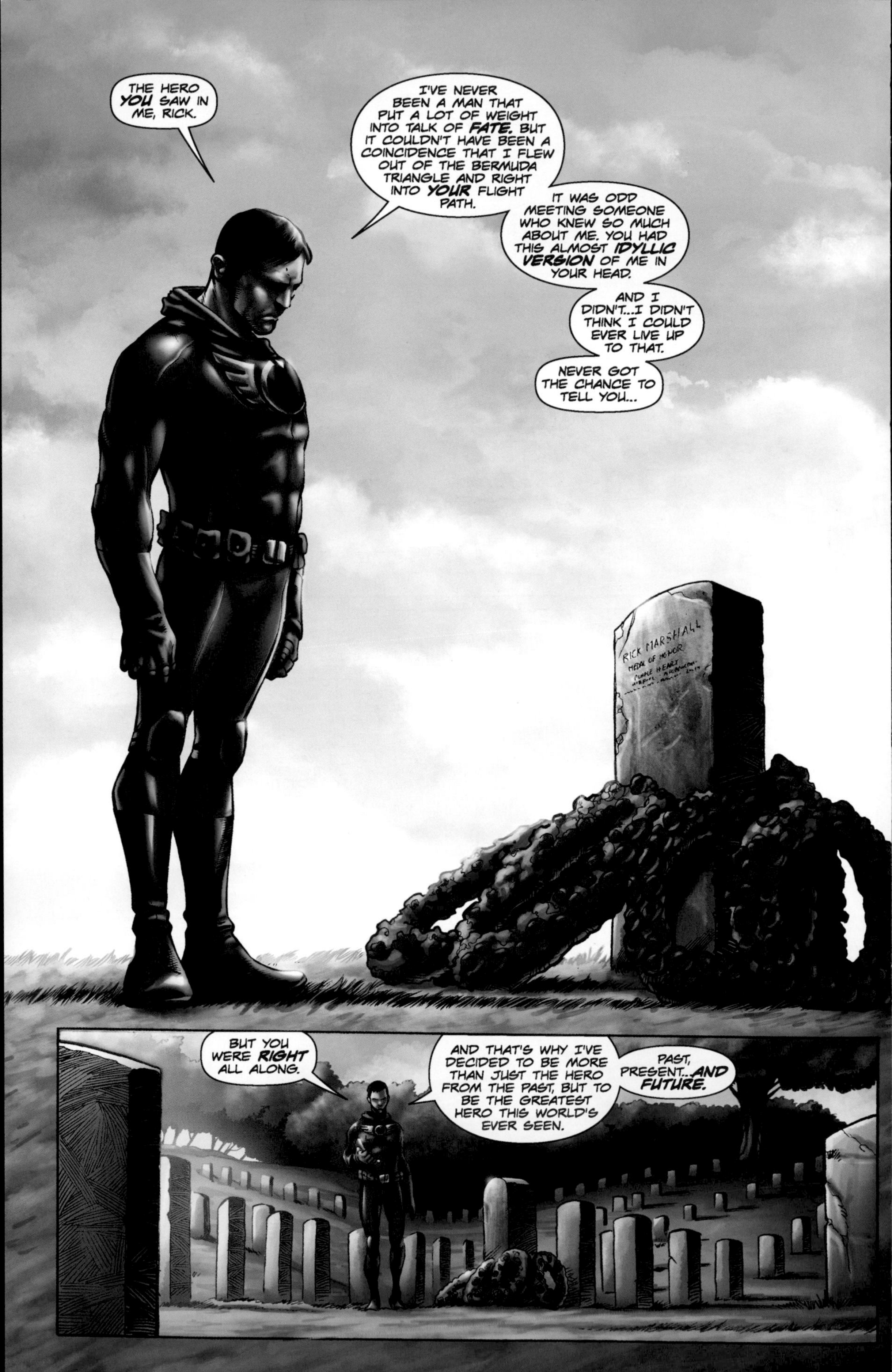
THE HERO YOU SAW IN ME, RICK.
I'VE NEVER BEEN A MAN THAT PUT A LOT OF WEIGHT INTO TALK OF FATE. BUT IT COULDN'T HAVE BEEN A COINCIDENCE THAT I FLEW OUT OF THE BERMUDA TRIANGLE AND RIGHT INTO YOUR FLIGHT PATH.
IT WAS ODD MEETING SOMEONE WHO KNEW SO MUCH ABOUT ME. YOU HAD THIS ALMOST IDYLLIC VERSION OF ME IN YOUR HEAD.
AND I DIDN'T...I DIDN'T THINK I COULD EVER LIVE UP TO THAT.
NEVER GOT THE CHANCE TO TELL YOU...
RICK MARSHALL
MEDAL OF HONOR
PURPLE HEART
BUT YOU WERE RIGHT ALL ALONG.
AND THAT'S WHY I'VE DECIDED TO BE MORE THAN JUST THE HERO FROM THE PAST, BUT TO BE THE GREATEST HERO THIS WORLD'S EVER SEEN.
PAST, PRESENT...AND FUTURE.

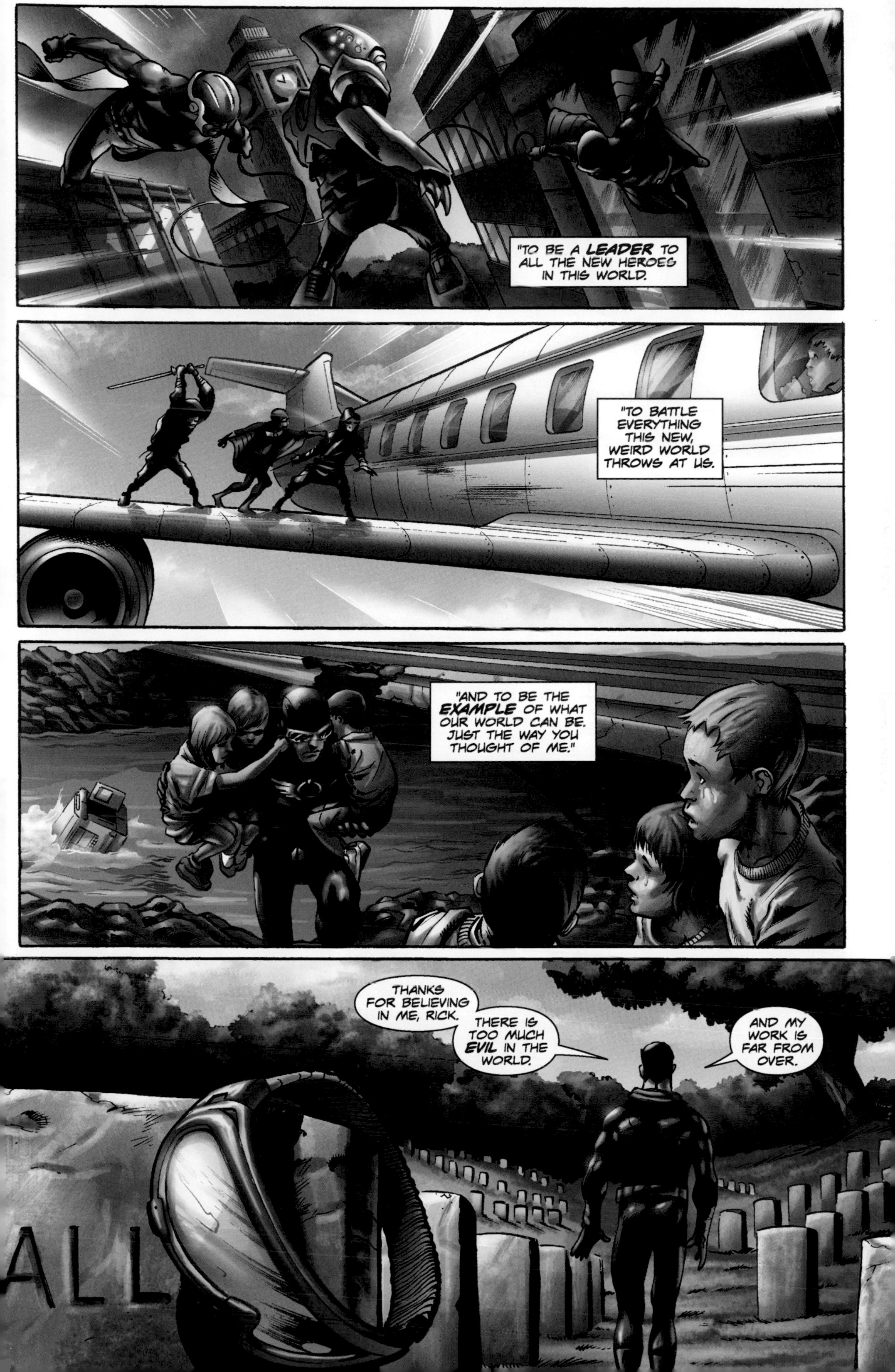
"TO BE A LEADER TO ALL THE NEW HEROES IN THIS WORLD.
"TO BATTLE EVERYTHING THIS NEW, WEIRD WORLD THROWS AT US.
"AND TO BE THE EXAMPLE OF WHAT OUR WORLD CAN BE. JUST THE WAY YOU THOUGHT OF ME."
THANKS FOR BELIEVING IN ME, RICK.
THERE IS TOO MUCH EVIL IN THE WORLD.
AND MY WORK IS FAR FROM OVER.
ALL

KRAKTT

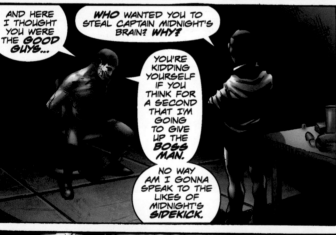

AND HERE I THOUGHT YOU WERE THE *GOOD GUYS*...

WHO WANTED YOU TO STEAL CAPTAIN MIDNIGHT'S BRAIN? *WHY?*

YOU'RE KIDDING YOURSELF IF YOU THINK FOR A SECOND THAT I'M GOING TO GIVE UP THE *BOSS MAN.*

NO WAY AM I GONNA SPEAK TO THE LIKES OF MIDNIGHT'S *SIDEKICK.*

SEE, I WAS *HOPING* YOU'D SAY THAT.

THEN I CAN STEAL A MOVE FROM *YOUR* PLAYBOOK.

BZZZ

BBZZZZZZ

YOU WOULDN'T *DARE*...

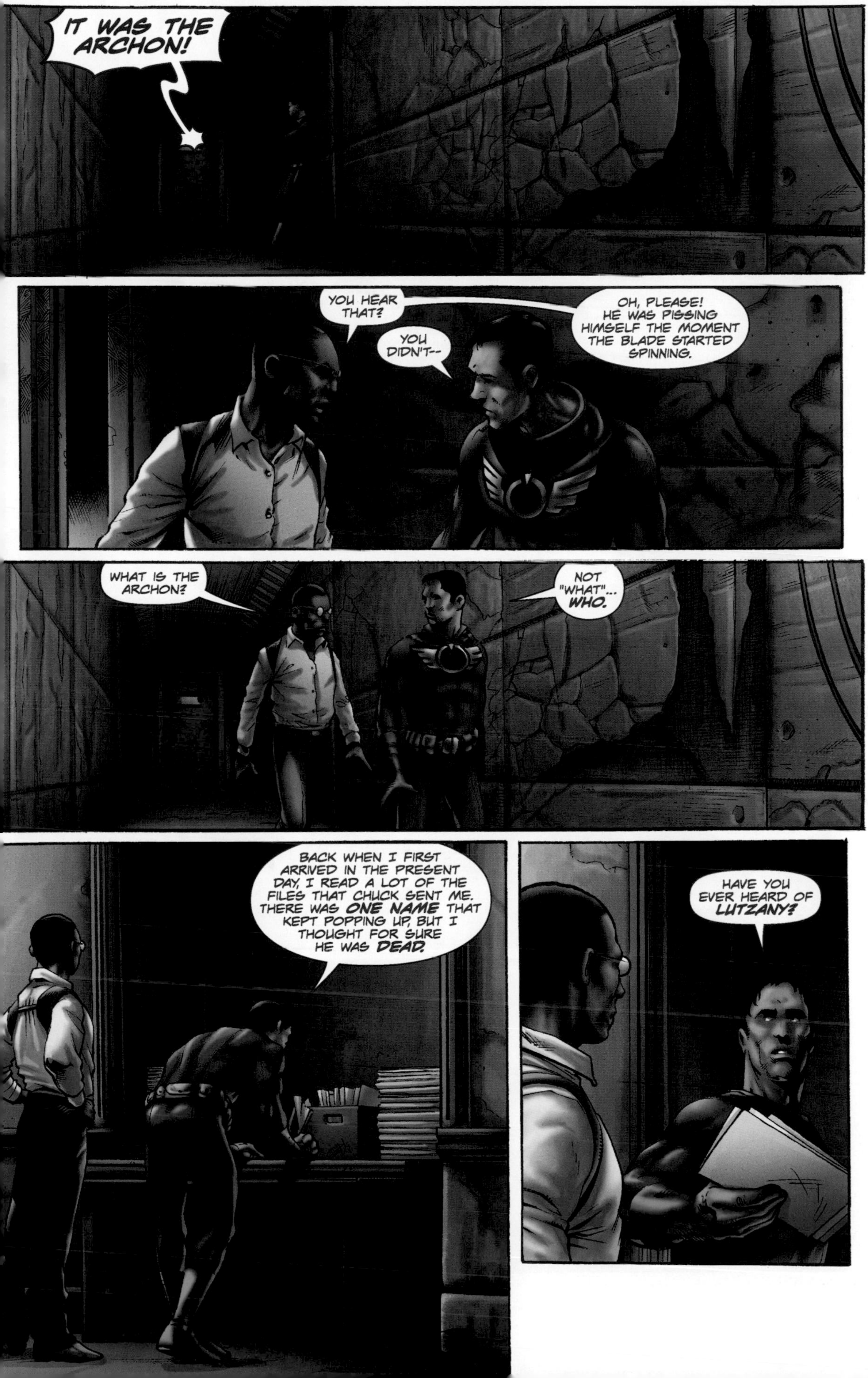
IT WAS THE ARCHON!
YOU HEAR THAT?
YOU DIDN'T--
OH, PLEASE! HE WAS PISSING HIMSELF THE MOMENT THE BLADE STARTED SPINNING.
WHAT IS THE ARCHON?
NOT "WHAT"... WHO.
BACK WHEN I FIRST ARRIVED IN THE PRESENT DAY, I READ A LOT OF THE FILES THAT CHUCK SENT ME. THERE WAS ONE NAME THAT KEPT POPPING UP, BUT I THOUGHT FOR SURE HE WAS DEAD.
HAVE YOU EVER HEARD OF LUTZANY?

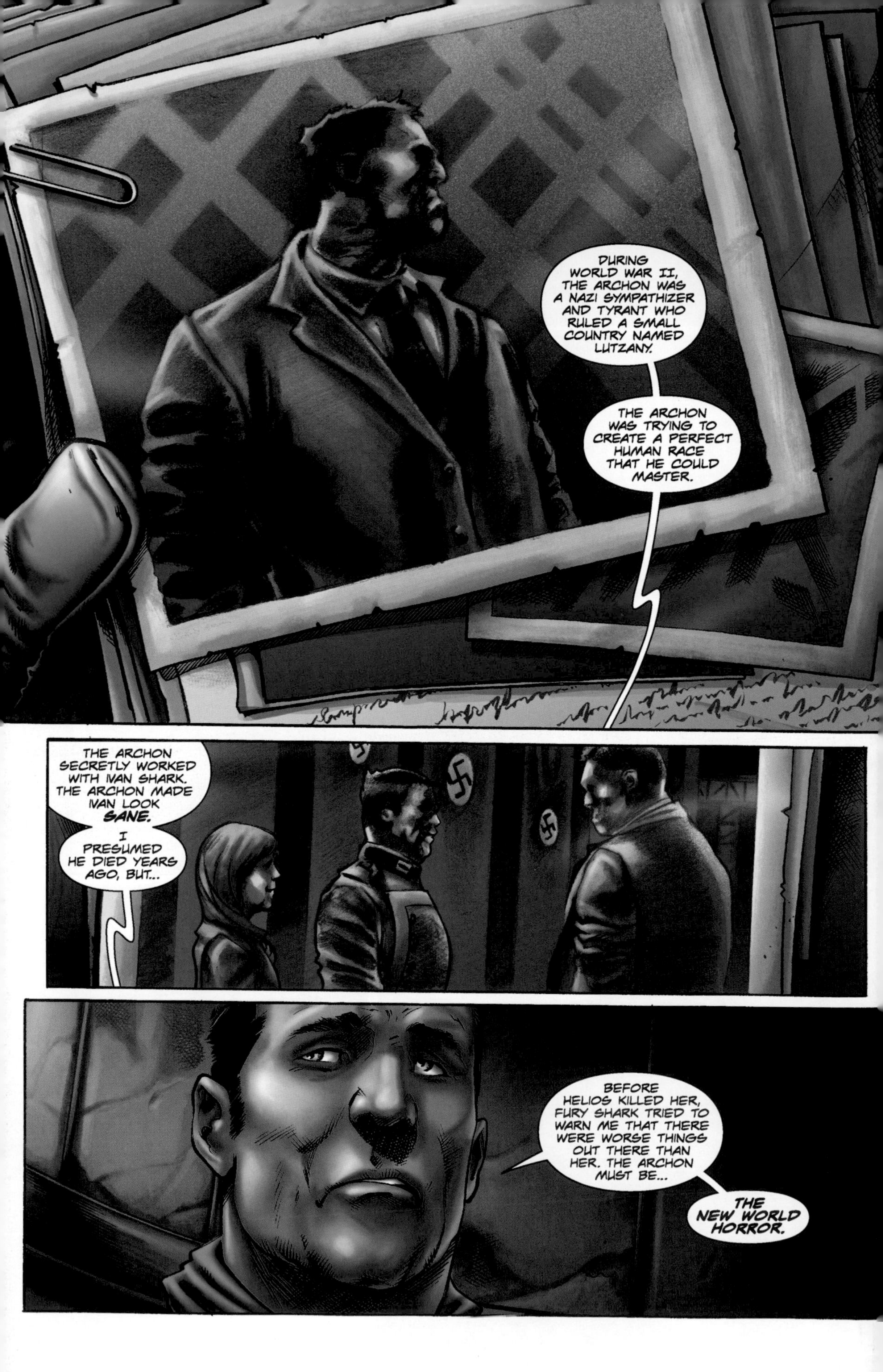
DURING WORLD WAR II, THE ARCHON WAS A NAZI SYMPATHIZER AND TYRANT WHO RULED A SMALL COUNTRY NAMED LUTZANY.
THE ARCHON WAS TRYING TO CREATE A PERFECT HUMAN RACE THAT HE COULD MASTER.
THE ARCHON SECRETLY WORKED WITH IVAN SHARK. THE ARCHON MADE IVAN LOOK SANE.
I PRESUMED HE DIED YEARS AGO, BUT...
BEFORE HELIOS KILLED HER, FURY SHARK TRIED TO WARN ME THAT THERE WERE WORSE THINGS OUT THERE THAN HER. THE ARCHON MUST BE...
THE NEW WORLD HORROR.

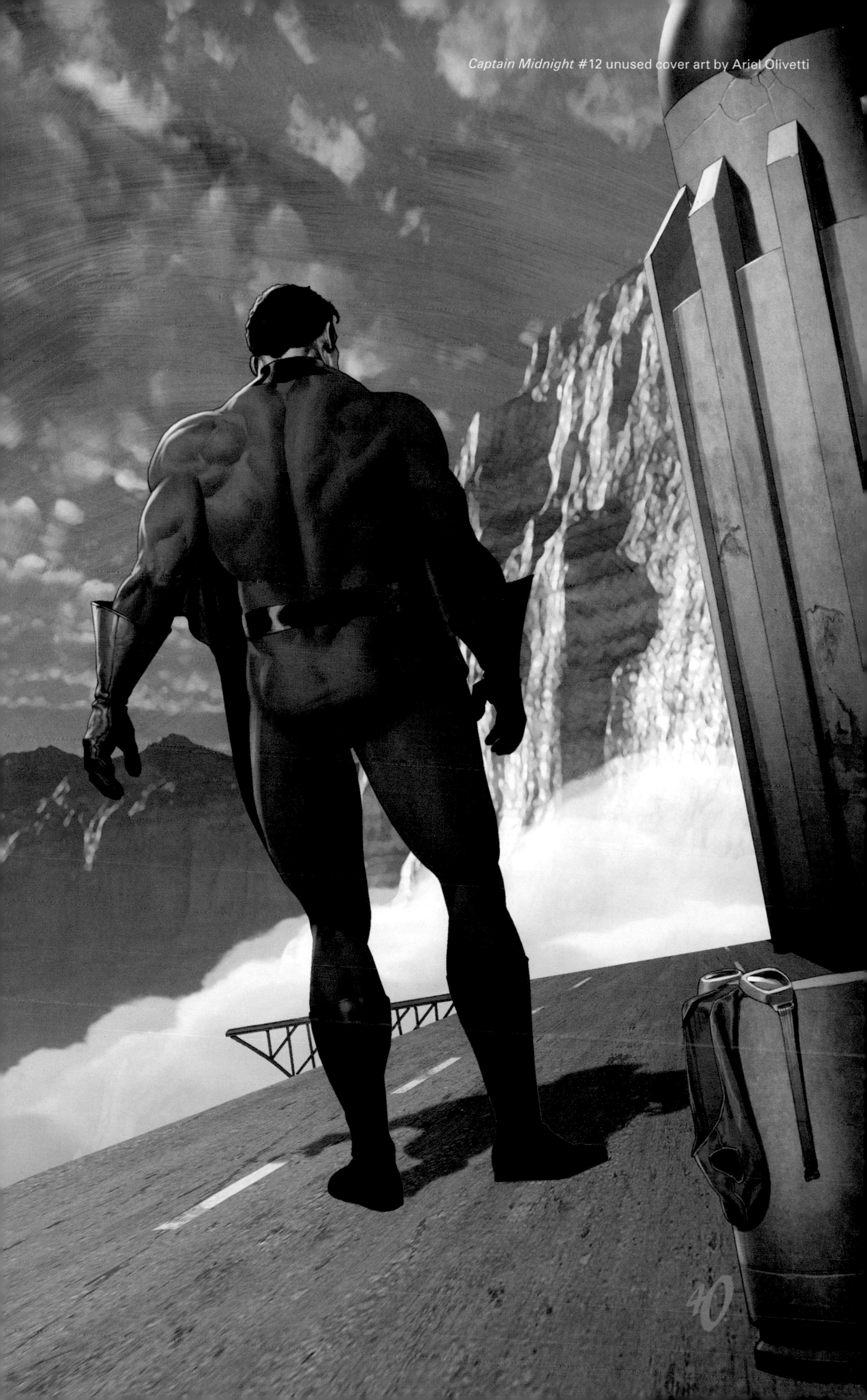

Captain Midnight #12 unused cover art by Ariel Olivetti

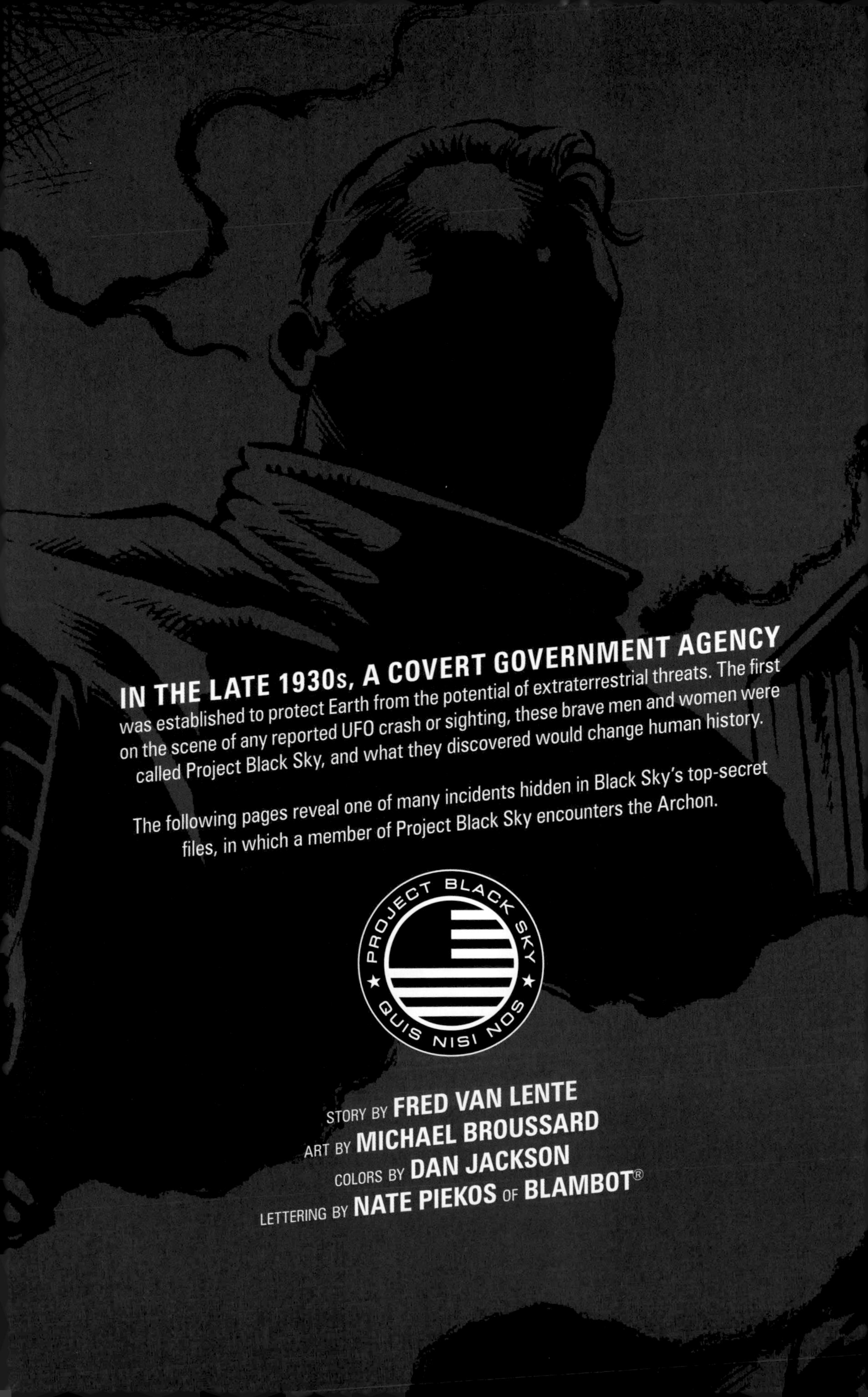

IN THE LATE 1930s, A COVERT GOVERNMENT AGENCY was established to protect Earth from the potential of extraterrestrial threats. The first on the scene of any reported UFO crash or sighting, these brave men and women were called Project Black Sky, and what they discovered would change human history.

The following pages reveal one of many incidents hidden in Black Sky's top-secret files, in which a member of Project Black Sky encounters the Archon.

PROJECT BLACK SKY ★ QUIS NISI NOS ★

STORY BY **FRED VAN LENTE**
ART BY **MICHAEL BROUSSARD**
COLORS BY **DAN JACKSON**
LETTERING BY **NATE PIEKOS** OF **BLAMBOT®**

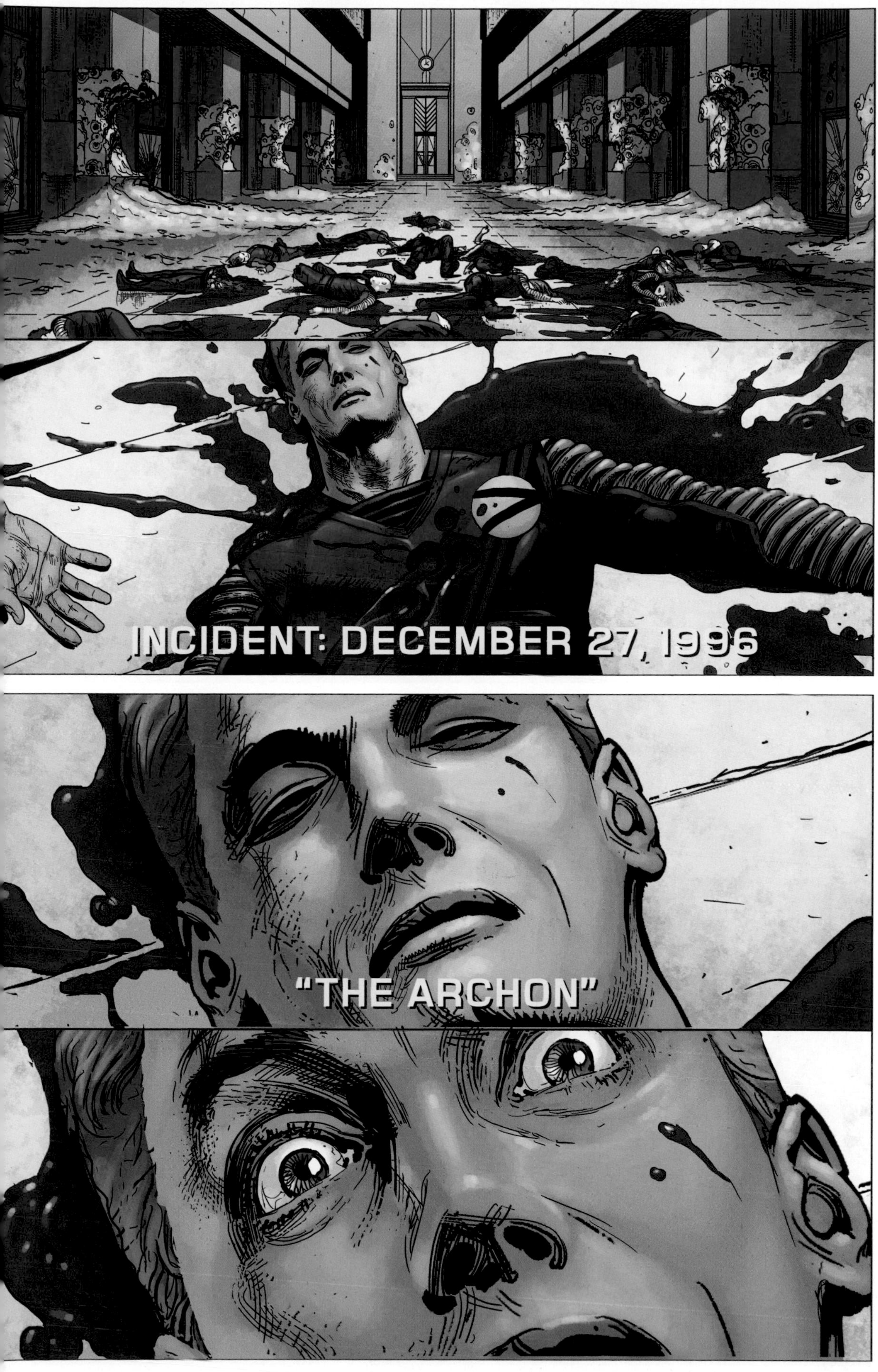
INCIDENT: DECEMBER 27, 1996
"THE ARCHON"

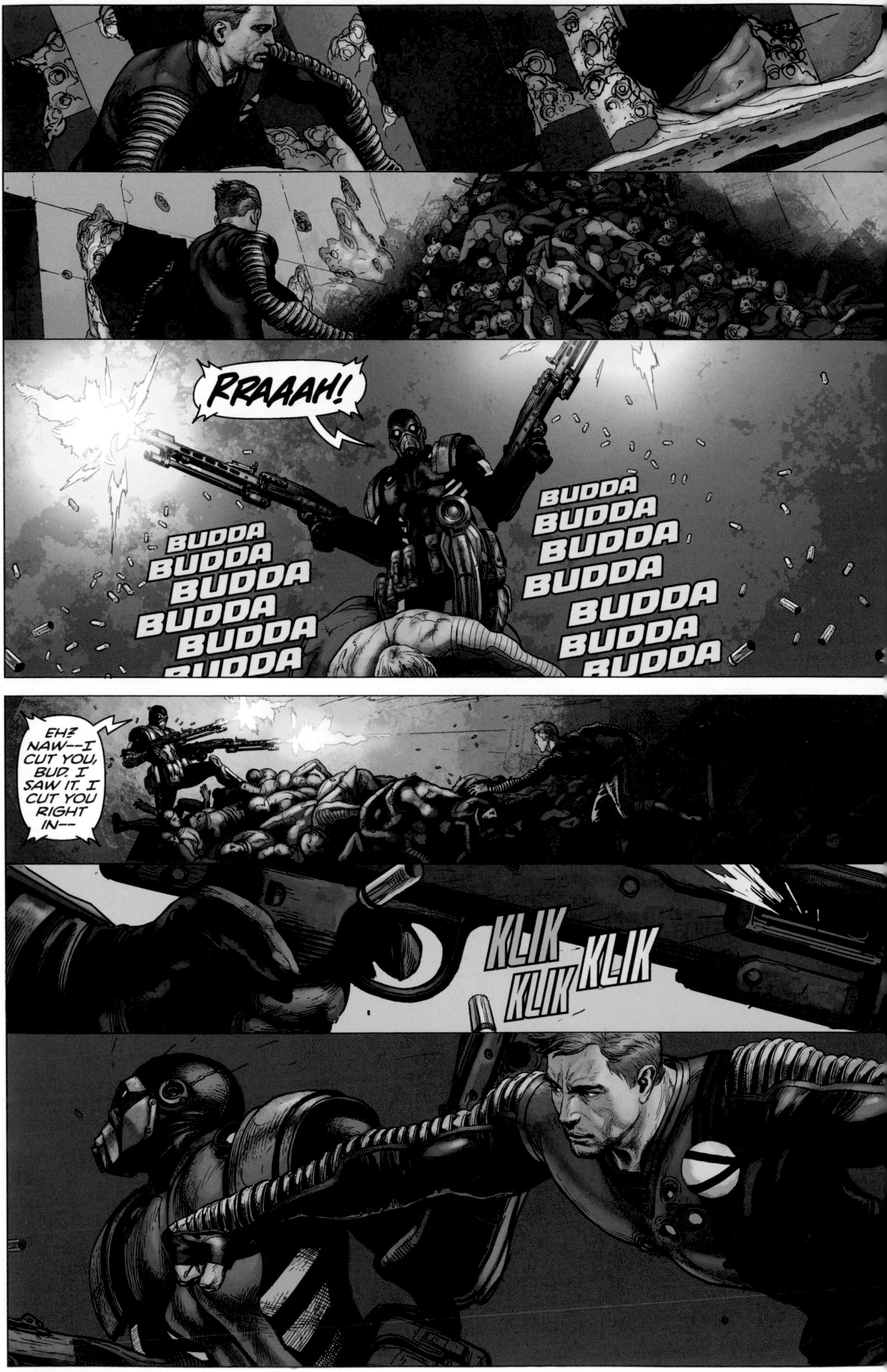
RRAAAH!
BUDDA BUDDA BUDDA BUDDA BUDDA
BUDDA BUDDA BUDDA BUDDA BUDDA BUDDA
EH? NAW--I CUT YOU, BUD. I SAW IT. I CUT YOU RIGHT IN--
KLIK KLIK KLIK

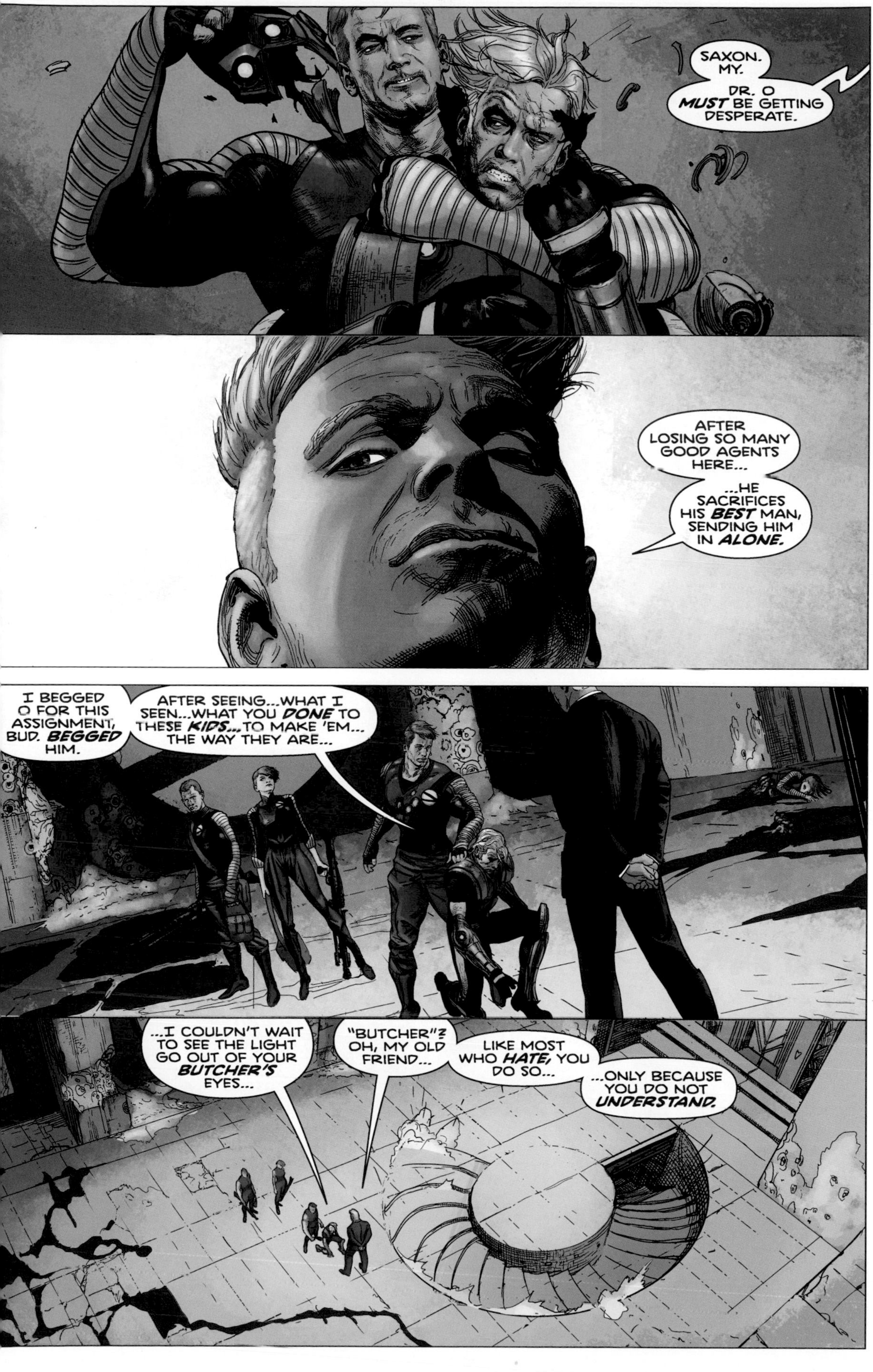
SAXON. MY.
DR. O *MUST* BE GETTING DESPERATE.
AFTER LOSING SO MANY GOOD AGENTS HERE...
...HE SACRIFICES HIS *BEST* MAN, SENDING HIM IN *ALONE.*
I BEGGED O FOR THIS ASSIGNMENT, BUD. *BEGGED* HIM.
AFTER SEEING...WHAT I SEEN...WHAT YOU *DONE* TO THESE *KIDS*...TO MAKE 'EM... THE WAY THEY ARE...
...I COULDN'T WAIT TO SEE THE LIGHT GO OUT OF YOUR *BUTCHER'S* EYES...
"BUTCHER"? OH, MY OLD FRIEND...
LIKE MOST WHO *HATE,* YOU DO SO...
...ONLY BECAUSE YOU DO NOT *UNDERSTAND.*

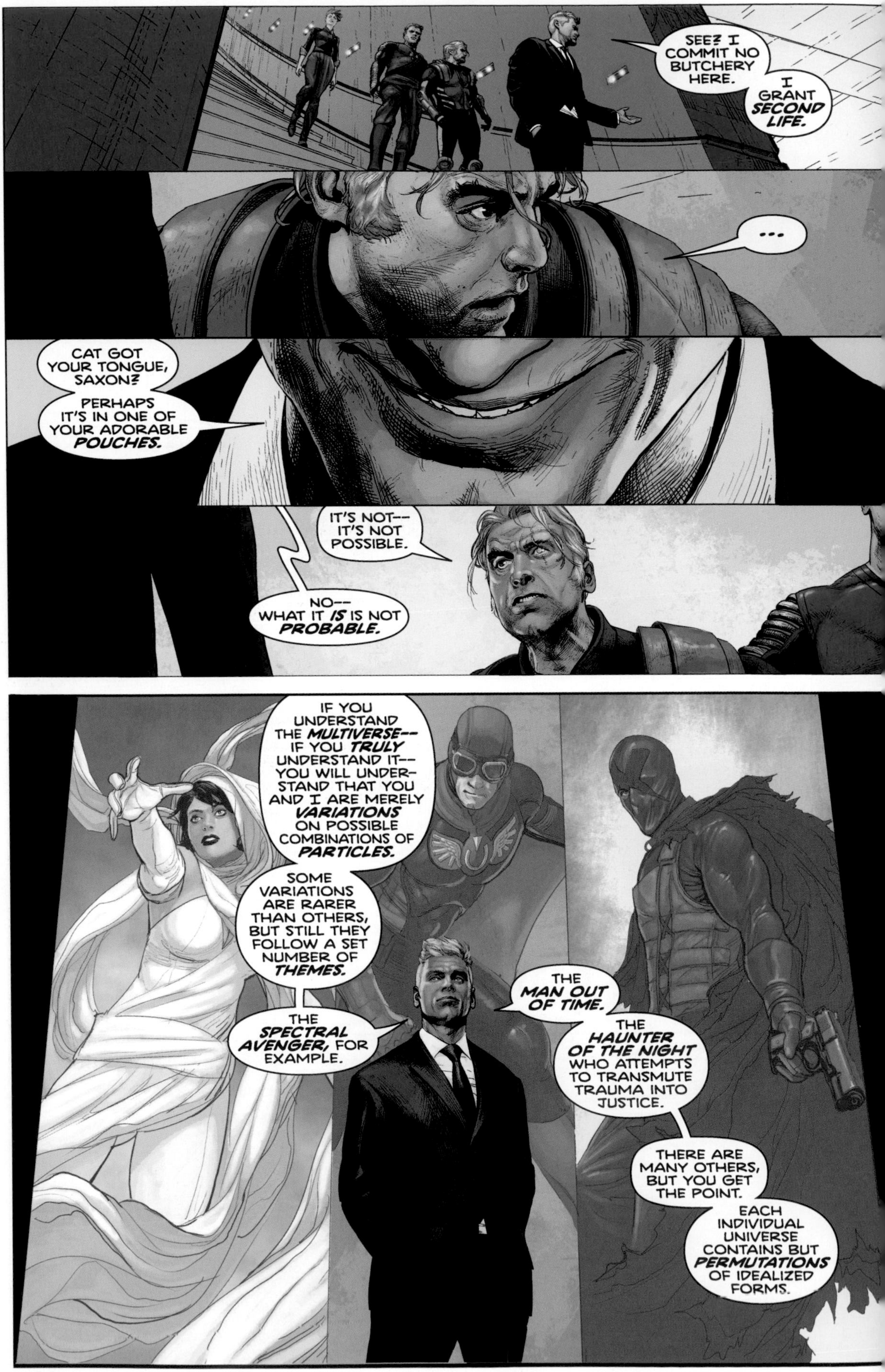
SEE? I COMMIT NO BUTCHERY HERE.
I GRANT *SECOND LIFE.*
...
CAT GOT YOUR TONGUE, SAXON?
PERHAPS IT'S IN ONE OF YOUR ADORABLE *POUCHES.*
IT'S NOT-- IT'S NOT POSSIBLE.
NO-- WHAT IT *IS* IS NOT *PROBABLE.*
IF YOU UNDERSTAND THE *MULTIVERSE*-- IF YOU *TRULY* UNDERSTAND IT-- YOU WILL UNDER-STAND THAT YOU AND I ARE MERELY *VARIATIONS* ON POSSIBLE COMBINATIONS OF *PARTICLES.*
SOME VARIATIONS ARE RARER THAN OTHERS, BUT STILL THEY FOLLOW A SET NUMBER OF *THEMES.*
THE *SPECTRAL AVENGER,* FOR EXAMPLE.
THE *MAN OUT OF TIME.*
THE *HAUNTER OF THE NIGHT* WHO ATTEMPTS TO TRANSMUTE TRAUMA INTO JUSTICE.
THERE ARE MANY OTHERS, BUT YOU GET THE POINT.
EACH INDIVIDUAL UNIVERSE CONTAINS BUT *PERMUTATIONS* OF IDEALIZED FORMS.

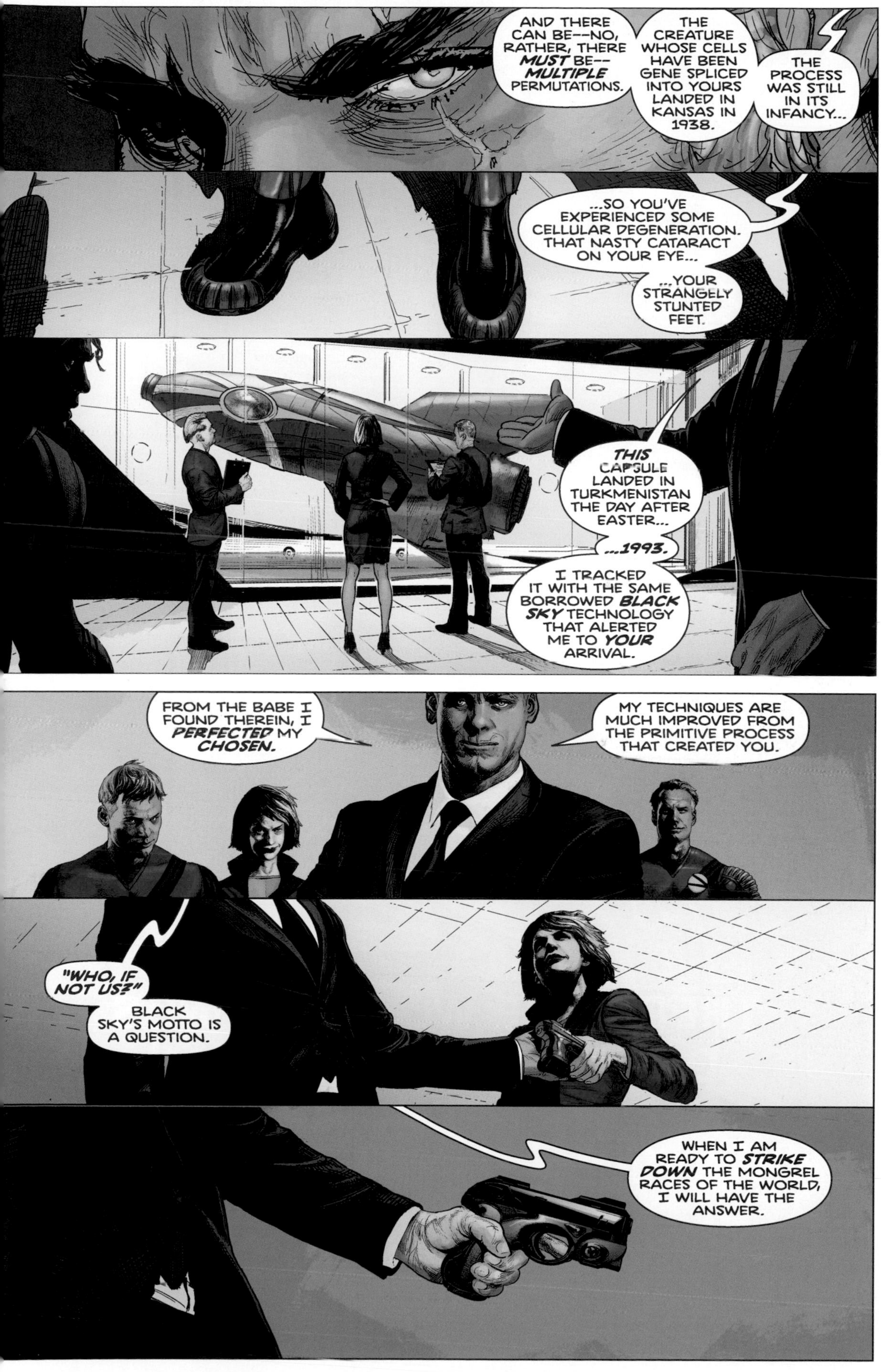
AND THERE CAN BE--NO, RATHER, THERE MUST BE--MULTIPLE PERMUTATIONS.
THE CREATURE WHOSE CELLS HAVE BEEN GENE SPLICED INTO YOURS LANDED IN KANSAS IN 1938.
THE PROCESS WAS STILL IN ITS INFANCY...
...SO YOU'VE EXPERIENCED SOME CELLULAR DEGENERATION. THAT NASTY CATARACT ON YOUR EYE...
...YOUR STRANGELY STUNTED FEET.
THIS CAPSULE LANDED IN TURKMENISTAN THE DAY AFTER EASTER...
...1993.
I TRACKED IT WITH THE SAME BORROWED BLACK SKY TECHNOLOGY THAT ALERTED ME TO YOUR ARRIVAL.
FROM THE BABE I FOUND THEREIN, I PERFECTED MY CHOSEN.
MY TECHNIQUES ARE MUCH IMPROVED FROM THE PRIMITIVE PROCESS THAT CREATED YOU.
"WHO, IF NOT US?"
BLACK SKY'S MOTTO IS A QUESTION.
WHEN I AM READY TO STRIKE DOWN THE MONGREL RACES OF THE WORLD, I WILL HAVE THE ANSWER.

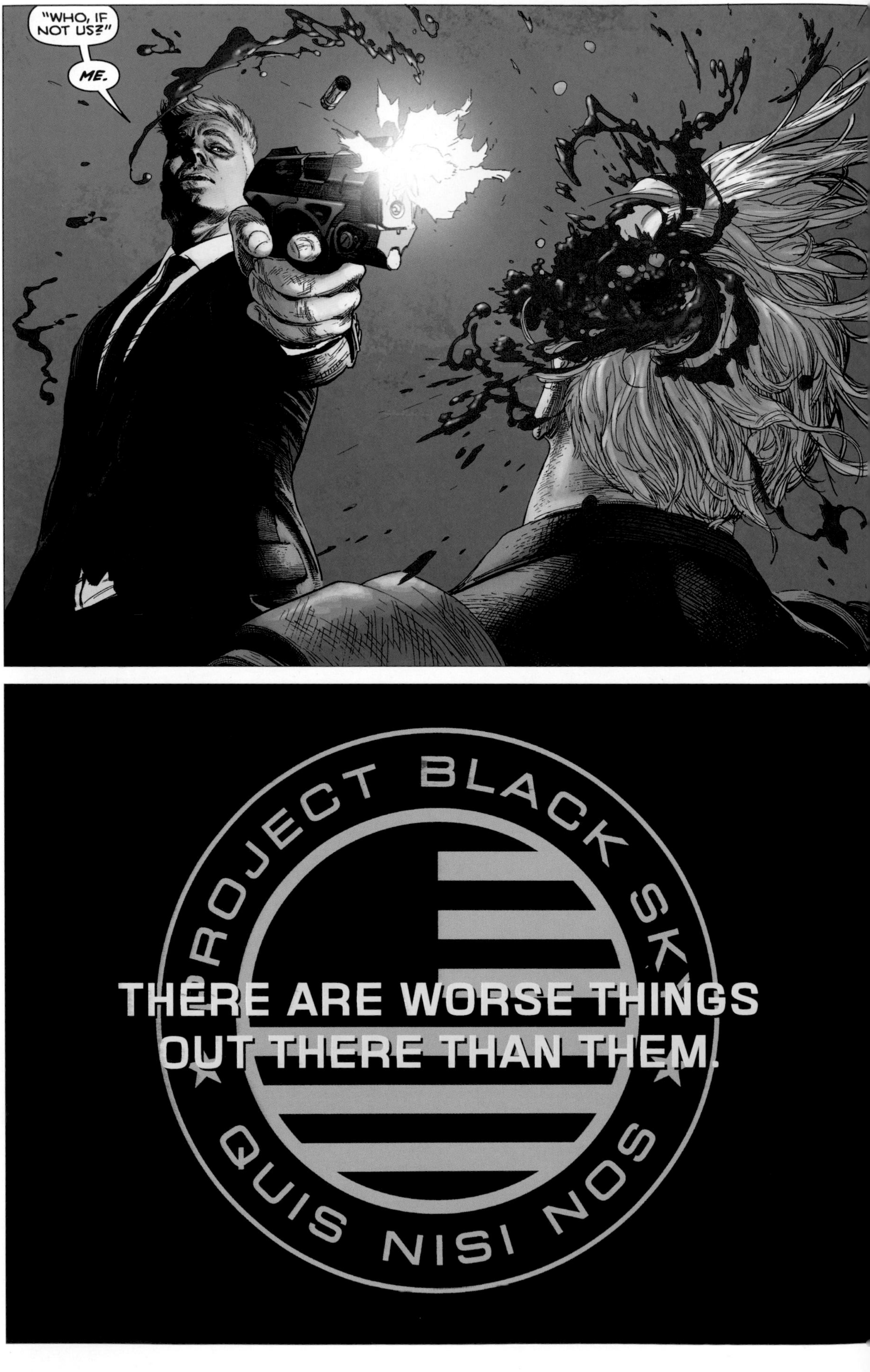
"WHO, IF NOT US?"
ME.
PROJECT BLACK SKY
QUIS NISI NOS
THERE ARE WORSE THINGS OUT THERE THAN THEM.

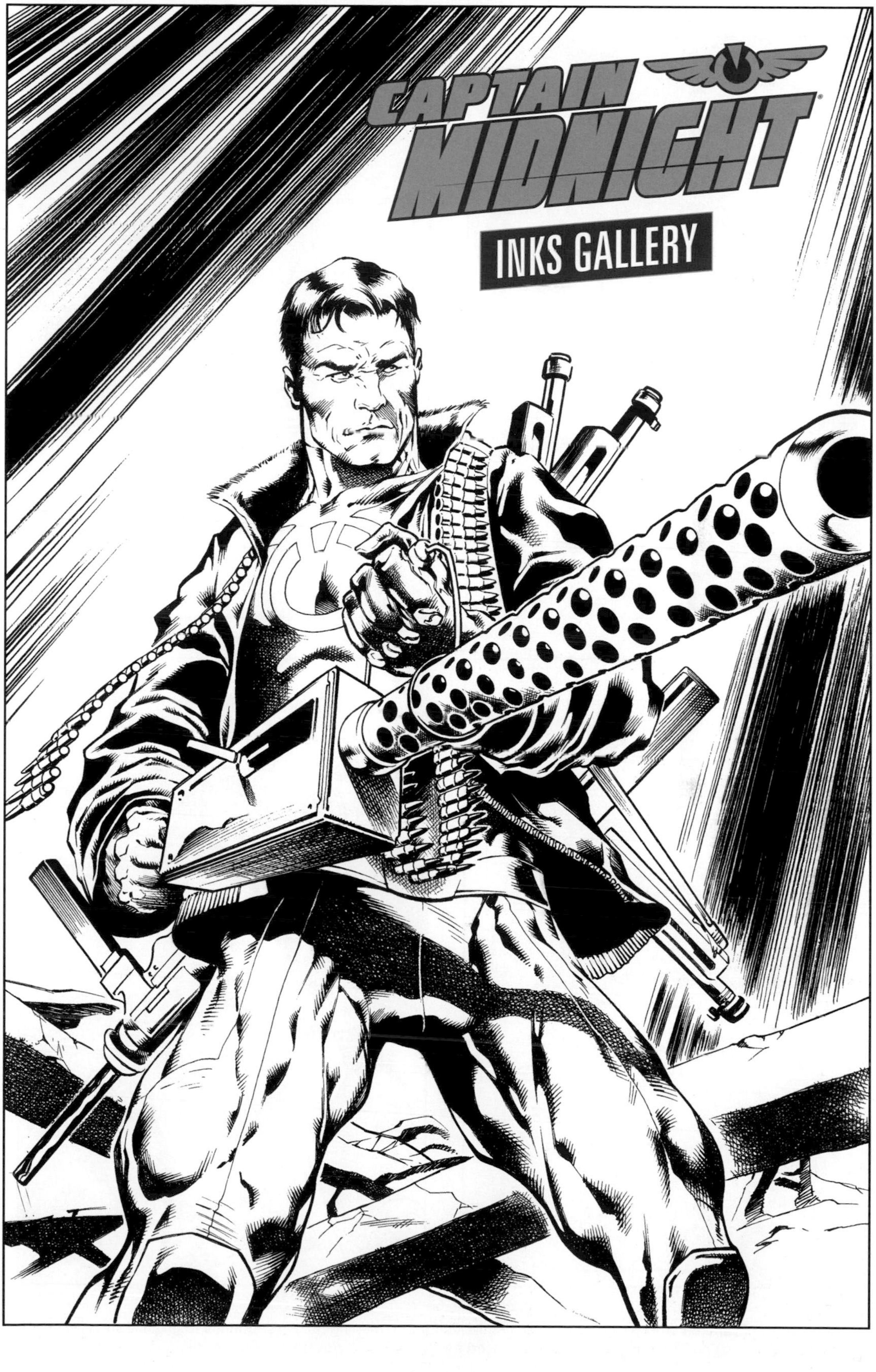
CAPTAIN MIDNIGHT
INKS GALLERY

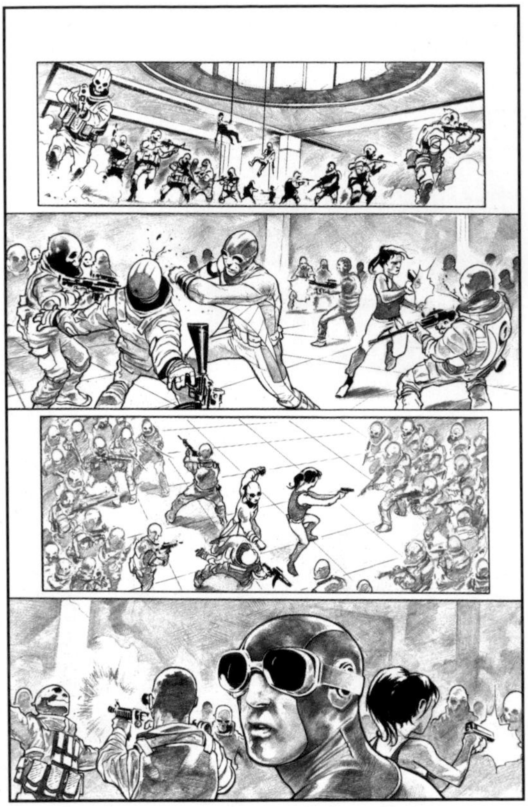
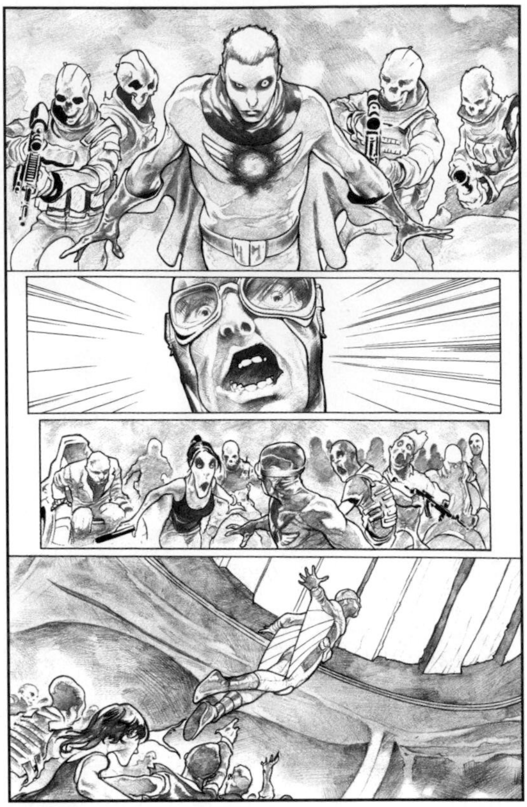
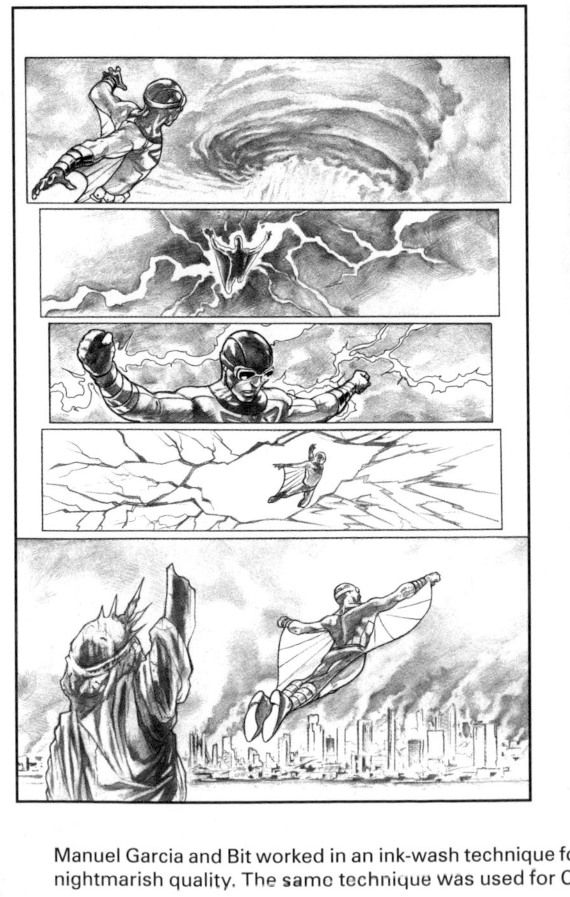
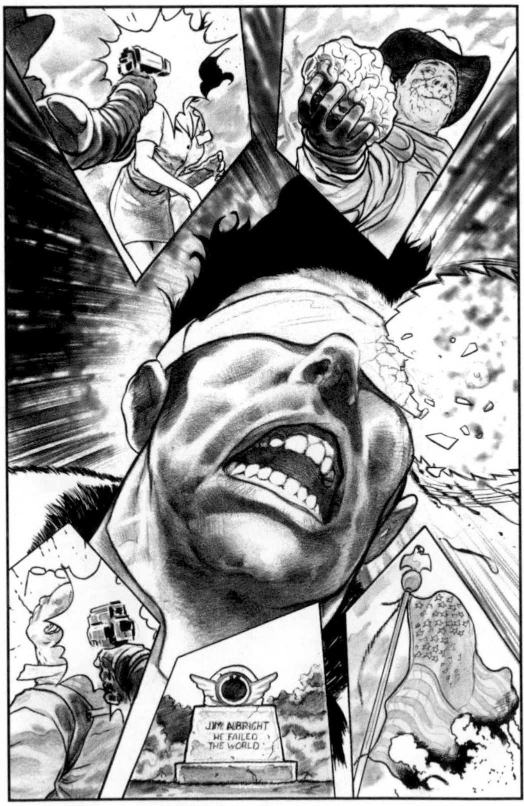
JIM ALBRIGHT
HE FAILED
THE WORLD

Manuel Garcia and Bit worked in an ink-wash technique for the opening dream sequence to give it a surreal and nightmarish quality. The same technique was used for Cap's "every possible scenario" visions in issue #15.

PROJECT BLACK SKY

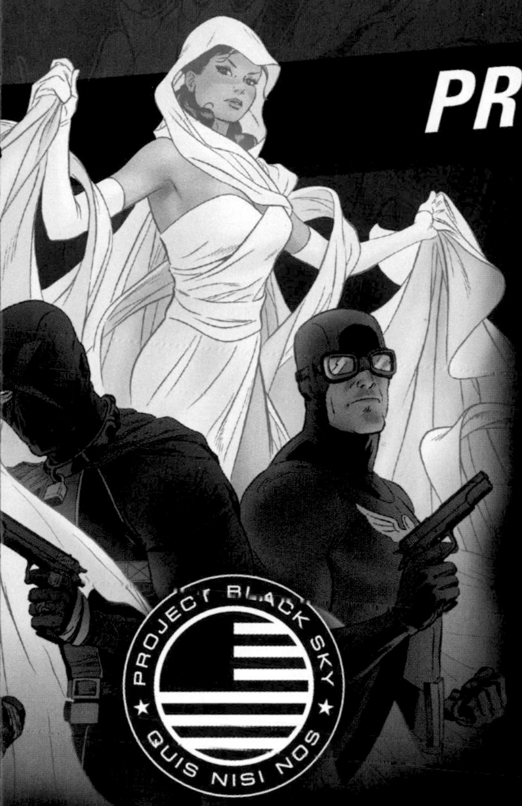
PROJECT BLACK SKY
QUIS NISI NOS

X

Duane Swierczynski and Eric Nguyen

A masked vigilante dispenses justice without mercy to the criminals of the decaying city of Arcadia. Nonstop, visceral action, with Dark Horse's most brutal and exciting character—X!

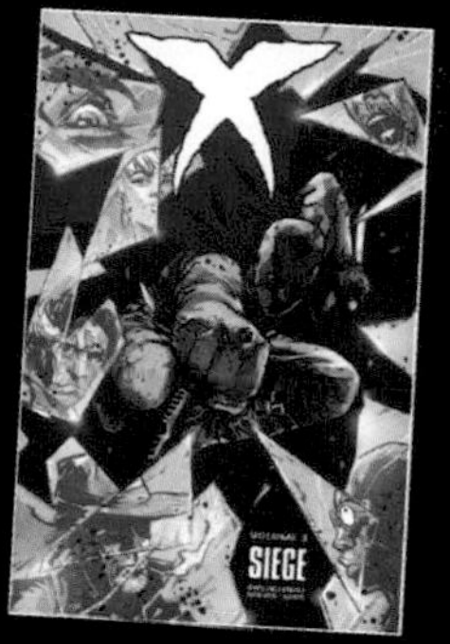
SIEGE

VOLUME 1: BIG BAD
978-1-61655-241-1 | $14.99

VOLUME 2: THE DOGS OF WAR
978-1-61655-327-2 | $14.99

VOLUME 3: SIEGE
978-1-61655-458-3 | $14.99

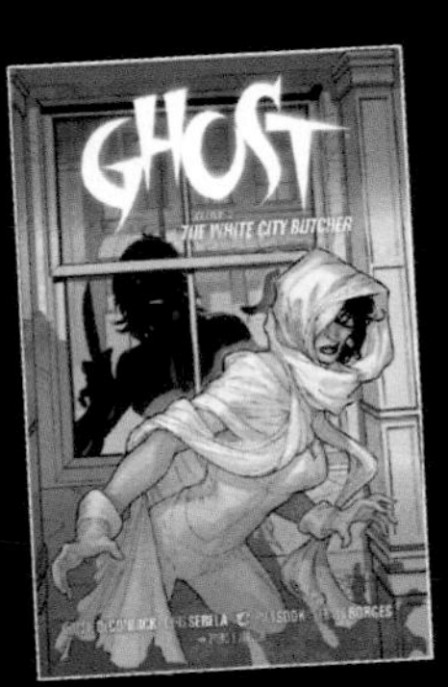
GHOST
THE WHITE CITY BUTCHER

GHOST

Kelly Sue DeConnick, Chris Sebela, Phil Noto, and Ryan Sook

Paranormal investigators accidentally summon a ghostly woman. The search for her identity uncovers a deadly alliance between political corruption and demonic science! In the middle stands a woman trapped between two worlds!

VOLUME 1: IN THE SMOKE AND DIN
978-1-61655-121-6 | $14.99

VOLUME 2: THE WHITE CITY BUTCHER
978-1-61655-420-0 | $14.99

THE OCCULTIST

Mike Richardson, Tim Seeley, and Victor Drujiniu

With a team of hit mages hired by a powerful sorcerer after him, it's trial by fire for the new Occultist, as he learns to handle his powerful magical tome, or suffer at the hands of deadly enemies. From the mind of Dark Horse founder Mike Richardson (*The Secret*, *Cut*, *The Mask*)!

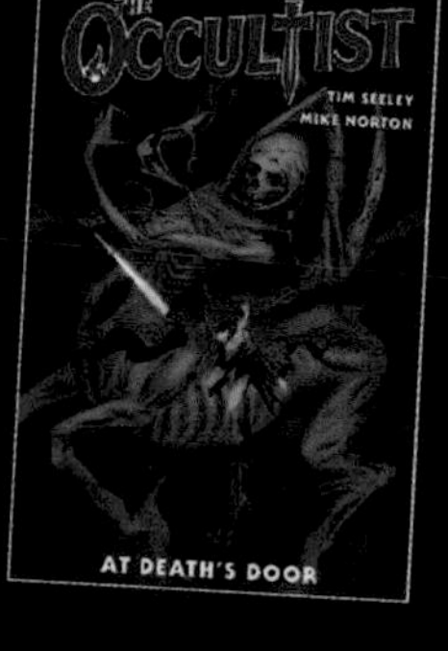
THE OCCULTIST
TIM SEELEY
MIKE NORTON
AT DEATH'S DOOR

VOLUME 1
978-1-59582-745-6 | $16.99

VOLUME 2: AT DEATH'S DOOR
978-1-61655-463-7 | $16.99

PROJECT BLACK SKY

CAPTAIN MIDNIGHT
BRAVE OLD WORLD

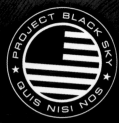

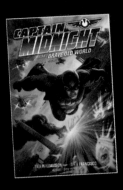

CAPTAIN MIDNIGHT

Joshua Williamson, Fernando Dagnino, Eduardo Francisco, Victor Ibáñez, Pere Pérez, and Roger Robinson

In the forties, he was an American hero, a daredevil fighter pilot, a technological genius . . . a superhero. Since he rifled out of the Bermuda Triangle and into the present day, Captain Midnight has been labeled a threat to homeland security. Can Captain Midnight survive in the modern world, with the US government on his heels and an old enemy out for revenge?

VOLUME 1: ON THE RUN
978-1-61655-229-9 | $14.99

VOLUME 2: BRAVE OLD WORLD
978-1-61655-230-5 | $14.99

BRAIN BOY

Fred Van Lente, Freddie Williams II, and R. B. Silva

Ambushed while protecting an important statesman, Matt Price Jr., a.k.a. Brain Boy, finds himself wrapped up in political intrigue that could derail a key United Nations conference and sets the psychic spy on a collision course with a man whose mental powers rival his own!

VOLUME 1: PSY VS. PSY
978-1-61655-317-3 | $14.99

BRAIN BOY
PSY VS. PSY

SKYMAN
THE RIGHT STUFF

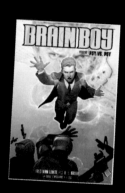

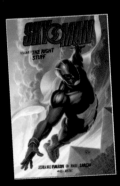

SKYMAN

Joshua Hale Fialkov and Manuel Garcia

The Skyman Program turns to US Air Force Sgt. Eric Reid: a wounded veteran on the ropes, looking for a new lease on life. *Ultimates* writer Joshua Hale Fialkov pens an all-new superhero series from the pages of *Captain Midnight*!

VOLUME 1: THE RIGHT STUFF
978-1-61655-439-2 | $14.99

BLACKOUT

Frank Barbiere, Colin Lorimer, and Micah Kaneshiro

Scott Travers possesses a special suit bearing technology that allows Travers to move in and out of our world through a shadowy parallel dimension–but he doesn't know how the device works or where it came from. With his benefactor missing, and powerful adversaries after his "Blackout" gear, Scott must master the suit's mysterious powers and find answers before the answers find him!

VOLUME 1: INTO THE DARK
978-1-61655-555-9 | $12.99

BLACKOUT
INTO THE DARK

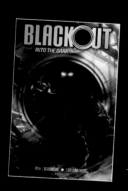